COOKING
THROUGH THE YEAR

COOKING
THROUGH THE YEAR

Audrey Ellis

TIGER BOOKS INTERNATIONAL
LONDON

Photography by Paul Kemp
Photographic styling by Mary Jane Kemp
Line illustrations by Joyce Tuhil

The publishers would like to thank
the following for kind loan of accessories for photography:
Designers Guild, Divertimenti, David Mellor,
Harvey Nichols.

This edition published in 1986 by
Tiger Books International Ltd, London

ISBN 0 600 32276 9

Phototypeset in Monophoto Garamond 10/11 pt
by Servis Filmsetting Limited, Manchester

Printed and bound by Graficromo s.a., Cordoba, Spain

Contents

——— Introduction 7 ———

— Freezing Seasonal Foods 8 —

——— January 10 ———

——— February 24 ———

——— March 36 ———

——— April 50 ———

——— May 66 ———

——— June 78 ———

——— July 92 ———

——— August 106 ———

——— September 120 ———

——— October 134 ———

——— November 146 ———

——— December 162 ———

Recipes for Round the Year 177

——— Index 190 ———

Introduction

This book has been planned to help you enjoy more than ever before the pleasure of eating seasonal dishes using easy, uncomplicated recipes and without incurring any daunting cost. Whatever the time of year some foods are at their best, and my experience has shown that good cooks are always on the lookout for new ways of using them.

Availability is not the only consideration. As the seasons change, so do our mealtime preferences. Hearty dishes are welcome in midwinter and it's a golden opportunity to offer a stew with delicious dumplings, or a filling baked pudding. Yet in midsummer, a sumptuous salad followed by a delicate fruit mousse would be more appropriate.

Somehow, we have to acquire a magic touch to create dishes which delight according to the weather and which make use of the fresh produce that's readily available in the shops, or causing a glut in our gardens. All too often busy housewives fall back on the same menus with little variation all round the year, when it would easily be possible to serve and enjoy really varied meals and make better use of foods at the peak of their seasons.

Here, a new approach is taken to meal planning, one chapter being devoted to each month from January through to December. To begin with, in every month you will find a special breakfast menu to give a new lift to what is often the most stereotyped meal of the day. Then there is a selection of starters, including many unusual savoury ones with fruit, and both hot and cold soups. Many of the recipes have variations or will provide a source of inspiration for you to create others.

A large section of each chapter is devoted to main dishes, because this is the most important course of a meal. All are designed to increase your expertise in blending together seasonal vegetables and fruit with meat, or the other substantial ingredients needed to make each dish a satisfying one.

The sweets which follow are fun to prepare and look almost too good to eat. Then there are other recipes for those light meals which most families seem to enjoy at some time of the day, to make a complete change from the everlasting snack of cheese or beans on toast.

In the spring, it seems particularly appropriate to think of making light-textured cakes. A whole section is given over to them here. And finally, each month has its own sparkling party plan – right in tune with both the mood and the food of the season.

There's a bonus at the end of the book; invaluable basics with a difference – sauces and so on; unusual bread and pastry recipes, to give a lift to your baking. I hope you'll refer to many of these again and again to complement your seasonal cooking.

Audrey Ellis

Freezing Seasonal Foods

Many freezer owners find it fun and financially rewarding to pick their surplus garden produce and store it for use later in the year. The army of freezer enthusiasts is swelled by those who do not grow fruit and vegetables, but enjoy picking farm produce when it is offered at a most attractive price.

However, since frozen food is kept far longer at a much lower temperature than it would be in the refrigerator, it requires special protection against dehydration by the cold, dry air inside the freezer cabinet.

Foods like fruit and vegetables with a relatively high water content are liable to suffer damage to their cell structure during the freezing process, so they need careful preparation and packing.

General Rules for Freezing

☐ Choose only perfect specimens, setting aside any that are slightly over-ripe for immediate serving, and prepare for freezing as soon as possible after picking.

☐ Keep your hands, any implements used, and the packing materials, perfectly clean, to prevent bacterial contamination between picking and freezing. Wash fruit only if absolutely necessary. Hull berry fruits after washing, to keep the interior as dry as possible.

☐ Use packing materials that are proof against invasion by the air inside the freezer, or loss of moisture from the pack itself into the cabinet. These include strong polythene bags or shaped containers with snap-on seals, freezer-proof boiling and roasting bags, heavy-duty cling wrap and foil containers or sheet foil. Bags should be sealed with twist ties and foil packs by crimping.

☐ Wrap or pack to eliminate air spaces, other than the necessary headspace to allow for the expansion of the water content of the food on freezing (1.25 cm/$\frac{1}{2}$ inch in rigid-based containers). Unnecessary air spaces allow moisture to be drawn out of the food and cause frost formation inside the pack. Use self-adhesive labels to identify contents.

☐ Freeze down fast, and keep packs fully frozen until required. Avoid partially defrosting and then refreezing.

Packing Fruit for the Freezer

Most fruits, other than very watery ones such as melon, freeze well. Fruit quickly loses vitamin c after picking, and some fruit tends to discolour when the flesh is exposed to the air. The addition of $\frac{1}{4}$ teaspoon ascorbic acid to 300 ml/$\frac{1}{2}$ pint cold water replaces lost vitamin c and prevents discoloration, however the following methods are more popular from the point of view of preserving the natural flavour. 450 g/1 lb fresh fruit, with its own juice or in a sugar syrup, makes an average serving for four.

Open freezing Use this method for soft juicy fruits especially delicate berries which damage easily, such as strawberries, raspberries, blackberries and loganberries. Ensure that, by spreading the fruit out on trays, each berry freezes separately, and therefore more quickly than if packed together. (Tight packing during freezing causes squashing and damage of the lower layers of fruit.) Spread dry, clean berries on trays, freeze at lowest temperature possible until hard; about 1 hour for small berries, 2 hours for strawberries. Pack at once, seal, label and return to freezer.

Note The frozen fruit will not at first appear any different, but do not wait to pack until a bloom caused by condensation appears on the surface, as it would do after a few minutes.

Dry sugar pack Use this method for most fruits. It is particularly suitable for soft juicy berries, currants and gooseberries. Also good for sliced apples, apricots, plums and greengages, although apples tend to discolour. Allow 450 g/1 lb sugar for 1.5–2.25 kg/3–5 lb fruit, according to its natural sweetness. Spoon alternate layers of fruit and sugar into containers, or place all the clean fruit with the sugar in a bowl. Turn the fruit gently with a wooden spoon until all is lightly coated, then pack, leaving a 1.25-cm/$\frac{1}{2}$-inch space. Snap on seal, or seal polythene bags with twist ties. Label and freeze. Foil or waxed cartons may be used but should be sealed with freezer tape.

Sugar syrup pack Use this method for less delicate fruits. It is particularly suitable for stone fruits such as plums, greengages, apricots and cherries and also for rhubarb, citrus fruit, apples, pears, currants, pineapples and peaches.

Prepare the fruit; if washing it, drain well. Remove stones from plums etc.; peel citrus fruits and divide into segments; blanch cut rhubarb, also peeled, cored and sliced apples, in boiling water for 1 minute; peel pineapple, remove core and eyes, and peel and stone peaches. Fruits which discolour quickly such as apples, peaches and apricots, should be dipped in lemon juice or put into salt water or ascorbic acid solution ($\frac{1}{4}$ teaspoon crystals in 4 tablespoons water). Pack into polythene containers. Pour over cold sugar syrup, allowing 150 ml/$\frac{1}{4}$ pint syrup to each 600-ml/1-pint pack of fruit. Syrup should just cover fruit. Allow 1.25 cm/$\frac{1}{2}$ inch headspace and, if necessary to hold fruit under syrup, place a layer of crumpled foil on top. Seal and label.

Cooked fruit purée pack Use this method for fresh soft berry fruits or other fruit that can be stewed and made into purée. Fresh berries can be puréed, uncooked, with sugar. Cook other fruits with sugar, and then purée. This can be done either with a sieve or electric blender. Some fruit purées such as apple, which may be required for unsweetened dishes, can be labelled and frozen separately. Stoned fruits should be sliced and cooked to a pulp over gentle heat with 4 tablespoons water to each 450 g/1 lb prepared fruit. Cool cooked purées quickly. Pack into suitable containers leaving 1.25 cm/$\frac{1}{2}$ inch headspace. Seal and label.

Packing Vegetables for the Freezer

All those vegetables which are usually served cooked freeze well. Vegetables, unlike fruit, are a non-acidic food, and require the extra precaution of blanching before freezing to halt destructive enzyme action. The blanching process is extremely easy to carry out, preserves the bright colour, softens vegetables and makes them easier to pack, and also shortens cooking time when thawed.

Blanching Vegetables

Prepare the vegetables as for cooking. You will need a large saucepan. Put vegetables into a wire basket and lower into fast-boiling water, or put straight into water. Allow water to return to the boil, then time blanching from that moment according to the chart on page 188. Accuracy of timing is important. Insufficient blanching time may not halt enzyme activity, and over-blanching may spoil the texture and flavour of vegetables. Remove wire basket from saucepan, place under running cold water from the tap, then plunge into a bowl of cold water, chilled if possible by the addition of ice cubes. Alternatively, transfer vegetables straight from the saucepan with a perforated draining spoon to a colander and cool as above. When vegetables are completely cold, drain thoroughly and pack as for fruit. That is, putting delicate vegetables like peas, whenever possible, in rigid-bottomed containers to distribute the weight, with 1.25 cm/$\frac{1}{2}$ inch headspace

and foil dividers half way up the packs. If using polythene bags, do not fill more than two-thirds full; to close, bring together and gently press out as much air as possible without damaging the contents. Seal with twist ties. Putting the date on the label is important to ensure that early processed packs are used up first.

Methods of Packing

As for fruit, there are various methods of packing vegetables after the essential blanching process.

Open Freezing Delicate vegetables can be open frozen in the same way as delicate fruits, but may require scraping off the freezing trays. The advantage is that small amounts of vegetables may be removed from the pack while still in the frozen state.

Dry Packs Simply pack well-drained vegetables into containers as soon as they are cold.

Using Frozen Fruit

All fruit other than purées should be allowed to thaw for about 3 hours (according to the size of the pack) at room temperature, or 6 hours in the refrigerator. The texture is best if eaten while slightly frozen or well-chilled. To hasten thawing, airtight packs such as sealed polythene containers can be placed under running cold water for about 30 minutes, then turned out and carefully broken up with a fork to thaw the centre of the pack. Purées, to be used in cooked dishes, can be thawed quickly by placing the airtight pack in a bowl of warm water.

Using Frozen Vegetables

Cook from the frozen state or partly-thawed. Blanched vegetables which were, ideally, young and tender when picked require very little further cooking. Cook with the minimum amount of water, covered, for half the usual cooking time or less. Delicate vegetables such as peas only require to be placed over moderate heat in a covered pan with salt, pepper and a knob of butter for about 5 minutes.

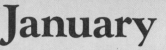

January

With the bite of frost upon the ground,
hot pies and casseroles are warming consolations

As the first snow comes whispering down, it usually heralds a long spell of cold weather. Hot soups, chowders and stews will be popular favourites with the family for months to come. Providing the ground isn't too hard to dig them, the old country saying that vegetables taste all the better for a touch of frost, may well be true. Winter vegetables when they are right in season are a joy, so make the most of them while they are at their best. The list of root and bulb vegetables is longer than you think – carrots, parsnips, turnips, swedes, beetroot, Jerusalem artichokes, potatoes, and their delectable companions, leeks, onions, fennel and celery. Onion dishes are particularly appropriate just now, so here are some new ideas to try out. And while you're at work in the inviting warmth of your kitchen, plan to celebrate by the cosy glow of candlelight and enjoy a hot buffet meal with your friends.

Oaty Herrings

BREAKFAST

(Illustrated on page 14)

4 small herrings, cleaned
salt and pepper
50 g/2 oz medium oatmeal
50 g/2 oz butter
1 tablespoon oil
1 tablespoon lemon juice

1 Split each herring and open out on a board with the cut sides downwards. Press along the backbone of each fish, turn over and remove the bones.

2 Sprinkle inside the fish with salt and pepper and fold each over to re-form the shape. Coat the herrings all over with oatmeal.

3 Heat the butter and oil in a large frying pan, put in the herrings and fry over moderate heat for 15 minutes, turning them carefully once. Test the flesh in the cavity gently with a fork to check that the fish is cooked. Place on warm serving plates and keep hot. Stir the lemon juice into the buttery pan juices and spoon over the fish. Serve immediately. **Serves 4**

Spiced Apple Compote

ACCOMPANIMENT

(Illustrated on page 14)

450 g/1 lb cooking apples
3 tablespoons pineapple juice
grated rind of 1 lemon
$\frac{1}{2}$ teaspoon ground mace
golden syrup to taste

1 Peel, core and slice the apples. Place in a small saucepan with the pineapple juice and the lemon rind. Cook gently until the apple is soft.

2 Beat the apple to a smooth pulp, mix in the mace and sweeten to taste with golden syrup. Continue cooking for 1 minute, stirring all the time. Serve with hot porridge or a cereal, if liked. **Serves 4**

Jerusalem Artichoke Soup with Anchovies

FIRST COURSE

350 g/12 oz large Jerusalem artichokes
1 tablespoon lemon juice
1 (56-g/2-oz) can anchovies
25 g/1 oz butter
1 medium onion, sliced
1 medium potato, diced
450 ml/$\frac{3}{4}$ pint chicken stock
salt and pepper
150 ml/$\frac{1}{4}$ pint milk
1 tablespoon chopped parsley to garnish

1 Scrub or peel the artichokes, then slice them. Place in a bowl with the lemon juice and just sufficient water to cover. Allow to stand for 30 minutes.

2 Drain the oil from the anchovies into a saucepan and add the butter. Chop the anchovies and reserve.

3 Drain the artichokes and pat dry with kitchen paper. Add to the pan with the onion and potato. Cook the vegetables over a low heat for about 5 minutes, without allowing them to take colour. Pour in the stock, add a little pepper and bring to the boil. Cover and simmer over a low heat for about 12–15 minutes.

4 Liquidise the mixture until smooth, or press through a sieve. Return to the pan and add the milk and chopped anchovies. Reheat the mixture, stirring all the time. Taste and adjust the seasoning, adding a little salt if necessary. Serve hot, sprinkled with parsley. **Serves 4**

Leek Chowder

FIRST COURSE

2 large leeks, trimmed
100 g/4 oz pickled belly of pork, diced
1 medium onion, grated
1 large potato, diced
450 ml/¾ pint milk
salt and pepper
4 tablespoons single cream

1 Slice the leeks finely and rinse well. Drain.

2 Place the pork in a large saucepan and fry gently until the fat runs. Add the onion and leek and stir over moderate heat for 2 minutes. Add the potato and just sufficient water to cover. Bring to the boil, cover and simmer over a low heat for 20 minutes.

3 Stir in the milk and season to taste. Bring back to boiling point, cover again and simmer for a further 15 minutes, until the pork is tender. Remove from the heat, swirl in the cream and serve hot. **Serves 4**

Smoked Haddock and Bean Salad

FIRST COURSE

450 g/1 lb smoked haddock
little milk and water
150 ml/¼ pint natural yogurt
2 teaspoons lemon juice
1 teaspoon curry powder
1 teaspoon ground ginger
salt and pepper
1 (425-g/15-oz) can haricot beans, drained
1 tablespoon chopped parsley
garnish
4 lettuce leaves
1 hard-boiled egg, sliced
1 tablespoon capers

1 Place the fish in a shallow pan with just enough milk and water to cover. Bring to the boil, lower the heat and simmer for 10 minutes. Drain well, remove any bones and skin, and flake the fish.

2 Combine the yogurt, lemon juice, curry powder, ginger and a little pepper in a bowl. Stir in the fish and haricot beans. Fold in the parsley. Taste and adjust the seasoning carefully, adding salt if necesary.

3 Serve portions of the salad in lettuce leaf cups, each garnished with slices of hard-boiled egg and a sprinkling of capers. **Serves 4**

Chinese-style Fish Strips

MAIN COURSE

450 g/1 lb plaice fillets
5 tablespoons oil
1 tablespoon lemon juice
salt and freshly ground black pepper
2 tablespoons seasoned flour
50 g/2 oz butter
450 g/1 lb beansprouts
100 g/4 oz button mushrooms, quartered
1 tablespoon soy sauce

1 Cut the plaice into 1-cm/½-inch wide strips. Marinate for 30 minutes in 1 tablespoon of the oil, the lemon juice and seasoning to taste.

2 Drain the fish and toss in the seasoned flour. Melt the butter and fry the fish strips until golden all over.

3 Meanwhile, heat the remaining oil and stir in the beansprouts and mushrooms. Cook briskly for 3 minutes, stirring all the time. Add the soy sauce, fold in the hot fish strips and adjust the seasoning. Serve with fluffy boiled rice. **Serves 4**

VARIATION
Chinese-style fish and prawns Use only 350 g/12 oz plaice fillets and add 100 g/4 oz peeled prawns with the soy sauce. Reheat thoroughly before adding the fish strips.

Glazed Ham Joint

MAIN COURSE

(Illustrated on page 15)

1 (1.5-kg/3-lb) middle gammon joint, soaked in
cold water for at least 2 hours
1 small onion, grated
4 tablespoons lemon juice
2 tablespoons clear honey
salt and pepper
150 ml/¼ pint chicken stock
1 teaspoon cornflour

1 Drain and rinse the gammon then place in a
saucepan and cover with cold water.

2 Bring to the boil, drain and cover with fresh cold
water. Bring to the boil, reduce the heat then cover and
simmer for 2–2¼ hours.

3 Drain and cool slightly then carefully remove the
rind and score the fat in a diagonal pattern.

4 Place the joint in a roasting tin. Combine the onion,
lemon juice, honey and seasoning then pour over the
joint and bake in a moderate oven (180 C, 350 F, gas 4)
for 30–40 minutes until golden brown.

5 Remove to a serving dish and keep hot.

6 Pour the stock into the roasting tin and stir well,
scraping up all the pan juices. Strain into a small
saucepan. Moisten the cornflour, add to the pan and
bring to the boil, stirring constantly. Simmer for 2
minutes. Check the seasoning, pour into a sauce boat
and serve with the ham joint. **Serves 4–6**

Baked Clove Oranges

ACCOMPANIMENT

(Illustrated on page 15)

6 medium oranges, peeled
18 whole cloves
4 tablespoons wine vinegar
150 ml/¼ pint dry cider
3 tablespoons soft brown sugar
¼ teaspoon ground mixed spice

1 Remove the white pith from the oranges and stud
each one with 3 cloves. Arrange them close together in
an ovenproof dish.

2 Place the remaining ingredients in a saucepan and
stir over gentle heat until the sugar dissolves. Pour
over the oranges, cover and cook in a moderate oven
(180 C, 350 F, gas 4) for 40 minutes.

3 Serve with the glazed ham joint or cool and serve
with plain boiled bacon. **Serves 6**

Oaty herrings and Spiced apple compote (page 12)

Glazed ham joint and Baked clove oranges;
Turkey-stuffed onions (page 18)

Bacon Hotpot

——— MAIN COURSE ———

(*Illustrated on page 10*)

675 g/1½ lb lean sweetcure bacon, soaked
50 g/2 oz butter
1 large onion, sliced
4 sticks celery, sliced
4 carrots, sliced
salt and freshly ground black pepper
600 ml/1 pint apple juice
1 tablespoon cider vinegar
100 g/4 oz button mushrooms
2 teaspoons cornflour
2 tablespoons chopped parsley

1 Cut the bacon into neat cubes, removing any excess fat.

2 Melt the butter in a flameproof casserole, add the bacon and the prepared vegetables. Season lightly and cook, stirring frequently, until the bacon is lightly browned.

3 Add the apple juice and cider vinegar then bring to the boil, cover and simmer gently for 40 minutes. Wipe the mushrooms and add to the casserole 15 minutes before the end of the cooking time.

4 Blend the cornflour to a smooth paste with cold water. Stir in a little of the hot cooking liquid then pour the cornflour mixture into the casserole and bring to the boil stirring continuously.

5 Simmer for 5 minutes, adjust the seasoning if necessary then stir in the chopped parsley before serving with Granary bread. **Serves 4**

Roast Pork with Parsnips

——— MAIN COURSE ———

1-kg/2-lb piece belly of pork
salt and pepper
250 ml/8 fl oz water
450 g/1 lb medium potatoes, quartered
450 g/1 lb medium parsnips, quartered
1 tablespoon redcurrant jelly
1 tablespoon flour

1 Score the skin of the pork and sprinkle with salt and pepper. Place in a roasting tin with the water.

2 Roast in a moderately hot oven (200 C, 400 F, gas 6) for 1 hour.

3 Meanwhile, parboil the potato and parsnip in salted water for 2 minutes. Drain and reserve the liquid. Arrange the vegetables round the meat and baste well.

4 Melt the redcurrant jelly in 125 ml/4 fl oz of the reserved vegetable liquid and pour over the pork skin. Return to the oven for a further hour, or until the vegetables are tender and golden brown.

5 Place the meat and vegetables on a warm dish.

6 Blend the flour with the pan juices in a small saucepan. Bring to the boil, stirring constantly. Simmer for a few minutes. Thin the gravy with a little more of the reserved vegetable liquid if necessary. Adjust the seasoning and strain into a sauce boat. **Serves 4**

Crofter's Roastie

——— MAIN COURSE ———

1 large breast of lamb
1 bay leaf
2 cloves
salt and pepper
225 g/8 oz carrots, diced
225 g/8 oz turnips, diced
225 g/8 oz parsnips, diced
1 large onion, chopped
4 large potatoes, quartered
1 tablespoon flour

1 Bone the breast of lamb and reserve bones. Use to make stock with the bay leaf, cloves, ½ teaspoon salt and sufficient water to cover. Use the strained stock to cook the vegetables, adding water if necessary.

2 Cut the breast of lamb into pieces and place them in a roasting tin. Sprinkle with salt and pepper and put into a hot oven (220 C, 425 F, gas 7) for 15 minutes.

3 Meanwhile, place the vegetables together in a saucepan. Add the strained stock to cover, bring to the boil, cover and simmer for 5 minutes. Drain well and reserve the cooking liquid.

4 Remove the meat from the fat in the roasting tin. Put in the vegetables and arrange the pieces of meat on top. Return the dish to the oven, reducing the temperature to moderate (180 C, 350 F, gas 4) and cook for 1¼ hours.

5 Drain 2 tablespoons of the fat from the roasting tin into a saucepan and blend in the flour. Gradually add 450 ml/¾ pint of the reserved bone and vegetable stock and bring to the boil, stirring constantly. Season to taste and simmer for 2 minutes, pour into a sauce boat and serve with the roastie. **Serves 4**

Veal Stew
with Potato Dumplings

—————— MAIN COURSE ——————

25 g/1 oz dripping
1 medium onion, chopped
225 g/8 oz turnips or swede, diced
225 g/8 oz carrots, sliced
450 g/1 lb stewing veal, diced
300 ml/½ pint strong beef stock
salt and pepper
dumplings
100 g/4 oz self-raising flour
1 small onion, grated
1 egg, beaten
450 g/1 lb mashed potato
salt and pepper

1 Melt the dripping in a large saucepan and fry the onion, turnip and carrot for 5 minutes. Add the veal and fry until sealed. Pour in the stock and season well.

2 Bring to the boil, lower the heat, cover and simmer for 30 minutes.

3 Meanwhile, make the dumplings. Combine the flour, onion, egg, potato and plenty of seasoning and mix together well.

4 Form into eight balls with floured hands.

5 Adjust the seasoning in the stew, place the dump-lings on top, bring back to boiling point, cover and simmer over a low heat for a further 30 minutes.
Serves 4

Lamb's Liver with Fennel

—————— MAIN COURSE ——————

25 g/1 oz seasoned flour
¼ teaspoon cayenne pepper
450 g/1 lb lamb's liver, sliced
3 tablespoons oil
2 large onions, sliced
2 small heads fennel, trimmed and sliced
300 ml/½ pint cider
salt and pepper

1 Combine the flour and cayenne pepper. Coat the slices of liver with this flour mixture, reserving any left over. Heat the oil and fry the liver slices for 5 minutes on each side, until just cooked through. Remove from the pan and place in a warm ovenproof dish. Keep hot.

2 Add the onion and fennel to the oil remaining in the pan and fry until golden. Stir in the remaining flour mixture, then blend in the cider. Stir until the sauce boils and thickens. Simmer for about 2 minutes. Adjust the seasoning and pour the sauce over the liver.
Serves 4

Lemon sultana pudding and Yorkshire apple pie (page 23)

Baked Chicken in Sharp Sauce

MAIN COURSE

4 chicken portions
1 tablespoon soy sauce
2 teaspoons Worcestershire sauce
1 small onion, grated
salt and pepper
5 tablespoons water
450 g/1 lb potatoes
225 g/8 oz Jerusalem artichokes
2 tablespoons dripping, melted

1 Place the chicken portions, skin side downwards, in a roasting tin. Combine the soy sauce, Worcestershire sauce, onion and seasoning with the water and pour this mixture over the chicken. Cook in a moderately hot oven (200 C, 400 F, gas 6) for 15 minutes.

2 Meanwhile, cut the potatoes and artichokes into even-sized pieces and parboil in boiling salted water for 10 minutes. Drain.

3 Turn the chicken pieces and baste with the pan juices. Arrange the vegetables around the outside of the chicken and spoon over the dripping. Return to the oven for a further 30 minutes, or until the vegetables are tender and golden brown. **Serves 4**

American Turkey and Rice Salad

MAIN COURSE

25 g/1 oz butter
2 tablespoons oil
1 small onion, sliced
175 g/6 oz long-grain rice
450 ml/$\frac{3}{4}$ pint chicken stock
225 g/8 oz cooked turkey breast meat, cubed
100 g/4 oz canned water chestnuts, sliced
100 g/4 oz cooked or canned sweet corn kernels
$\frac{1}{2}$ teaspoon ground ginger
4 tablespoons mayonnaise (page 186)
salt and pepper
few lettuce leaves, shredded
1 tablespoon flaked almonds, toasted, to garnish

1 Heat the butter and oil and use to fry the onion and rice until golden brown. Add the stock and bring to the boil. Stir once, lower the heat, cover and simmer for 15 minutes, or until the rice is tender and the liquid absorbed. Turn into a large bowl and allow to cool.

2 Stir the turkey, water chestnuts and sweet corn into the rice mixture. Beat the ginger into the mayonnaise and adjust the seasoning. Add to the bowl and stir well.

3 Arrange a bed of shredded lettuce on four salad plates and spoon the rice salad over the top. Garnish with flaked almonds. **Serves 4**

VARIATION

Chicken and rice salad Substitute 225 g/8 oz cooked chicken breast for the turkey and use 100 g/4 oz canned bamboo shoot, cut into fine strips, instead of the water chestnuts. Omit the almonds and scatter the salad with 25 g/1 oz split cashew nuts.

Turkey-stuffed Onions

SUPPER OR SNACK

4 large Spanish onions
grated rind and juice of $\frac{1}{2}$ lemon
1 chicken stock cube
350 g/12 oz cooked turkey meat, diced
100 g/4 oz fresh white breadcrumbs
40 g/1$\frac{1}{2}$ oz shredded suet
1 tablespoon currants
2 tablespoons chopped parsley
salt and pepper
50 g/2 oz butter

1 Place the peeled onions in a saucepan with salted water to cover. Bring to the boil, cover and simmer for about 15 minutes, until the onions are tender but not soft. Drain and reserve the cooking liquid. Remove the centre of the onions with a grapefruit knife or teaspoon. Make the lemon juice up to 150 ml/$\frac{1}{4}$ pint with the reserved liquid and use to dissolve the stock cube.

2 Mix the onion pulp with the turkey meat. Stir in the breadcrumbs, suet, currants, lemon rind, parsley and seasoning. Add just sufficient stock to moisten and use this mixture to stuff the onions. (Any extra filling can be placed in a small ovenproof dish, moistened with stock and baked in the oven with the onions.)

3 Stand the onions upright in an ovenproof dish, dot with butter and pour the remaining stock around them. Cover with foil and cook in a moderately hot oven (190 C, 375 F, gas 5) for about 45 minutes, until the onions are soft and the stuffing is cooked. Uncover for the last 15 minutes to allow the onions to brown. **Serves 4**

Carrot and Haddie Flan

225 g/8 oz shortcrust pastry (page 184)
450 g/1 lb smoked haddock fillet
300 ml/½ pint milk
150 ml/¼ pint water
2 medium carrots, diced
25 g/1 oz butter
20 g/¾ oz flour
little prepared mustard
freshly ground black pepper

1 Roll out the pastry to line a 20-cm/8-inch flan tin. Line with greaseproof paper and baking beans and bake blind in a moderately hot oven (200 C, 400 F, gas 6) for 15 minutes. Remove the paper and beans.

2 Meanwhile, poach the haddock in the milk and water for 10 minutes and cook the carrot in boiling water until just tender. Drain and flake the fish, reserving the liquid and drain the carrot.

3 Strain the fish liquid into a clean saucepan and place over a moderate heat. Cream together the butter and flour and add a little at a time to the liquid, stirring constantly until the sauce thickens and boils. Season carefully with mustard and pepper. Stir in the fish and carrots and pour into the flan case. Return to the oven for a further 10 minutes. **Serves 4**

VARIATION

Corn and haddie flan Substitute a drained 198-g/7-oz can of sweet corn kernels for the carrot, and season the sauce with a few drops of Tabasco sauce instead of the mustard.

Pizza in the Pan

1 (396-g/14-oz) can tomatoes
12 spring onions, chopped
salt and freshly ground black pepper
8 stuffed green olives, sliced
175 g/6 oz self-raising flour
½ teaspoon baking powder
50 g/2 oz butter
about 150 ml/¼ pint milk
75 g/3 oz Cheddar cheese, grated

1 Combine the tomatoes and liquid from the can with the spring onions and seasoning in a saucepan. Bring to the boil and cook briskly for about 6 minutes, or until reduced by half. Stir in the olives.

2 Sift the flour and baking powder into a bowl and rub in the butter. Add sufficient milk to make a soft dough. Turn on to a floured surface and pat out into a round to fit a well greased 20-cm/8-inch heavy frying pan.

3 Cook over a very low heat for about 15 minutes, until risen and golden underneath.

4 Top with the tomato mixture, sprinkle with the cheese and grill until the cheese is golden and bubbling. **Serves 4**

VARIATION

Pan pizza with anchovy topping Drain a 56-g/2-oz can of anchovy fillets. Arrange over the tomato topping then sprinkle with just 25 g/1 oz grated cheese. Trickle over a little of the anchovy oil from the can before placing the pizza under the grill.

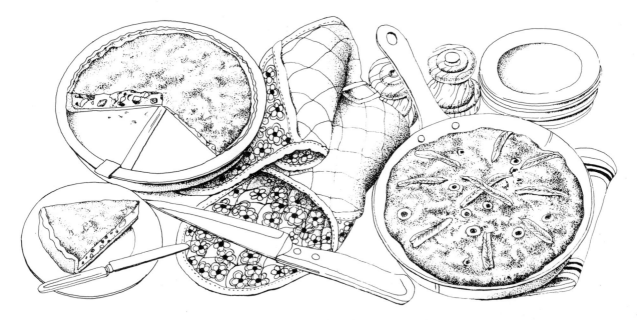

Fudge brownie pear flan (page 22)

Candlelight Supper Buffet

Beef and Chestnut Casserole

•

Red Cabbage Salad

•

Apple and Treacle Tart

Beef and Chestnut Casserole

CANDLELIGHT SUPPER BUFFET

(Illustrated on page 20)

2 large onions, sliced
3 tablespoons oil
1.25 kg/2½ lb chuck steak, cubed
2 cloves garlic, crushed
50 g/2 oz flour
600 ml/1 pint beef stock
450 ml/¾ pint red wine
100 g/4 oz dried chestnuts, soaked
1 red pepper, deseeded and sliced
1 tablespoon redcurrant jelly
2 bay leaves
salt and pepper
strip of orange rind

1 Fry the onion in the oil in a large saucepan for 2–3 minutes. Add the meat and garlic and fry briskly until the meat is browned on all sides. Stir in the flour and cook for 1 minute. Gradually add the stock and wine and bring to the boil, stirring constantly. Add the prepared chestnuts, red pepper, redcurrant jelly, bay leaves, seasoning and orange rind.

2 Transfer to an ovenproof casserole. Cover and cook in a moderate oven (160 C, 325 F, gas 3) for about 2 hours, until the beef is tender.

3 Remove the bay leaves and orange rind and serve the casserole with red cabbage salad and jacket potatoes. **Serves 8**

Note To prepare dried chestnuts, first cover them with boiling water and leave to soak for 4–6 hours.

VARIATIONS

Cidered beef and prune hotpot Substitute 450 ml/¾ pint strong cider for the red wine and 175 g/6 oz soaked prunes for the chestnuts. The redcurrant jelly can be omitted.

Beef and ale hotpot Substitute 450 ml/¾ pint stout for the red wine and 225 g/8 oz button onions for the chestnuts. Omit the redcurrant jelly and add 1 tablespoon French mustard and 1 tablespoon demerara sugar instead.

Red Cabbage Salad

CANDLELIGHT SUPPER BUFFET

(Illustrated on page 20)

1 medium red cabbage
50 g/2 oz chopped walnuts
50 g/2 oz seedless raisins
150 ml/¼ pint French dressing (page 186)

1 Quarter the cabbage and remove any damaged outer leaves. Cut out the hard core and shred about 675 g/1½ lb of the leaves into a bowl.

2 Mix the red cabbage with the walnuts and raisins and toss lightly in the dressing. **Serves 8**

Apple and Treacle Tart

CANDLELIGHT SUPPER BUFFET

(Illustrated on page 20)

225 g/8 oz shortcrust pastry (page 184)
350 g/12 oz cooking apples, peeled
8 tablespoons golden syrup
2 tablespoons black treacle
3 egg yolks
grated rind of 1 lemon
4 tablespoons fresh white breadcrumbs
2 tablespoons double cream
whipped cream to decorate (optional)

1 Roll out the pastry and use to line a 23-cm/9-inch flan tin.

2 Core and grate the apples. Beat the golden syrup and treacle with the egg yolks and lemon rind. Stir in the breadcrumbs, apple and cream. Spoon the mixture into the pastry case.

3 Bake in a moderately hot oven (190 C, 375 F, gas 5) for 35–40 minutes. If the filling starts to brown too much, cover with a circle of greased greaseproof paper for the last few minutes of cooking time. Serve warm with cream or chill and decorate with piped, whipped cream if liked. **Serves 8**

VARIATION

Fudge brownie pear flan *(Illustrated on page 21)* Make up the filling as in the main recipe, omitting the grated apple. Put 6 small pear halves into the pastry case and cover with the filling. Dot the surface with butter and bake as above.

Hazelnut Pear Pie

—— DESSERT ——

350 g/12 oz shortcrust pastry (page 184)
450 g/1 lb firm pears
1 tablespoon lemon juice
50 g/2 oz castor sugar
1 tablespoon ground cinnamon
100 g/4 oz hazelnuts, chopped
100 ml/4 fl oz single cream
1 tablespoon milk

1 Roll out three-quarters of the pastry to line a 20-cm/8-inch fluted flan ring. Place on a baking sheet.

2 Peel, core and slice the pears and mix with the lemon juice, sugar and cinnamon.

3 Spoon half the pear mixture into the pastry case, sprinkle with half the hazelnuts then add the rest of the pear mixture and hazelnuts. Spoon the cream evenly over the top.

4 Roll out the remaining pastry to make a lid for the pie. Dampen the edges and seal well together. Cut several slits in the pastry and brush all over with milk.

5 Bake in a moderately hot oven (190 C, 375 F, gas 5) for about 40 minutes, until golden brown. Serve warm. **Serves 6**

Yorkshire Apple Pie

—— DESSERT ——

(*Illustrated on page 17*)

450 g/1 lb puff pastry (page 185)
675 g/1½ lb cooking apples
175 g/6 oz Cheddar cheese, diced
50 g/2 oz seedless raisins
2–3 tablespoons soft brown sugar
grated rind and juice of ½ lemon
1 egg, beaten

1 Roll out the pastry and cut out two 23-cm/9-inch circles. Place one circle of pastry on a dampened baking sheet.

2 Peel, core and slice the apples and arrange on the pastry base, leaving a border of 1 cm/½ inch all round. Place the cheese and raisins on the apple and sprinkle over the sugar, lemon rind and juice. Brush the exposed pastry edges with beaten egg, place the remaining pastry circle on top and seal the edges

together well. Brush the pie with beaten egg and use pastry trimmings to decorate. Brush again with egg to glaze. Score the top surface of the pastry lightly with a sharp knife, but do not cut a steam vent.

3 Bake in a moderately hot oven (200 C, 400 F, gas 6) for about 40 minutes, until well risen and golden brown. **Serves 6**

Lemon Sultana Pudding

—— DESSERT ——

(*Illustrated on page 17*)

100 g/4 oz self-raising flour
pinch of salt
50 g/2 oz shredded suet
25 g/1 oz castor sugar
50 g/2 oz sultanas
grated rind and juice of 1 lemon
1 egg
3 tablespoons milk
4 tablespoons lemon curd (page 178)
pared lemon rind to decorate

1 Sift the flour and salt into a bowl and stir in the suet, sugar, sultanas and lemon rind. Beat the egg, lemon juice and milk together, add to the dry ingredients and mix to a soft dropping consistency.

2 Divide between six greased dariole moulds, cover with greased foil and steam for 30 minutes.

3 Warm the lemon curd and add a very little boiling water to thin to a pouring consistency. Turn out the puddings, spoon a little of the lemon curd sauce over each one and decorate with strips of pared lemon rind. **Serves 6**

VARIATION

Coconut raisin pudding Use 75 g/3 oz self-raising flour and 25 g/1 oz desiccated coconut instead of all flour, and substitute 25 g/1 oz seedless raisins for the sultanas. Turn into a greased 600-ml/1-pint pudding basin, cover with foil and steam for 1½ hours.

February

The fill-dyke month when rain falls tirelessly
and it's best to stay indoors,
enjoying the riches of a winter menu

We can expect fill-dyke weather from this month when the rain is often a non-stop daily event. While it's too wet to tempt you out of doors, spend a little extra time at home making your marmalade and other citrus fruit jams for the year. Lemons, oranges and grapefruit are all superb, and pineapples make a welcome appearance when there's very little other fruit to be found in the shops. If by any chance you have no time to do your preserving just now, put the fruit into bags and freeze it until the right moment arrives. Beef is the meat of the month and several entirely different ways to cook it are given in this section. Also here are many ideas for using our wonderful root vegetables, particularly the adaptable parsnip which is so sweet in flavour and smooth in texture when cooked. To satisfy the romantic members of the family, offer a special menu on St Valentine's day, ending with an unusual Winter fruit salad.

Paprika Baked Eggs

BREAKFAST

(*Illustrated on page 28*)

15 g/½ oz butter
50 g/2 oz ham, diced
2 eggs
salt and pepper
pinch of paprika pepper
chopped parsley to garnish

1 Grease two small ramekin dishes or one small ovenproof gratin dish with the butter. Arrange the ham leaving hollows for the eggs.

2 Carefully break an egg into each dish, keeping the yolks whole. Sprinkle with salt and pepper to taste and a pinch of paprika.

3 Place the ramekins or gratin dish on a baking sheet and cook in a moderately hot oven (200 C, 400 F, gas 6) for 15 minutes, or until the whites of the eggs are set. Garnish with a little chopped parsley. **Serves 2**

Hot Rolls

Make white rolls, following the recipe on page 182. Take frozen rolls straight from the freezer, place on an ovenproof plate and put in the coolest part of the oven to defrost and reheat while the eggs are baking. If the rolls are not frozen and merely need refreshing and warming, sprinkle lightly with cold water and place on the same oven shelf as the eggs for about 8 minutes.

Saffron Fennel Soup

FIRST COURSE

(*Illustrated on page 29*)

450 ml/¾ pint chicken stock
1 small packet saffron strands
2 medium heads fennel, trimmed
50 g/2 oz lean bacon
25 g/1 oz butter
1 tablespoon oil
25 g/1 oz flour
salt and pepper
2 tablespoons double cream (optional)

1 Heat the stock until boiling, add the saffron, remove from the heat and allow to stand for 30 minutes.

2 Finely dice the fennel and chop the bacon. Heat the butter and oil together in a large saucepan. Add the fennel and bacon and toss over moderate heat until golden. Sprinkle in the flour and stir well. Season lightly.

3 Gradually pour in the stock, stirring all the time. Return to the boil, stirring constantly, then reduce the heat, cover and simmer for 15 minutes, or until the fennel is tender. Taste and adjust the seasoning. If the bacon is fairly salty, extra salt will probably not be needed.

4 Serve hot in soup plates. If using the cream, swirl a little into each portion. **Serves 4**

VARIATION

Saffron fennel cream Liquidise the cooked soup or press through a sieve and stir in 4 tablespoons double cream instead of swirling with the 2 tablespoons. Reheat the soup but do not allow to boil. Serve sprinkled with paprika pepper.

Viennese Mushroom Puffs

———— FIRST COURSE ————

tartare sauce
2 teaspoons finely chopped onion
2 teaspoons chopped capers
2 teaspoons chopped pickled gherkin
2 teaspoons chopped parsley
3 tablespoons mayonnaise (page 186)
puffs
100 g/4 oz plain flour
pinch of salt
1 egg
150 ml/¼ pint pale ale
225 g/8 oz button mushrooms
seasoned flour to coat
oil for deep frying

1 First make the tartare sauce. Stir the onion, capers, gherkin and parsley into the mayonnaise. Place in a serving dish and chill while you prepare the puffs.

2 Sift the flour and salt into a bowl. Add the egg and half the ale and beat until smooth. Gradually beat in the remaining ale.

3 Wipe the mushrooms and trim the stalks level with the caps if necessary. Turn in seasoned flour and coat in the batter. Deep fry in hot oil, a few at a time, for about 3 minutes, or until golden brown and crisp. Drain well on kitchen paper and serve hot with the sauce. **Serves 4**

Kohlrabi Croquettes

———— FIRST COURSE ————

300 ml/½ pint savoury white sauce (page 186)
450 g/1 lb peeled and diced kohlrabi, blanched
100 g/4 oz mixed nuts, finely chopped
pinch of grated nutmeg
salt and freshly ground pepper
1 egg
2 tablespoons water
flour for coating
dry white breadcrumbs for coating
oil for deep frying

1 Combine the white sauce, kohlrabi, nuts and nutmeg and season generously with salt and pepper. The mixture should be very stiff and highly seasoned. Chill for about 1 hour and then divide the mixture into 24 equal portions. Shape each into a croquette.

2 Beat the egg with the water. Coat the croquettes with flour, dip in the egg mixture and cover all over with breadcrumbs. If necessary, repeat the egg and breadcrumb coating.

3 Deep fry the croquettes in batches in hot oil for 2–3 minutes, until crisp and golden brown all over. Drain well on kitchen paper and serve hot. **Makes 24**

Celeriac with Mustard Mayonnaise

———— FIRST COURSE ————

2 medium roots celeriac
2 teaspoons French mustard
150 ml/¼ pint mayonnaise (page 186)
2 tablespoons double cream
paprika pepper

1 Scrub the celeriac. Place in a saucepan with salted water to cover. Bring to the boil, cover and cook for 20 minutes or until tender. Drain thoroughly, peel and slice thinly. Arrange the slices, overlapping, on a serving dish and allow to cool.

2 Meanwhile, beat the mustard into the mayonnaise with the cream. Spoon over the celeriac to cover completely. Chill for at least 1 hour, then serve sprinkled with paprika. **Serves 4–6**

Grapefruit Baskets

———— FIRST COURSE ————

2 large grapefruit
4 tablespoons mayonnaise (page 186)
2 hard-boiled eggs
8 stuffed green olives
100 g/4 oz celery, chopped
100 g/4 oz peeled prawns
salt and pepper

1 Cut the grapefruit in half, scoop out and chop the flesh. Drain off any excess juice and reserve. Remove the core and any remaining tough membrane from the grapefruit and reserve the shells.

2 Place the mayonnaise in a large bowl and beat in the reserved grapefruit juice.

3 Roughly chop the eggs and half the olives. Fold into the mayonnaise mixture with the celery, prawns and grapefruit pieces. Season to taste with salt and pepper.

4 Pile up the prawn mixture in the grapefruit 'baskets' and garnish each with a stuffed olive. **Serves 4**

Pork with Swede Cream

MAIN COURSE

(Illustrated on page 29)

450 g/1 lb swede, diced
50 g/2 oz butter
1 large onion, grated
1 tablespoon flour
pinch of ground mace
salt and pepper
4 tablespoons single cream
4 pork chops
watercress to garnish

1 Cook the swede in boiling salted water for 10–15 minutes, until tender. Drain and mash well.

2 Melt the butter and fry the onion gently until soft. Stir in the flour and when smoothly blended, add the mace, mashed swede and seasoning. Cook gently for 5 minutes, stirring all the time. Add the cream and beat well.

3 Meanwhile, cook the pork chops under a moderately hot grill for 7–10 minutes on each side until cooked through.

4 Place the swede cream in a warm serving dish, arrange the chops on top and garnish with sprigs of watercress. **Serves 4**

Beef and Pickled Walnut Pot

MAIN COURSE

2 tablespoons flour
salt and pepper
pinch of ground ginger
450 g/1 lb braising steak, cubed
50 g/2 oz beef dripping
450 g/1 lb medium onions, quartered
2 beef stock cubes
3 pickled walnuts, quartered

1 Season the flour generously with salt, pepper and the ginger. Use to coat the meat.

2 Melt the dripping and fry the quartered onions until golden. Add the steak and fry briskly, stirring, until sealed. Crumble in the stock cubes, add the pickled walnuts and just sufficient water to cover. Bring to the boil, stirring, then cover and simmer for 2–2½ hours, stirring occasionally, until the meat is tender. Adjust the seasoning if necessary. **Serves 4**

VARIATION

Beef and pickled beetroot pot Substitute 75 g/3 oz drained and diced pickled beetroot for the pickled walnuts and add this about 30 minutes before the end of the cooking time.

Paprika baked eggs (page 26)

Saffron fennel soup (page 26) and Pork with swede cream

Beef Spice Boats

—— MAIN COURSE ——

25 g/1 oz fresh root ginger
2–4 whole cloves
50 g/2 oz dripping or lard
450 g/1 lb braising steak, cubed
225 g/8 oz swede, diced
2 large onions, sliced
2 tablespoons flour
1 tablespoon vinegar
150 ml/$\frac{1}{4}$ pint orange juice
450 ml/$\frac{3}{4}$ pint hot beef stock
good pinch ground cinnamon
salt and pepper

1 Bruise the piece of ginger with a rolling pin to release the flavour. Tie the ginger and cloves together in a piece of muslin.

2 Melt the dripping and fry the steak briskly until brown on all sides. Remove the meat from the pan and place in an ovenproof casserole. Add the swede and onion to the pan and fry until the onion is golden. Remove from the pan with a slotted draining spoon and place in the casserole with the meat. Sprinkle the flour into the fat remaining in the pan and stir until smooth. Gradually add the vinegar, orange juice, stock, cinnamon and the bag of spices. Bring to the boil, stirring constantly.

3 Add seasoning and pour over the meat mixture. Cover and cook in a moderate oven (160 C, 325 F, gas 3) for 2–2$\frac{1}{4}$ hours, until the meat is tender. Remove the bag of spices and adjust the seasoning if necessary before serving. **Serves 4**

Boiled Brisket with Parsnips

—— MAIN COURSE ——

1 (1 to 1.25-kg/2 to 2$\frac{1}{2}$-lb) brisket of beef joint
4 whole cloves
1 large onion, peeled
450 g/1 lb medium parsnips
2 beef stock cubes, crumbled
1 bay leaf
450 /1 lb medium potatoes
2 teaspoons cornflour
salt and pepper

1 Put the brisket into a large saucepan and add sufficient cold water to just cover. Bring slowly to the boil and skim. Stick the cloves into the onion and add to the pan with the parsnips, stock cubes and bay leaf.

Bring back to the boil, lower the heat, cover and simmer gently for 2 hours. Halve the potatoes and add to the pan. Cover and continue cooking for a further 30 minutes, or until the vegetables and meat are tender.

2 Place the vegetables on a warm serving dish. Slice the meat and arrange on top. Keep hot. Skim any excess fat from the stock and measure 600 ml/1 pint of the cooking liquid into a small saucepan. Moisten the cornflour with a little cold water, add to the pan and bring to the boil, stirring constantly. Reduce the heat and simmer for 2 minutes. Taste and adjust seasoning if necessary. Spoon a little of this sauce over the meat and hand the remainder separately in a sauce boat. **Serves 4–6**

Double-crust Pork Pie

—— MAIN COURSE ——

25 g/1 oz lard
750 g/1$\frac{1}{2}$ lb minced lean pork
25 g/1 oz fresh white breadcrumbs
1 small onion, finely chopped
1 clove garlic, finely chopped
$\frac{1}{2}$ teaspoon salt
pinch of freshly ground black pepper
pinch of ground nutmeg
1 egg, lightly beaten
350 g/12 oz shortcrust pastry (page 184)
1 egg yolk

1 To make the filling: melt the lard in a frying pan, add the pork and fry, stirring, until it changes colour. Continue cooking gently, stirring frequently, for a further 5 minutes.

2 Stir in the breadcrumbs, onion, garlic, salt, pepper and nutmeg. Add the egg and mix well.

3 Roll out half the pastry and use to line a greased 27.5-cm/9-inch shallow flan tin. Pack the pork filling evenly in the pastry case. Roll out the rest of the pastry to make a lid. Beat the egg yolk, use to brush the pastry edges and seal them well together. Mark the top surface of the pie with the tip of a sharp knife to look like the spokes of a wheel. Brush all over with egg yolk.

4 Bake in a moderately hot oven (200 C, 400 F, gas 6) for about 40 minutes, or until the top is deep golden brown. Serve hot or cold. **Serves 6**

Fruity Apple Batter Pudding

Dessert

100 g/4 oz plain flour
pinch of salt
1 egg
300 ml/½ pint milk
1 tablespoon oil
450 g/1 lb cooking apples
50 g/2 oz sultanas
25 g/1 oz chopped mixed peel
50 g/2 oz butter
100 g/4 oz castor sugar
1 teaspoon ground cinnamon

1 Sift the flour and salt into a bowl. Make a well in the centre and drop in the egg and half the milk. Beat well until the batter is smooth, then gradually beat in the remaining milk and the oil. Allow the batter to stand.

2 Peel, core and slice the apples and mix with the sultanas and chopped peel.

3 Place the butter in a baking tin measuring about 25 × 30 cm/10 × 12 inches. Put into a hot oven (220 C, 425 F, gas 7) until the butter is hot but not brown.

4 Add the apple mixture to the hot butter and stir until coated. Sprinkle with the sugar and cinnamon then pour over the batter. Return the tin to the oven for 30 minutes. Reduce the oven temperature to moderately hot (200 C, 400 F, gas 6) and bake for a further 15–20 minutes, until the pudding is well risen and golden brown. **Serves 4**

Note This basic recipe can be adapted to use other fruits according to season.

Orange Croissants

Dessert

675 g/1½ lb puff pastry (page 185)
175 g/6 oz ground almonds
1 egg yolk
100 g/4 oz castor sugar
3 oranges
1 egg, beaten
6 tablespoons apricot jam, warmed and sieved
flaked almonds

1 Roll out the pastry thinly and cut 10 triangles with equal sides measuring 15 cm/6 inches. Chill.

2 Combine the ground almonds with the egg yolk and sugar. Grate the rind from two of the oranges and squeeze the juice. Stir into the almond mixture.

3 Divide this orange mixture between the pastry triangles, placing it in the centres. Brush all the pastry edges with beaten egg. With one straight edge towards you, roll up towards the opposite point of the triangle. Press the edges to seal and curve round to make a crescent shape. Repeat with the remaining pastry triangles. Arrange the pastry crescents on a dampened baking sheet.

4 Grate the rind from the remaining orange and squeeze the juice. Combine with the jam. Use to brush the pastry crescents and sprinkle with flaked almonds.

5 Bake in a moderately hot oven (200 C, 400 F, gas 6) for about 25 minutes, until well risen and golden brown. **Makes 10**

Variation
Lemon croissants Substitute 2 lemons for the oranges in the filling and use 6 tablespoons lemon jelly marmalade for the glaze. Omit the fruit rind and juice from the glaze.

Biscuit Hearts

Accompaniment

(*Illustrated on page 33*)

175 g/6 oz soft margarine
25 g/1 oz icing sugar, sifted
100 g/4 oz self-raising flour
25 g/1 oz cornflour
25 g/1 oz cocoa powder
icing sugar to sprinkle

1 Cream the margarine and icing sugar together until really light and creamy. Sift the flour with the cornflour and cocoa powder and gradually beat into the creamed mixture.

2 Place in a piping bag fitted with a star nozzle and pipe in heart shapes on to greased baking sheets, keeping them well apart.

3 Bake in a moderate oven (180 C, 350 F, gas 4) for about 15 minutes, until the edges just begin to brown. Cool on the sheet for about 4 minutes, until the biscuit hearts are firm, then lift carefully on to a wire rack to cool completely. Dredge with icing sugar while still warm. Serve with fruit desserts such as the Winter fruit salad (see page 33). **Makes about 12**

Avocado with Herb Dressing

St. Valentine's day party

(*Illustrated on page 33*)

3 avocado pears
3 tablespoons dry white wine
2 teaspoons lemon juice
4 tablespoons olive oil
2 tablespoons chopped parsley
salt and freshly ground black pepper
$\frac{1}{2}$ teaspoon castor sugar
$\frac{1}{2}$ teaspoon garlic granules
$\frac{1}{2}$ teaspoon dried dill

1 Halve the avocado pears, remove the stones and slice thinly. Arrange the slices on individual plates in heart shapes.

2 Whisk the remaining ingredients together, or shake them in a screw-topped jar and pour over the avocado slices.

3 Serve with crisp toast. (The toast may be cut into heart shapes using a biscuit cutter.) **Serves 6**

Lovers' Pie

St. Valentine's day party

(*Illustrated on page 33*)

1 medium onion, sliced
2 tablespoons oil
2 chicken breasts, boned
450 g/1 lb pork fillet, cubed
25 g/1 oz butter
175 g/6 oz button mushrooms, sliced
150 ml/$\frac{1}{4}$ pint white wine
150 ml/$\frac{1}{4}$ pint chicken stock
1 tablespoon cornflour
salt and pepper
2 tablespoons chopped parsley
225 g/8 oz shortcrust pastry (page 184)
1 egg, beaten
100 ml/4 fl oz double cream

1 Fry the onion gently in the oil for 2–3 minutes. Cube the chicken meat, add to the pan with the pork and fry until browned on all sides. Melt the butter in a separate saucepan and fry the mushrooms gently for 2–3 minutes. Transfer the meat mixture and mushrooms to a large ovenproof pie dish.

2 Heat the wine and stock in the pan in which you have cooked the mushrooms. Blend the cornflour with a little cold water, add to the wine and bring to the boil, stirring constantly. Season to taste and stir in the parsley. Pour over the meat mixture in the pie dish.

3 Roll out the pastry and cut a lid and a strip to fit the rim of the dish. Place the strip around the moistened edge of the dish, moisten it and cover the whole pie with the lid, sealing the edges well together. Cut small heart shapes from the pastry trimmings. Brush the pastry lid with beaten egg, decorate with the heart-shaped pastry pieces, and brush with egg again. Cut a steam vent in the centre of the pie crust.

4 Bake in a moderately hot oven (200 c, 400 f, gas 6) for 30 minutes. Reduce the oven temperature to moderate (180 c, 350 f, gas 4) and cook for a further 20 minutes.

5 Remove the pie from the oven and pour the cream through the hole in the pastry crust. Return to the oven for a few minutes to warm through.

6 Serve hot with carrot and celery salad. **Serves 6**

VARIATIONS

Welsh pie Use 2 sliced leeks in place of the mushrooms and add 50 g/2 oz grated cheese to the sauce. **Crusted coq au vin** Use 4 chicken breasts, boned and cubed, and omit the pork fillet. Use 150 ml/$\frac{1}{4}$ pint red wine instead of the white wine.

Carrot and Celery Salad

St. Valentine's day party

(*Illustrated on page 33*)

rind and juice of 1 small lemon
1 tablespoon oil
150 ml/$\frac{1}{4}$ pint natural yogurt
1 oz chopped walnuts
salt and freshly ground black pepper
3 small carrots
1 head celery

1 Combine the lemon juice, oil and yogurt by whisking well together. Stir in lemon rind and walnuts.

2 Scrape the carrots and grate them into a bowl. Remove the outer stalks from the celery and finely dice the heart. Add to the carrot and stir in the dressing. Mix well and season to taste with salt and freshly ground black pepper. Serve chilled. **Serves 6**

Winter Fruit Salad

ST. VALENTINE'S DAY PARTY

(Illustrated on page 33)

350 g/12 oz dried fruit, for example, apricots and
prunes
1 (397-g/14-oz) can green figs
300 ml/½ pint sweet cider
1 cinnamon stick
juice of 1 lemon
2 tablespoons clear honey
50 g/2 oz seedless raisins (optional)
1 red and 1 green dessert apple, halved, cored and
sliced

1 Soak the dried fruit overnight in hot water.

2 Drain the figs and place the syrup in a saucepan with
the cider, cinnamon, lemon juice and honey. Drain the
dried fruit and add to the cider mixture.

3 Bring to the boil, reduce the heat and cover closely.
Cook gently for 15 minutes then add the raisins, apples
and figs.

4 Leave to cool, remove the cinnamon stick and serve
warm with Biscuit hearts (see page 31). **Serves 6**

*St Valentine's Day party: Avocado with herb dressing, Lovers' pie, Carrot and celery salad,
Winter fruit salad and Biscuit hearts (page 31)*

Salmon Flan with Crumb Crust

SUPPER OR SNACK

tailpiece of fresh salmon, about 225 g/8 oz
225 g/8 oz shortcrust pastry (page 184)
50 g/2 oz butter
1 medium Spanish onion, chopped
50 g/2 oz mushrooms, chopped
50 g/2 oz fresh white breadcrumbs
pinch of grated nutmeg
pinch of ground cloves
1 egg
4 tablespoons milk
salt and freshly ground black pepper
2 tablespoons port
3 tablespoons lemon juice

1 Wrap the salmon in a foil parcel and cook in a moderately hot oven (190 C, 375 F, gas 5) for 15 minutes. Remove skin and bones and flake roughly.

2 Roll out the pastry and use to line a lightly floured 20-cm/8-inch flan tin. Chill while you prepare the topping.

3 Melt half the butter and fry the onion gently until soft. Add the mushroom and breadcrumbs and cook for 2 minutes, stirring. Remove from the heat and stir in the nutmeg, cloves, egg and milk. Season to taste with salt and pepper.

4 Arrange the pieces of salmon in the pastry case and cover evenly with the mushroom topping.

5 Place the port, remaining butter and lemon juice in a pan and bring to the boil. Remove from the heat and spoon over the ingredients in the pastry case. Bake in the oven for 35 minutes and serve hot. **Serves 6**

Piquant Fish Puffs

SUPPER OR SNACK

15 g/$\frac{1}{2}$ oz butter
150 ml/$\frac{1}{4}$ pint water
100 g/4 oz plain flour
salt and pepper
2 eggs, separated
225 g/8 oz cooked smoked fish, flaked
3 tablespoons lemon juice
2 tablespoons chopped capers
oil for frying
300 ml/$\frac{1}{2}$ pint white sauce (page 186)

1 Place the butter and water in a saucepan and heat until the butter melts. Cool to lukewarm.

2 Sift the flour, a pinch of salt and $\frac{1}{4}$ teaspoon pepper into a bowl. Add the egg yolks and the butter mixture and beat until the batter is smooth. Stir in the fish, 1 tablespoon of the lemon juice and the capers. Whisk the egg whites until stiff and fold in.

3 Drop spoonfuls of the mixture into hot oil, a few at a time, and fry until golden brown and crisp. Drain well on kitchen paper.

4 Meanwhile, heat the white sauce with the remaining lemon juice and season well. Serve with the hot fish puffs. **Serves 4**

Thatched Sausage Bake

SUPPER

675 g/1$\frac{1}{2}$ lb potatoes
2 teaspoons dry mustard
450 g/1 lb pork sausagemeat
$\frac{1}{2}$ teaspoon dried sage
150 ml/$\frac{1}{4}$ pint natural yogurt
50 g/2 oz Cheddar cheese, grated

1 Parboil the potatoes in salted water for about 5 minutes, until beginning to soften. Drain and cut into slices.

2 Mix the mustard with just enough water to make a paste and add to the sausagemeat with the sage. Blend in evenly. Spread this mixture over the base of a shallow ovenproof dish. Spoon over the yogurt, cover with the potato slices and sprinkle with the cheese.

3 Bake in a moderately hot oven (190 C, 375 F, gas 5) for 35 minutes. **Serves 4**

Beefy Pop~over

100 g/4 oz plain flour
pinch of salt
1 egg
300 ml/½ pint milk
50 g/2 oz dripping or lard
350 g/12 oz minced beef
1 large onion, grated
75 g/3 oz fresh breadcrumbs
salt and pepper
1 teaspoon dried mixed herbs
1 egg, beaten

1 Sift the flour and salt into a bowl. Add the egg and half the milk and beat well until smooth. Beat in the remaining milk. Allow to stand.

2 Place the dripping in a roasting tin and melt in a moderately hot oven (200 C, 400 F, gas 6).

3 Combine the remaining ingredients to form twelve meatballs. Arrange these evenly in the roasting tin and bake for 10· minutes.

4 Pour the batter over the meatballs and return to the oven for about 30 minutes, until well risen and golden brown. **Serves 4**

Cheese~crusted Fish

4 (175-g/6-oz) portions white fish fillet
75 g/3 oz butter
1 large onion, chopped
1 large leek, chopped
salt and pepper
4 tablespoons toasted breadcrumbs
50 g/2 oz Cheddar cheese, grated

1 Place the fish portions side by side in a greased shallow ovenproof dish. Melt the butter and fry the onion and leek until golden. Drain the vegetables and spoon over the fish. Season to taste.

2 Combine the breadcrumbs and cheese with the buttery juices and spread over the onion and leek.

3 Bake in a moderately hot oven (200 C, 400 F, gas 6) for 25–20 minutes, until the fish is cooked and the cheese crust is golden brown. **Serves 4**

Rice Ring with Brussel Sprouts

100 g/4 oz long-grain rice
175 g/6 oz white bread
75 g/3 oz butter, melted
300 ml/½ pint hot milk
350 g/12 oz Cheddar cheese, grated
3 eggs, beaten
1 small onion, grated
½ teaspoon dried mixed herbs
salt and pepper
450 g/1 lb Brussels sprouts
2 tablespoons flaked almonds, toasted

1 Cook the rice in boiling salted water for 12 to 15 minutes, until tender. Drain well. Meanwhile remove the crusts from the bread and cut into small even-sized dice. Combine all the ingredients except the Brussels sprouts and almonds and mix well. Pour into a large greased ring mould or ovenproof dish.

2 Place the mould in a roasting tin half filled with warm water and bake in a moderate oven (180 C, 350 F, gas 4) for 1 hour, or until brown on top.

3 Meanwhile cook the prepared sprouts in boiling salted water until just tender. Drain well.

4 Loosen the edges of the ring mould and turn out on to a warm serving dish. Pile the sprouts in the centre, and sprinkle with the toasted almonds. **Serves 4**

March

A hot soup is welcome in the crisp cool days
which herald early spring

Bright and showery days alternate in this exhilarating month when it can be bitterly cold and deceptively mild by turns. But it is the beginning of spring and just the right time to shop for lamb, so here we have plenty of good lamb recipes including a seasonal hotpot with kidneys as well. If you are beginning to find root vegetables monotonous, shop around for broccoli, cabbage and spring greens to bulk out the main course, but keep your eyes open also for the appearance of tiny new potatoes and that early spring taste-treat, a bunch of delicate young carrots. Fortunately, pale pink 'forced' rhubarb should be available to give excitement to puddings and sweets. It deserves more than the stewed fruit treatment – try it as suggested here, combined with ginger or with apple. If you are not having turkey for Easter Sunday lunch, make the appropriate choice of a leg of lamb; cooked en croûte, nothing could be nicer.

Bacon and Chicken Liver Rolls with Mushrooms

— BREAKFAST —

225 g/8 oz chicken livers
salt and pepper
8 small rashers streaky bacon
25 g/1 oz lard or bacon dripping
225 g/8 oz button mushrooms

1 Divide the chicken livers into eight equal portions. Sprinkle with salt and pepper. Roll each in a bacon rasher, and thread four rolls on to a short skewer, making sure that the rolls are secured. Thread the remaining four rolls on to a second skewer.

2 Melt the fat in a frying pan, add the skewers, and fry gently, turning several times with cooking tongs until the bacon is crisp, about 8 minutes. Drain and place on a warm plate.

3 Add the mushrooms to the pan, and toss over moderate heat until just cooked on all sides.

4 Carefully remove the skewers, pressing off the bacon rolls with a fork. Serve each person with 2 bacon rolls and some mushrooms. **Serves 4**

Lemon Curd Toasts

— BREAKFAST —

4 large slices brown bread
a little butter
2–4 tablespoons lemon curd (page 178)

1 Lightly toast the slices of brown bread on one side. Spread the untoasted side very sparingly with butter and then thickly with lemon curd. Place under a hot grill for about 2 minutes, until the lemon curd is bubbling and hot. Serve cut into fingers. **Serves 4**

Chicken Liver Terrine

— FIRST COURSE —

(*Illustrated on page 41*)

225 g/8 oz streaky bacon
225 g/8 oz chicken livers
100 g/4 oz pork sausagemeat
50 g/2 oz fresh white breadcrumbs
2 tablespoons lemon juice
grated rind of 1 lemon
175 g/6 oz cooked chicken meat, diced
salt and pepper

1 Remove the rind from the bacon and stretch the rashers with the back of a knife. Use to line a 0.5-kg/1-lb loaf tin.

2 Finely chop the livers and combine with the sausagemeat. Soak the breadcrumbs in the lemon juice and work evenly into the sausagemeat mixture with the lemon rind. Press half this mixture into the prepared tin, then cover with the chicken. Season generously and top with the remaining sausagemeat mixture. Press down evenly.

3 Cover with foil, place in a roasting tin half-filled with warm water and cook in a moderate oven (180 C, 350 F, gas 4) for $1\frac{3}{4}$ hours.

4 Cool and leave until the terrine shrinks away from the sides of the tin. Turn out and serve with crusty French bread. **Serves 4–6**

Chilled Carrot Cream

FIRST COURSE

25 g/1 oz butter
1 small onion, sliced
2 cloves garlic, crushed
450 g/1 lb carrots, chopped
900 ml/1½ pints chicken stock
salt and pepper
150 ml/¼ pint double cream
fried bread croûtons to garnish

1 Melt the butter, add the onion and garlic, cover the pan and cook until soft. Add the carrot and cook, covered, for about 5 minutes. Add the stock and bring to the boil, stirring. Cover and simmer over a low heat for about 25 minutes, until the carrot is soft.

2 Liquidise the soup or press through a sieve, season to taste and allow to cool. Whip the cream until beginning to thicken and fold into the carrot mixture. Taste and add more seasoning if necessary. Chill and serve in bowls garnished with croûtons. **Serves 4**

Bacon and Celery Soup

FIRST COURSE

25 g/1 oz butter
175 g/6 oz streaky bacon rashers chopped
1 small head celery, sliced
1 small onion, chopped
450 g/1 lb potatoes, sliced
1 litre/1¾ pints chicken stock
150 ml/¼ pint single cream
salt and pepper

1 Melt the butter in a large heavy-based saucepan and use to fry two-thirds of the bacon, the celery and onion for 2 minutes. Cover and cook gently for 10 minutes. Add the potato and stock and bring to the boil, stirring. Lower the heat, cover and simmer for 30 minutes.

2 Meanwhile, fry the remaining bacon gently until crisp. Drain on kitchen paper.

3 Liquidise the soup or press through a sieve and return to the pan. Blend in the cream and reheat but do not allow to boil. Taste and adjust the seasoning.

4 Serve portions of the soup piping hot, garnished with the bacon pieces. **Serves 4-6**

Chicken Mousse Towers

FIRST COURSE

2 teaspoons powdered gelatine
300 ml/½ pint hot strong chicken stock
225 g/8 oz cooked chicken meat, minced
½ teaspoon finely grated lemon rind
150 ml/¼ pint double cream
salt and pepper
finely shredded lettuce

1 Dissolve the gelatine in the hot stock and add two thirds of this mixture to the chicken with the lemon rind. Allow to cool until beginning to thicken. Keep the remaining jellied stock warm to prevent it setting.

2 Whip the cream until thick but not stiff. Fold into the chicken mixture and season well. Divide between four rinsed dariole moulds and chill in the refrigerator until set. Pour the remaining jellied stock on top and return to the refrigerator until firmly set.

3 Arrange a bed of lettuce on a serving dish and unmould the mousses on to this. **Serves 4**

Spinach Custard Tartlets

FIRST COURSE

350 g/12 oz shortcrust pastry (page 184)
filling
2 eggs, separated
225 g/8 oz well-drained spinach purée
225 g/8 oz cottage cheese, sieved
2 tablespoons grated Parmesan cheese
¼ teaspoon grated nutmeg
4 tablespoons single cream
salt and freshly ground black pepper

1 Roll out the pastry and use to line 12 deep patty tins.

2 Beat the egg yolks with the spinach purée, cottage cheese, Parmesan, nutmeg and cream. Season well to taste. Whisk the egg whites until stiff and fold into the spinach mixture.

3 Spoon into the pastry cases and bake in a moderately hot oven (190 C, 375 F, gas 5) for about 25 minutes, or until the pastry is golden and the filling well risen and browned. Serve hot. **Makes 12**

Smoked fish bake and Mustard-glazed chicken (page 43)

Smoked Fish Bake

MAIN COURSE

(Illustrated on page 40)

450 g/1 lb smoked cod, haddock or whiting
25 g/1 oz butter
100 g/4 oz button mushrooms, sliced
300 ml/½ pint white sauce (page 186)
450 g/1 lb freshly boiled potatoes, diced
100 g/4 oz Cheddar cheese, grated
salt and freshly ground black pepper

1 Place the fish in a saucepan and add sufficient water to cover. Poach for 20 minutes, until the fish is cooked. Drain and reserve the stock. Remove any skin and bones from the fish and flake roughly.

2 Melt the butter and fry the mushrooms lightly. Add these to the white sauce with the fish and 250 ml/8 fl oz of the reserved stock. Fold in the hot diced potato and half the cheese. Taste and season carefully. Pour the fish mixture into a greased ovenproof pie dish and sprinkle with the remaining cheese.

3 Bake in a hot oven (220 C, 425 F, gas 7) for 20 minutes. **Serves 4**

Veal Casserole with Chinese Leaves

MAIN COURSE

50 g/2 oz butter
450 g/1 lb stewing veal, cubed
1 medium onion, sliced
175 g/6 oz elbow macaroni
2 teaspoons soy sauce
600 ml/1 pint beef stock
2 teaspoons cornflour
175 g/6 oz Chinese leaves
salt and pepper

1 Melt the butter and fry the veal until sealed on all sides. Remove the meat to an ovenproof casserole. Add the onion to the pan and stir over a brisk heat for 2 minutes. Remove with a slotted draining spoon and place in the casserole with the meat. Stir in the dry macaroni, the soy sauce and the stock.

2 Cover and cook in a moderate oven (180 C, 350 F, gas 4) for 1 hour.

3 Moisten the cornflour with a little cold water, stir well into the casserole. Chop the Chinese leaves roughly and add to the casserole. Return to the oven for a further 15 minutes. Taste and season if necessary before serving. **Serves 4**

Chicken liver terrine (page 38)

Roast Pork with Souffléed Vegetables

MAIN COURSE

1 (1-kg/2¼-lb) boned hand of pork joint
300 ml/½ pint dry cider
salt and pepper
450 g/1 lb floury potatoes, sliced
450 g/1 lb carrots, sliced
1 small onion, grated
2 egg yolks
1 teaspoon dried sage
2 teaspoons cornflour
1 teaspoon yeast extract

1 Score the skin of the pork, place the joint in a roasting tin and pour over the cider. Allow to stand for at least 2 hours. Sprinkle with salt and roast in a moderately hot oven (190 C, 375 F, gas 5) for 45 minutes.

2 Meanwhile, cook the potato and carrot in boiling salted water until tender. Drain well and mash until smooth. Beat in the onion, egg yolks, sage and plenty of seasoning.

3 Take 2 tablespoons fat from the roasting tin and place in an ovenproof pie dish. Turn in the vegetable mixture and place the dish on a shelf beneath the joint. Continue cooking the joint and vegetables for a further 35 minutes.

4 Spoon out most of the pork fat from the roasting tin, leaving the meat juices. Strain these into a saucepan and make up to about 450 ml/¾ pint with water. Moisten the cornflour, add to the pan with the yeast extract and bring to the boil, stirring constantly. Simmer for 2 minutes, adjust the seasoning if necessary, then pour into a sauce boat and serve with the roast. **Serves 6**

Braised Bacon with Sherry Gravy

MAIN COURSE

1 (1-kg/2-2¼-lb) bacon collar joint
25 g/1 oz lard
1 large carrot, chopped
1 medium parsnip, chopped
1 medium turnip, chopped
1 large onion, chopped
salt and pepper
2 teaspoons cornflour
2 tablespoons dry sherry

1 Soak the joint overnight in cold water to cover. Drain well and dry with kitchen paper.

2 Melt the lard, add the joint and brown all over in the hot fat. Remove from the pan. Add the vegetables to the fat remaining in the pan and fry for 5 minutes. Turn this mixture into an ovenproof casserole and place the joint on top. Season well and pour in sufficient boiling water to come halfway up the sides of the joint. Cover and cook in a moderate oven (180 C, 350 F, gas 4) for 1¾ hours.

3 Remove the joint, strip off the skin and place on a warm serving dish. Strain the liquid from the casserole into a saucepan and skim off excess fat. Blend the cornflour with the sherry. Add to the pan and bring to the boil, stirring constantly. Boil for 2 minutes and season carefully. Serve the joint, vegetables and gravy separately. **Serves 4**

VARIATION

Braised bacon with Madeira gravy Substitute 2 tablespoons Madeira for the sherry and add 2 teaspoons redcurrant jelly to the liquid from the casserole. Whisk till the jelly melts before adding the cornflour.

Lamb and Apple Casserole

MAIN COURSE

450 g/1 lb potatoes, sliced
1 large cooking apple, peeled
1 large onion sliced
675 g/1½ lb best end of neck lamb cutlets
1 clove garlic, crushed
pinch of dried rosemary
grated rind of 1 lemon
450 ml/¾ pint beef stock
salt and pepper
chopped parsley to garnish

1 Parboil the potato in boiling salted water for 5 minutes. Drain. Core and thickly slice the apple.

2 Layer the potato, apple and onion with the cutlets in an ovenproof casserole. Mix together the garlic, rosemary, lemon rind and stock. Season well and pour into the casserole.

3 Cover and cook in a moderate oven (180 C, 350 F, gas 4) for 1¼ hours, or until the meat and potatoes are tender. Adjust the seasoning and serve sprinkled with plenty of chopped parsley. **Serves 4**

VARIATION

Lamb and plum casserole Substitute 4 large halved and stoned plums for the apple and use the grated rind of 1 orange instead of the lemon rind.

Sweet and Spicy Lamb

———— MAIN COURSE ————

50 g/2 oz butter
4 large lamb chops
1 (425-g/15-oz) can pineapple chunks
1 medium onion, chopped
2 large carrots, sliced
2 teaspoons brown sugar
1 tablespoon Worcestershire sauce
salt and pepper
1 tablespoon cornflour

1   Melt the butter and brown the chops on both sides. Add the pineapple chunks with the syrup from the can, the onion, carrot, sugar, Worcestershire sauce and seasoning to taste. Bring to the boil, stirring constantly. Reduce the heat, cover and simmer for 20 minutes, until the chops are tender.

2   Moisten the cornflour with a little cold water, add to the pan and stir until the sauce boils. Cook for a further 3 minutes. Check and adjust the seasoning if necessary. **Serves 4**

Note You can use fresh pineapple instead of canned but add extra water and brown sugar to taste as a substitute for the syrup.

Lamb and Kidney Hotpot

———— MAIN COURSE ————

2 lamb's kidneys
350 g/12 oz boneless lamb, diced
25 g/1 oz seasoned flour
25 g/1 oz dripping
1 medium onion, chopped
450 ml/¾ pint chicken stock
1 tablespoon brown table sauce
salt and pepper
675 g/1½ lb potatoes
1 tablespoon oil

1   Skin, core and slice the kidneys. Coat the kidney and lamb in seasoned flour. Melt the dripping and fry the onion until soft. Add the kidney and lamb to the pan and fry briskly until sealed. Stir in any remaining seasoned flour. Blend in the stock, brown sauce and seasoning, and bring to the boil, stirring constantly. Transfer the mixture to an ovenproof dish.

2   Thinly slice the potatoes and arrange, overlapping, on the lamb mixture. Brush with oil and cook in a moderately hot oven (190 C, 375 F, gas 5) for 1 hour, or until the potatoes are cooked and golden brown. **Serves 4**

VARIATION

Lamb, kidney and mushroom hotpot Add 100 g/4 oz button mushrooms to the pan with the stock and use 1 tablespoon tomato ketchup instead of the brown table sauce.

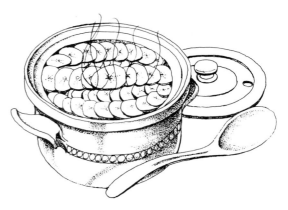

Mustard-glazed Chicken

———— MAIN COURSE ————

(*Illustrated on page 40*)

4 chicken portions
50 g/2 oz butter
1–2 teaspoons clear honey
½ teaspoon dried oregano
1 teaspoon tomato purée
1 teaspoon salt
2 tablespoons wholegrain mustard
½ teaspoon freshly ground black pepper
300 ml/½ pint chicken stock
2 teaspoons cornflour

1   Place the chicken portions, skin side downwards, in the grill pan. Cook under moderate heat for about 20 minutes. Meanwhile, cream together the butter, honey, oregano, tomato purée, salt, mustard and pepper. Turn the chicken portions and spread with the mustard glaze. Cook for a further 20 minutes, or until the chicken is cooked through, basting frequently with the juices in the pan. Place the chicken on a warm serving dish and keep hot.

2   Pour the stock into the grill pan and stir well, scraping up all the pan juices. Strain into a small saucepan. Moisten the cornflour with a little cold water, add to the pan and bring to the boil, stirring constantly. Simmer over a low heat for 2 minutes, add extra seasoning if necessary, then pour into a sauce boat and hand separately with the chicken. **Serves 4**

Easter Sunday Lunch

Caramelised Pink Grapefruit

Lamb en Croûte

Broccoli in Lemon Butter

Rhubarb Kissel

Caramelised Pink Grapefruit

EASTER SUNDAY LUNCH

(Illustrated on page 44)

4 large pink grapefruit
50 ml/2 fl oz rum
25 g/1 oz butter
50 g/2 oz demerara sugar

1 Cut the grapefruit in half. Sprinkle each cut surface with rum and allow to stand for at least 15 minutes.

2 Heat the grill to its hottest setting. Melt the butter in a small saucepan and combine with the sugar. Spread this mixture over the cut grapefruit. Place under the grill until the topping bubbles and caramelises. **Serves 8**

Lamb en Croûte

EASTER SUNDAY LUNCH

(Illustrated on page 44)

1 (1.75-kg/3¾ to 4-lb) leg of lamb
salt and pepper
2 cloves garlic
3 tablespoons mint jelly
50 g/2 oz butter
675 g/1½ lb puff pastry (page 185)
1 egg, beaten

1 Trim the leg of lamb to a neat shape. Rub all over with salt and pepper. Cut the cloves of garlic into slivers. Make small slits over the leg of lamb with a sharp knife and press a sliver of garlic into each one. Stand the joint on a rack in a roasting tin. Spread the mint jelly over the surface and top with knobs of butter.

2 Roast in a moderately hot oven (190 C, 375 F, gas 5) for 1¼ hours. Allow the meat to cool completely.

3 Roll out the pastry quite thinly. Stand the joint in the centre of the pastry and fold over 'parcel fashion' to completely enclose the joint. Trim off excess pastry and seal the joins with beaten egg.

4 Bake in a moderately hot oven (200 C, 400 F, gas 6) for about 40 minutes, until well risen and golden brown.

5 Serve with Broccoli in lemon butter, creamed potatoes and extra mint jelly. A green salad may also be served, if liked. **Serves 8**

VARIATIONS
Lamb with rosemary Insert small sprigs of fresh rosemary into the lamb in place of the garlic, and use redcurrant jelly instead of the mint jelly.
Apricot-stuffed lamb Ask your butcher to bone the leg of lamb for you. Combine 75 g/3 oz fresh white breadcrumbs with 1 teaspoon dried marjoram, 1 tablespoon chopped chives, ½ teaspoon salt and ¼ teaspoon freshly ground black pepper. Stir in 150 ml/¼ pint boiling water and add 1 egg yolk and 100 g/4 oz dried apricots, chopped and plumped in boiling water, then drained. Fill the pocket in the lamb with the stuffing and sew up. Roast for the first 1¼ hours, glazing the joint with apricot jam in place of the mint jelly. Cool, enclose in pastry and cook as above.

Broccoli in Lemon Butter

EASTER SUNDAY LUNCH

(Illustrated on page 44)

1 kg/2 lb broccoli
50 g/2 oz butter
finely grated rind and juice of 1 lemon
salt and freshly ground black pepper

1 Cook the broccoli spears in boiling salted water until just tender. Drain well and place in a warm serving dish.

2 Soften the butter and beat in the lemon rind and juice. Season to taste and spoon over the hot broccoli. **Serves 8**

Rhubarb Kissel

EASTER SUNDAY LUNCH

(Illustrated on page 45)

1 kg/2 lb rhubarb
grated rind and juice of 1 orange
100 g/4 oz sugar
2 tablespoons cornflour
2 tablespoons brandy
150 ml/¼ pint double cream

1 Wash the rhubarb and chop roughly. Place in a pan with the orange rind and juice and the sugar. Cook gently until the rhubarb is soft. Moisten the cornflour with a little cold water and add to the rhubarb. Bring to the boil, stirring constantly.

2 Purée the rhubarb mixture in a liquidiser until smooth or press through a sieve. Add the brandy and allow to cool.

3 Pour the rhubarb kissel into a glass bowl. Lightly whip the cream and stir gently through the fruit to give a rippled effect. **Serves 8**

VARIATION

Ginger and rhubarb kissel Use 2 tablespoons ginger wine in place of the brandy, and stir 2 tablespoons chopped preserved stem ginger through the cooled kissel.

Beef and Paprika Pancakes

SUPPER OR SNACK

pancakes
100 g/4 oz plain flour
pinch of salt
1 egg
150 ml/¼ pint milk
150 ml/¼ pint water
oil for frying
filling
50 g/2 oz butter
40 g/1½ oz flour
450 ml/¾ pint beef stock
2 tablespoons vinegar
2 teaspoons paprika pepper
350 g/12 oz cooked minced beef
salt and pepper
1 tablespoon fresh white breadcrumbs

1 First make the pancakes. Sift the flour and salt into a bowl and make a well in the centre. Drop in the egg and add the milk. Beat well until smooth. Gradually add the water, beating all the time, until the batter is the consistency of thin cream.

2 Brush an omelette pan with oil and pour in about 2 tablespoons of batter. Cook until golden underneath, then turn and cook the other side. Repeat with the remaining batter, adding more oil to the pan only when necessary. Layer the pancakes with pieces of grease-proof or kitchen paper and keep them warm.

3 To make the filling, place the butter, flour and stock in a saucepan and whisk over moderate heat until the sauce boils and thickens. Stir in the vinegar, paprika, beef and seasoning to taste.

4 Fill the pancakes with the beef mixture, roll them up and place close together in a greased ovenproof dish. Spoon any remaining filling over the top and sprinkle with the breadcrumbs. Place under a moderate grill for about 10 minutes, until piping hot and the bread-crumbs are golden. **Serves 4**

Sausage and Vegetable Turnovers

SUPPER OR SNACK

350 g/12 oz shortcrust pastry (page 184)
2 medium potatoes
1 large onion, grated
1 large carrot, grated
1 teaspoon yeast extract
2 tablespoons boiling water
salt and pepper
450 g/1 lb large pork sausages
1 egg, beaten

1 Roll out the pastry thinly and cut into eight circles using a saucer as a guide. Finely dice the potatoes and combine with the onion, carrot, yeast extract, water and seasoning.

2 Place a sausage on one side of each pastry circle and divide the vegetable mixture between them. Brush the pastry edges with beaten egg, fold over and seal well together. Arrange the turnovers on a greased baking sheet and brush with beaten egg.

3 Bake in a moderately hot oven (190 C, 375 F, gas 5) for about 35 minutes, until golden brown. Serve hot with a salad. **Makes 8**

Mexicali Liver

SUPPER

1 medium red pepper, deseeded
2 tablespoons oil
1 medium onion, chopped
350 g/12 oz pig's liver, cut in strips
25 g/1 oz flour
1 (396-g/14-oz) can tomatoes
1 (220-g/7¾-oz) can red kidney beans, drained
2 teaspoons mild chilli powder
1 teaspoon dried mixed herbs
salt
225 g/8 oz tagliatelli

1 Chop the pepper. Heat the oil and fry the onion and pepper gently together until the onion is transparent. Add the liver and cook gently, stirring, until sealed on all sides. Stir in the flour and cook for 1 minute. Add the tomatoes with the juice from the can, the kidney beans, chilli powder and herbs. Bring to the boil, stirring constantly, then simmer for 10 minutes. Add salt to taste.

2 Meanwhile, cook the tagliatelli in plenty of boiling salted water until tender, about 10–12 minutes. Drain well and divide between four warm serving dishes. Spoon the liver mixture over. **Serves 4**

Fried Ham and Gherkin Sandwiches

SUPPER OR SNACK

8 slices white bread from a large sandwich loaf
4 small pickled gherkins, finely chopped
1 egg, beaten
75 g/3 oz Cheddar cheese, grated
4 slices lean ham
oil for frying

1 Trim the crusts from the slices of bread. Mix together the gherkin, egg and cheese and spread on the bread slices. Put them together, two at a time, with a slice of ham in between, and press well to seal.

2 Shallow fry, one at a time, in a little hot oil until golden brown on each side. Drain well on kitchen paper and serve hot, cut into quarters. **Serves 4**

Orange and almond pudding

Scalloped Bread Dice

SUPPER OR SNACK

50 g/2 oz butter
4 large slices white bread, diced
4 eggs, beaten
150 ml/¼ pint milk
100 g/4 oz Cheddar cheese, grated
1 large carrot, grated
2 tablespoons chopped parsley
¼ teaspoon grated nutmeg
salt and pepper

1 Melt the butter and fry the bread dice until golden brown. Transfer to an ovenproof pie dish. Beat together the eggs, milk, cheese, carrot, parsley and nutmeg with plenty of seasoning. Pour over the fried bread dice.

2 Cook in a moderate oven (180 C, 350 F, gas 4) for about 30 minutes, until set and golden brown on top. Serve immediately. **Serves 4**

Rhubarb Flapjack

DESSERT

1 large orange
675 g/1½ lb rhubarb, sliced
1 tablespoon flour
3 tablespoons raspberry jam
50 g/2 oz butter
2 tablespoons golden syrup
50 g/2 oz demerara sugar
100 g/4 oz rolled oats

1 Peel and chop the orange removing all the pith. Place in a greased ovenproof dish with the rhubarb. Sprinkle on the flour and stir in. Spread the jam over the rhubarb mixture as evenly as possible.

2 Melt the butter and syrup in a saucepan and stir in the sugar and oats. Spoon this mixture over the rhubarb to cover it completely.

3 Bake in a moderate oven (180 C, 350 F, gas 4) for 50 minutes, or until the rhubarb is tender and the topping crisp and golden brown. Serve warm with cream. **Serves 4**

Orange and Almond Pudding

DESSERT

(*Illustrated on page 48*)

100 g/4 oz soft margarine
100 g/4 oz castor sugar
2 eggs, beaten
grated rind and juice of 1 orange
100 g/4 oz self-raising flour, sifted
50 g/2 oz ground almonds
orange slices to decorate (optional)
sauce
2 teaspoons cornflour
300 ml/½ pint orange juice
1 tablespoon golden syrup

1 Cream the margarine and sugar together until soft and light. Gradually beat in the eggs and orange rind and juice, then fold in the flour and almonds. Pour the mixture into a greased 1.15-litre/2-pint pudding basin, cover with greased foil and steam over a pan of simmering water for 1½ hours.

2 Meanwhile make the sauce. Moisten the cornflour with a little of the orange juice. Place the remaining juice in a saucepan with the syrup and bring to boiling point. Add the moistened cornflour and bring back to the boil, stirring constantly. Simmer for 2 minutes and serve poured over the pudding. Decorate with orange slices, if using. **Serves 4**

Caramel Bananas with Rum

DESSERT

50 g/2 oz butter
175 g/6 oz light soft brown sugar
4 tablespoons single cream
4 tablespoons rum
4 bananas

1 Place the butter, sugar, cream and rum in a saucepan. Stir over gentle heat until the sugar has dissolved. Bring to the boil, reduce the heat and cook gently for about 4 minutes, or until the mixture forms a thick caramel sauce.

2 Peel the bananas and cut in half crossways, then split them lengthways. Add to the caramel and simmer for 3 minutes. Serve hot or allow to cool then chill for 30 minutes before serving. **Serves 4**

April
Hot cross buns and freshly made bread
reflect the scent of Easter baking

Here comes the sun at last to welcome the first fresh green shoots on the trees, and the shy emergence of our kitchen garden seedlings. This means home-grown spring onions, spinach and lettuce will soon be available. Eggs, of course, are abundant this month, so here are all sorts of egg dishes including pancakes and omelettes. It is also a month when poultry, which is good value for money all round the year, seems particularly appropriate. Try some of the delicious chicken liver recipes in this section. If there's to be a spring wedding or other celebration in the family, and the main dish must be cold, try Chicken tonnato or Chicken breasts in tarragon aspic as the centrepiece for the menu, with a rich cheesecake for the dessert.

Hot Cross Buns

BREAKFAST

(Illustrated on page 50)

450 g/1 lb strong white flour
1 teaspoon salt
50 g/2 oz butter
50 g/2 oz castor sugar
$\frac{1}{2}$ teaspoon mixed spice (optional)
100 g/4 oz currants
25 g/1 oz fresh yeast *or* 15 g/$\frac{1}{2}$ oz dried yeast
250 ml/8 fl oz lukewarm milk
1 egg, lightly beaten
50 g/2 oz plain flour
25 g/1 oz butter
glaze
50 g/2 oz sugar
150 ml/$\frac{1}{4}$ pint water

1 Sift the flour and salt into a bowl, add the butter and rub in until the mixture resembles fine breadcrumbs. Stir in the sugar, spice if used, and currants.

2 Cream the fresh yeast, if using, with a little of the milk, add the remaining milk and leave in a warm place until frothy. If using dried yeast, sprinkle it over the milk, stir gently then leave until frothy.

3 Add the yeast liquid to the dry ingredients together with the egg and mix well to form a dough. Knead thoroughly on a well-floured surface for approximately

10 minutes until smooth and elastic. Place the dough in a lightly oiled bowl, cover with cling film and leave to rise in a warm place for 40–50 minutes or until doubled in volume.

4 Knock back the dough by kneading lightly on a well-floured surface. Cut into twelve equal portions and shape each piece into a round bun. Place the buns well apart on greased baking trays, cover with lightly oiled cling film or polythene and leave to rise in a warm place for 15–20 minutes.

5 Sift the flour for the cross shapes into a bowl, add the butter and rub in lightly until the mixture resembles fine breadcrumbs. Mix to a soft pastry with a little cold water. Roll out the pastry and cut into thin strips. Form these into the shape of a cross on each bun.

6 Bake the buns in a moderately hot oven (200 C, 400 F, gas 6) for 15–20 minutes, until golden brown. Meanwhile make a sugar glaze by dissolving the sugar in the water over a low heat. Boil until a thick syrup is formed. Remove the hot buns to a wire rack and brush immediately with the sugar syrup. Serve warm with butter. **Makes 12**

Grilled Mustard Kidneys

BREAKFAST

8 lamb's kidneys
salt and pepper
50 g/2 oz butter
1 tablespoon prepared mustard
4 large slices white bread

1 Remove the skin from the kidneys and cut through carefully crossways, without quite separating. Sprinkle with salt and pepper on both sides.

2 Soften the butter and combine with the mustard. Spread over the kidneys to coat them thoroughly.

3 Place a sheet of foil on the grid of the grill pan, and arrange the kidneys on this, cut surfaces downwards to prevent them from curling up.

4 Cook under a moderate grill for about 8 minutes, turning the kidneys at least once, until they cooked through.

5 Remove to a warm plate, shape the foil into a funnel and pour the mustard butter over the kidneys.

6 Toast the bread on both sides and serve each person with two kidneys on a slice of toast. **Serves 4**

Minted Fennel Starters

— FIRST COURSE —

2 medium heads fennel
300 ml/$\frac{1}{2}$ pint chicken stock
2 teaspoons sugar
2 teaspoons concentrated mint sauce
3 tablespoons oil

1 Trim the heads of fennel and cut each one in half. Place in a saucepan with the stock and bring to the boil. Cover and simmer for about 20 minutes, or until just tender.

2 Dissolve the sugar in 2 tablespoons hot fennel stock, beat in the mint sauce and then the oil. Drain the cooked fennel well, pour over the mint dressing and allow to stand until cold, turning once.

3 Place each fennel half on a small plate, rounded side upwards, and spoon over any remaining dressing. **Serves 4**

Pasta Cocktail with Avocado Sauce

— FIRST COURSE —

175 g/6 oz large pasta shells
6 tablespoons French dressing (page 186)
1 large ripe avocado
grated rind and juice of 1 lemon
1 clove garlic, crushed
2 teaspoons castor sugar
4 tablespoons chicken stock
salt and pepper
1 canned red pimiento, diced
4 spring onions, chopped
2 tablespoons chopped parsley

1 Cook the pasta shells in plenty of boiling salted water for about 10 minutes, or until just tender. Drain well and stir the French dressing into the hot shells.

2 Halve and stone the avocado. Scoop out the flesh and purée in a liquidiser with the lemon rind and juice, garlic, sugar and stock. Taste and add salt and pepper if necessary. Stir in the pimiento, spring onion and parsley.

3 Fold the avocado sauce into the cooled pasta shells and serve in cocktail glasses. **Serves 4**

Tuna and Cod Cream

— FIRST COURSE —

(*Illustrated on page 54*)

15 g/$\frac{1}{2}$ oz powdered gelatine
2 tablespoons water
1 (198-g/7-oz) can tuna, mashed
175 g/6 oz cooked cod, mashed
300 ml/$\frac{1}{2}$ pint mayonnaise (page 186)
salt and pepper
1 (170-g/6-oz) can evaporated milk, chilled
1 tablespoon lemon juice
filling
2 teaspoons oil
2 teaspoons lemon juice
450 g/1 lb tomatoes, peeled and quartered
6 spring onions, chopped
garnish
cucumber slices
radish slices

1 Dissolve the gelatine in the water in a basin over a pan of hot water.

2 Combine the tuna and liquid from the can with the cod and mayonnaise and season well. Stir in the dissolved gelatine.

3 Whisk the evaporated milk with the lemon juice until thick, then fold into the fish mixture. Pour into a 1.15-litre/2-pint ring mould or shallow dish and chill until set.

4 Mix together the oil and lemon and toss the tomatoes and spring onions in the dressing. Fill the centre of the ring with the tomatoes and garnish with slices of radish and cucumber. **Serves 4**

Lemon Sole in Spinach Sauce

MAIN COURSE

225 g/8 oz spinach
25 g/1 oz butter
350 ml/¾ pint milk
15 g/½ oz flour
salt and pepper
4 (175-g/6-oz) lemon sole fillets
100 g/4 oz shelled prawns
25 g/1 oz cheese, grated
25 g/1 oz dry breadcrumbs

1 Wash the spinach well and cook gently in the water clinging to the leaves for 5 minutes, or until tender. Drain and sieve or purée in a liquidiser.

2 Combine the butter, milk and flour in a saucepan and whisk over moderate heat until the sauce thickens. Cook for 1 minute, stir in the spinach and season.

3 Season the fish fillets and fold each one over. Arrange them in alternate directions in a well-buttered shallow ovenproof dish. Sprinkle over the prawns and pour the spinach sauce evenly on top. Scatter the cheese and breadcrumbs over the surface.

4 Cover lightly with foil and cook in a moderately hot oven (190 C, 375 F, gas 5) for 20 minutes. Remove the cover and cook for a further 5–10 minutes, until the topping is golden brown. **Serves 4**

Casseroled Lamb Noisettes

MAIN COURSE

8 lamb cutlets
25 g/1 oz seasoned flour
2 tablespoons oil
½ green pepper, deseeded
1 large onion, sliced
1 tablespoon brown sugar
1 teaspoon French mustard
300 ml/½ pint orange juice
garnish
1 small orange
sprigs of watercress

1 Remove the bone from each cutlet and shape the meat into a neat round. Tie securely with string. Coat the noisettes with seasoned flour. Heat the oil and fry the chops until sealed on both sides. Remove from the pan and keep hot. Cut the pepper into strips and add to the fat remaining in the pan with the onion. Fry for 2 minutes. Stir in the sugar, mustard and orange juice and bring to the boil, stirring constantly.

2 Return the noisettes to the pan and baste with the sauce. Bring back to the boil, cover and simmer for about 30 minutes, until the noisettes are tender. Place the noisettes on a warm serving dish, remove the string and spoon over the pan juices and vegetables. Garnish with orange wedges and sprigs of watercress. **Serves 4**

Tuna and cod cream (page 53)

Turkey kebabs with raisin rice (page 56)
and Spring soufflé omelette (page 57)

Three-meat Family Loaf

MAIN COURSE

175 g/6 oz chicken livers
3 spring onions, chopped
225 g/8 oz pork sausagemeat
225 g/8 oz minced beef
2 teaspoons dried mixed herbs
1 teaspoon salt
$\frac{1}{2}$ teaspoon pepper
4 tablespoons strong beef stock
12 stuffed green olives, sliced

1 Place the livers in a saucepan with water to cover and poach until just firm. Drain well and mince, or purée in a liquidiser, with the onion. Mix well with all the remaining ingredients and press into a well-greased 0.5-kg/1-lb loaf tin.

2 Stand the tin in a roasting tin half-filled with hot water and bake in a moderate oven (180 C, 350 F, gas 4) for 1$\frac{1}{4}$ hours. Turn out the loaf and serve hot or cold. **Serves 4–6**

Duckling with Green Pea Sauce

MAIN COURSE

1 (1.7-kg/4-lb) duckling
salt
2 tablespoons clear jellied marmalade (page 178)
2 teaspoons lemon juice
sauce
25 g/1 oz flour
$\frac{1}{4}$ teaspoon ground mace
225 g/8 oz shelled or frozen peas
6 outside lettuce leaves
$\frac{1}{2}$ teaspoon dried mixed herbs
1 sprig fresh mint
1 tablespoon double cream
salt and freshly ground black pepper

1 Simmer the giblets in lightly salted water to cover for 30 minutes. Strain the stock and reserve.

2 Prick the skin of the duckling lightly with a fork and sprinkle with salt. Place on a grid in a roasting tin and cook in a moderately hot oven (200 C, 400 F, gas 6) for 1 hour.

3 To prepare the glaze, heat the marmalade with half the lemon juice and beat until blended.

4 Remove the bird from the oven and spoon 2 tablespoons of the duck fat into a saucepan for the sauce. Spoon the glaze over the duckling and return to the oven for a further 30 minutes.

5 Meanwhile, make the sauce. Stir the flour into the duck fat and cook for 1 minute. Gradually add 450 ml/$\frac{3}{4}$ pint of the reserved stock, the rest of the lemon juice and the mace and bring to the boil, stirring. Add the peas, lettuce and herbs, cover and cook gently for 20 minutes. Remove the mint and purée the sauce in a liquidiser or press through a sieve. Return to the pan, stir in the cream, season to taste and reheat.

5 Drain off the juices, place the duckling on a warm dish and hand the sauce separately. **Serves 4**

Turkey Kebabs with Raisin Rice

MAIN COURSE

(Illustrated on page 55)

450 g/1 lb boned turkey or chicken
2 tablespoons soy sauce
$\frac{1}{2}$ teaspoon ground ginger
$\frac{1}{2}$ teaspoon dry mustard
juice of 1 lemon
1 clove garlic, crushed
3 tablespoons dry sherry
salt and pepper
12 pickling onions
2 green peppers, roughly chopped
225 g/8 oz long-grain rice
600 ml/1 pint turkey or chicken stock
75 g/3 oz seedless raisins
2 tablespoons chopped parsley

1 Cut the turkey into 2.5-cm/1-inch cubes. Mix together the soy sauce, ginger, mustard, lemon juice, garlic, sherry and seasoning. Pour this marinade over the turkey. Cover and chill for about 3 hours.

2 Drain the turkey from the marinade and thread on to four kebab skewers together with the onions and green pepper. Cook under a moderately hot grill, turning frequently, for about 15 minutes. Baste with the marinade during cooking.

3 Meanwhile, place the rice and stock in a saucepan and bring to the boil. Stir once, cover and simmer for 7 minutes. Add the raisins and season to taste. Bring back to boiling point, cover and continue cooking for another 5 minutes, or until the rice is tender.

4 Fork up the rice, stir in the chopped parsley and place on a warm serving dish. Arrange the kebab skewers on top and serve hot. **Serves 4**

Turkey and Ham Cassoulet

—— MAIN COURSE ——

100 g/4 oz dried haricot beans
1 clove garlic, crushed
1 bouquet garni
50 g/2 oz butter
1 medium onion, chopped
1 tablespoon tomato purée
300 ml/½ pint turkey or chicken stock
225 g/8 oz cooked turkey meat diced
225 g/8 oz ham, diced
salt and pepper
50 g/2 oz fresh breadcrumbs

1 Place the beans in a saucepan and add cold water to cover. Allow to soak overnight. The following day, cover with fresh water and add the garlic and bouquet garni. Bring to the boil, cover and simmer for about 2 hours, or until the beans are tender but not mushy.

2 Meanwhile, melt half the butter and fry the onion until soft. Stir in the tomato purée and stock. Bring to the boil and add the turkey and ham. Cook gently for 10 minutes.

3 Drain the beans, season to taste and place a layer in the bottom of a well-greased casserole. Spoon over some of the turkey mixture and continue filling the dish with layers, ending with turkey mixture. Cover the surface with the breadcrumbs and dot with the rest of the butter.

4 Place in a moderately hot oven (190 C, 375 F, gas 5) for 30 minutes, until the crumb topping is crisp and golden brown. Serve straight from the casserole. **Serves 4**

VARIATION
Bacon and chicken cassoulet Substitute 225 g/8 oz diced boiled bacon and 225 g/8 oz diced cooked chicken for the ham and turkey.

Spring Soufflé Omelette

—— SUPPER OR SNACK ——

175 g/6 oz cottage cheese
4 eggs, separated
salt and pepper
4 spring onions, chopped
20 g/¾ oz butter
chopped parsley to garnish

1 Beat the cottage cheese into the egg yolks and season well. Stir in the onion. Whisk the egg whites until stiff and fold quickly into the egg yolk mixture.

2 Melt the butter in a large frying pan until foamy. Turn in the egg mixture and level the top. Cook gently for 6–7 minutes until golden brown underneath. Slip the frying pan under a moderately hot grill and cook for 4–5 minutes until the omelette is well risen and golden brown on top. Serve hot, cut in half and sprinkled with parsley, with a green salad. **Serves 2**

VARIATION
Mushroom soufflé omelette (*Illustrated on page 55*) Lightly sauté 100 g/4 oz button mushrooms in 25 g/1 oz butter to top the omelette before serving.

Ham and Broccoli Pancakes

—— SUPPER OR SNACK ——

350 g/12 oz broccoli spears
175 g/6 oz ham, thinly sliced
1 (326-g/11½-oz) can sweet corn kernels, drained
8 cooked pancakes (page 47)
175 g/6 oz Cheddar cheese, grated
300 ml/½ pint cheese sauce (page 186)

1 Cook the broccoli in boiling salted water to cover until just tender. Drain and chop roughly. Cut the ham into strips and mix with the broccoli and sweet corn.

2 Divide this mixture between the pancakes and sprinkle with half the cheese. Roll up the pancakes and place side by side in a shallow ovenproof dish. Spoon over the cheese sauce and sprinkle with the remaining cheese. Bake in a moderate oven (180 C, 350 F, gas 4) for 15 minutes. **Serves 4**

VARIATION
Corn and cauliflower pancakes Instead of the broccoli spears substitute 350 g/12 oz cauliflower florets and add ¼ teaspoon grated nutmeg to the cheese sauce before pouring over the pancakes.

Spring Wedding Breakfast

Jellied Beef Consommé

•

Miniature Bread Knots

•

Chicken Breasts in Tarragon Aspic

•

Chicken Tonnato

•

Mocha Cheesecake

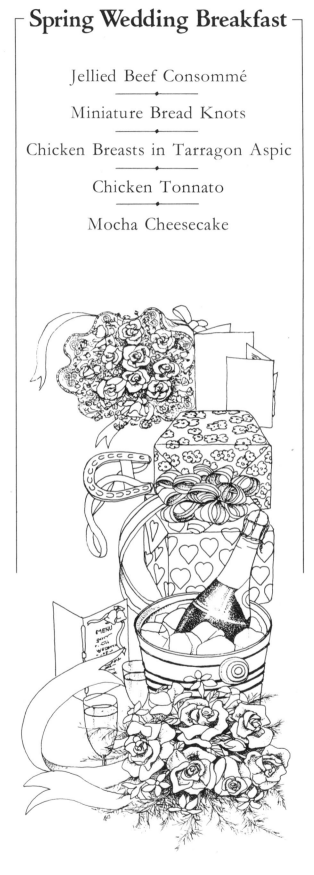

Jellied Beef Consommé

SPRING WEDDING BREAKFAST

(Illustrated on page 58)

10 (425-g/15-oz) cans consommé
600 ml/1 pint dry sherry
150 g/5 oz gelatine
garnish
bunch of radishes, trimmed
sprigs of parsley

1 Heat the consommé gently then add the sherry.

2 Dissolve the gelatine in 300 ml/½ pint hot water in a basin over a pan of boiling water. Add to the consommé, stirring well, and chill until set.

3 Roughly chop the jellied consommé and divide between individual serving dishes. Garnish with thinly sliced radishes and sprigs of parsley. **Serves 20**

Miniature Bread Knots

SPRING WEDDING BREAKFAST

(Illustrated on page 58)

1 Make up 1.5 kg/3 lb of milk bread dough (page 182).

2 Pinch off pieces of dough weighing about 25 g/1 oz. Roll each into a sausage shape and tie in a single knot. Arrange the 'knots' on greased baking sheets, cover with oiled polythene and allow to rise in a warm place until doubled in size. Brush the rolls with milk and sprinkle with poppy seeds. Bake in a hot oven (220 C, 425 F, gas 7) for 15–20 minutes, until golden brown. **Serves 20**

VARIATION

Sesame shapes Form each portion of dough into a sausage as above, then curve into an 'S' shape and place on greased baking sheets. Cover and allow to rise until doubled in size, then brush with beaten egg and sprinkle with sesame seeds. Baking time will probably be only 15 rather than 20 minutes.

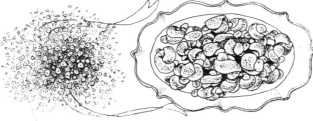

Chicken Breasts in Tarragon Aspic

SPRING WEDDING BREAKFAST

20 boned chicken breast portions
750 ml/1¼ pints strong chicken stock
450 ml/¾ pint ruby port
2 tablespoons paprika pepper
fresh tarragon leaves
900 ml/1½ pints liquid aspic jelly
(made from packet crystals)
shredded lettuce
lemon slices

1 Form the chicken breasts into neat oval shapes by tucking irregular edges underneath. Arrange them side by side in 2 large roasting tins.

2 Heat the stock and port with the paprika to boiling point and stir well. Pour over the chicken breasts and cover each tin with foil. Cook in a moderately hot oven (190 C, 375 F, gas 5) for 30 minutes.

3 Strain the liquid from both roasting tins into a saucepan and reduce, by rapid boiling if necessary, to make 450 ml/¾ pint. Spoon a little of the reduced liquid over each chicken breast, cover again and leave until cold.

4 Spread the chicken breasts out on racks over trays for coating. Arrange 3 tarragon leaves diagonally across the centre of each chicken breast. Allow the aspic jelly to become syrupy and then spoon it carefully over each breast to coat. Leave until set.

5 Serve on a bed of shredded lettuce and garnish with thin slices of lemon. **Serves 20**

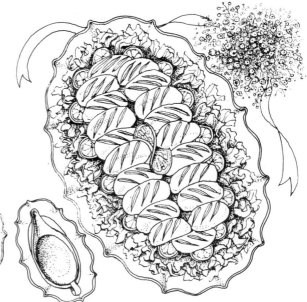

Chicken Tonnato

(Illustrated on page 58)

4 large roasting chickens
600 ml/1 pint white wine
600 ml/1 pint chicken stock
2 medium onions, sliced
bouquet garni
600 ml/1 pint mayonnaise (page 186)
grated rind and juice of 1 lemon
3 cloves garlic, crushed
3 (198-g/7-oz) cans tuna, drained
4 tablespoons capers
3 (56-g/2-oz) cans anchovies, drained
salt and pepper
garnish
4 tablespoons chopped parsley
rind of 1 lemon

1 Place the chickens in one or two large roasting tins. Add the wine, stock, onion and bouquets garnis. Cover with foil and cook in a moderate oven (180 C, 350 F, gas 4) for 2 hours.

2 Meanwhile, make the sauce. Place the mayonnaise, lemon rind and juice, garlic, tuna, capers and anchovies in a liquidiser and purée until smooth. Do this in batches if your liquidiser is not sufficiently large. Adjust the seasoning.

3 When the chickens are cool, remove all the flesh from the bones in quite large pieces, discarding the skin. Arrange the chicken meat on two large plates.

4 Add sufficient of the strained chicken cooking liquid to the sauce to give a coating consistency. Spoon the sauce evenly over the chicken and chill thoroughly.

5 Garnish with chopped parsley and thinly pared strips of lemon rind. Serve with a green salad and the miniature bread knots. **Serves 20**

VARIATIONS
Egg tonnato Make up the tonnato sauce as above, adding chicken stock or wine to thin the sauce. Spoon over 30 halved hard-boiled eggs instead of the chicken.
Plaice tonnato Poach 40 rolled plaice fillets. Spoon the tonnato sauce, thinned with the fish poaching liquid, over the cooked and cooled plaice fillets.

Mocha Cheesecake

(Illustrated on page 58)

base
225 g/8 oz margarine
175 g/6 oz castor sugar
450 g/1 lb plain chocolate digestive biscuits, crushed
cheesecake mixture
1 kg/2 lb cream cheese
8 eggs, separated
600 ml/1 pint soured cream
50 g/2 oz powdered gelatine
150 ml/$\frac{1}{4}$ pint hot water
150 ml/$\frac{1}{4}$ pint strong black coffee
1 tablespoon coffee essence
350 g/12 oz castor sugar
decoration
whipped cream
chocolate caraque

1 Grease two 25-cm/10-inch loose-bottomed cake tins. To make the crumb base, melt the margarine and stir in the sugar and crushed biscuit. Press this mixture evenly over the bases of both tins. Chill.

2 To make the cheesecake mixture, beat the cream cheese with the egg yolks and soured cream until smooth. Dissolve the gelatine in the hot water, then cool and mix with the coffee and coffee essence. Beat into the cheese mixture. Whisk the egg whites until stiff. Add the sugar and whisk again until thick. Fold the meringue into the cheese mixture.

3 Spoon the cheese mixture evenly over the biscuit bases and chill until set.

4 Unmould the cheesecakes carefully and serve decorated with swirls of whipped cream and chocolate caraque. **Serves 20**

VARIATIONS
Black Forest cheesecake Substitute 450 g/1 lb digestive biscuits for the plain chocolate digestive biscuits. Use 150 ml/$\frac{1}{4}$ pint Maraschino or brandy in place of the coffee and coffee essence. Top the set cheesecakes with fresh cherries poached in syrup and thickened with cornflour.
Lemon and ginger cheesecake Use crushed gingernuts for the base and substitute 150 ml/$\frac{1}{4}$ pint lemon juice for the black coffee and coffee essence. Top the cheesecakes with a thick layer of whipped cream and decorate with crystallised lemon slices.

Sherried Apple Dumplings

DESSERT

2 tablespoons sweet sherry
1 tablespoon castor sugar
50 g/2 oz sultanas
4 small cooking apples
100 g/4 oz almond paste
450 g/1 lb shortcrust pastry (page 184)
1 egg, beaten

1 Place the sherry in a covered container with the castor sugar and sultanas. Allow to soak for about 8 hours or overnight.

2 Peel and core the apples. Divide the almond paste into eight portions. Press a piece of almond paste over one end of each apple cavity to 'plug' it. Fill the holes in the apples with the sultana mixture and use the remaining pieces of almond paste to seal the tops of the holes.

3 Divide the pastry into four equal portions and roll each one out to a circle about 18 to 20 cm/7 to 8 inches in diameter, large enough to enclose an apple com-

pletely. Place a stuffed apple on each piece of pastry and bring the edges up to meet on top. Brush with beaten egg and seal well together. Roll out the pastry trimmings and cut four fluted circles with a small biscuit cutter. Place one on each dumpling.

4 Place on a greased baking sheet, brush all over with beaten egg and bake in a moderately hot oven (200 C, 400 F, gas 6) for about 20 minutes. Reduce the heat to moderate (180 C, 350 F, gas 4) and cook for a further 40 minutes. Serve hot or warm. **Serves 4**

VARIATIONS

Tipsy apple dumplings Substitute rum for the sherry and use seedless raisins instead of sultanas.
Maraschino apple dumplings Use 12 drained maraschino cherries, chopped, and 1 tablespoon Maraschino or Kirsch to make the filling, instead of the sultanas and sherry.

Lemon kiwi gateau and Glazed strawberry sponge (page 64)

Apricot Choux Puffs

DESSERT

choux paste
150 ml/¼ pint water
50 g/2 oz butter
75 g/3 oz plain flour
2 eggs
filling
150 ml/¼ pint whipping cream
50 g/2 oz castor sugar
1 (425-g/15-oz) can apricot halves
glaze
1 teaspoon lemon juice
syrup from the apricots
2 teaspoons arrowroot

1 First make the choux paste. Place the water and butter in a saucepan and bring to the boil, stirring to melt the butter. Remove from the heat and beat in the flour, which will almost immediately form a ball leaving the sides of the pan clean.

2 Allow to cool, then beat in the eggs one at a time.

3 Dampen two baking sheets with cold water. Arrange teaspoonfuls of the mixture well spaced out on the baking sheets, and bake in a moderately hot oven (190 C, 375 F, gas 5) for 15 minutes. Change the position of the two baking sheets, and cook for a further 5 minutes, or until all the puffs are evenly risen and golden brown. Cool on wire racks.

4 Meanwhile, whip the cream until thick, fold in the sugar and continue whipping until the mixture is stiff. Drain the apricots well, reserving the syrup. Chop the fruit finely and fold into the whipped cream. Slit the puffs and fill with the cream mixture.

5 Add the lemon juice to the reserved syrup, heat until nearly boiling, then stir in the arrowroot, mixed to a smooth paste with a little water. Cook, stirring continuously for a few minutes until clear and smooth. Cool and spoon the glaze over the puffs. **Serves 6**

VARIATION

Choux puffs with pineapple filling Drain a 382-g/13½-oz can crushed pineapple, reserving the syrup, and use the fruit and syrup as for the apricot puffs. Add 2 tablespoons orange juice to the reserved syrup instead of the lemon juice and proceed as above.

Rose petal fancies and Chocolate and orange layer cake (page 65)

Light~textured Cakes

These delicate cake mixtures are welcome at any time of the year, but particularly so in spring. Each of the four recipes demonstrates a different classic method, showing you how to achieve many variations on a basic theme. First a Victoria sandwich mixture, adapted to baking in a deep cake tin and soaked with a rich liqueur syrup. Then a fatless sponge, ideal for making flan cases to be filled with fruit. Next comes the famous Genoese 'pastry', which is really a fatless sponge enriched with melted butter, the perfect basis for small iced fancies. Finally there is a superb gâteau using feather cake batter, made with corn oil.

Lemon Kiwi Gâteau

DESSERT

(*Illustrated on page 62*)

175 g/6 oz self-raising flour
175 g/6 oz butter
175 g/6 oz castor sugar
3 large eggs, beaten
finely grated rind of 1 lemon
syrup
juice of 1 lemon
100 g/4 oz granulated sugar
150 ml/¼ pint water
2 tablespoons Kirsch or Cointreau
decoration
150 ml/¼ pint double or whipping cream
1 large ripe kiwi fruit, peeled

1 Grease a 16-cm/6½-inch, loose-bottomed cake tin and line the bottom with greaseproof paper. Heat the oven to moderate (180 C, 350 F, gas 4).

2 Sift the flour and set aside. Cream the butter with the sugar until pale and fluffy. Gradually add the egg, beating well. Beat in the lemon rind; fold in the flour.

3 Transfer to the prepared cake tin and bake for about 45 minutes, or until golden brown and firm.

4 Place the lemon juice, sugar and water in a saucepan and heat gently until the sugar dissolves. Bring to the boil, remove from the heat and add the liqueur.

5 Remove the cake from the oven and transfer to a plate. Prick all over and spoon over the hot syrup.

6 Leave the cake until quite cold before decorating, if possible overnight. Whip the cream until stiff and swirl over the cake. Thinly slice the kiwi fruit and use to decorate the cake. **Serves 6–8**

Glazed Strawberry Sponge

DESSERT

(*Illustrated on page 62*)

50 g/2 oz plain flour
pinch of salt
2 large eggs
65 g/2½ oz castor sugar
pastry cream filling
1 large egg
25 g/1 oz castor sugar
15 g/½ oz plain flour
150 ml/¼ pint milk
25 g/1 oz butter
few drops of vanilla essence
350 g/12 oz firm medium strawberries
glaze
100 g/4 oz strawberry jam
1 teaspoon lemon juice
1 tablespoon water

1 Butter and flour a 20-cm/8-inch sponge flan tin. Heat the oven to moderately hot (190 C, 375 F, gas 5).

2 Sift the flour with the salt and set aside. Place the eggs and sugar in a mixing bowl and whisk with an electric mixer until pale and firm enough to leave a thick 'ribbon' when the beaters are lifted. If whisking by hand, set the bowl over a pan of simmering water until the mixture thickens, then remove from the heat and whisk until cold. Fold in the dry ingredients with a metal spoon until evenly blended.

3 Transfer to the prepared flan tin and bake for 15 to 20 minutes, or until golden brown and firm to the touch. Leave in the tin for 1 minute then turn out carefully and cool on a wire rack.

4 Meanwhile, make the pastry cream. Place the egg, sugar and flour in a basin and beat well together. Heat the milk to boiling point and gradually whisk into the egg mixture. Return it to the pan and stir constantly until it comes just to boiling point and is smooth and thick. Continue to stir over the lowest possible heat for 2 minutes. Remove from the heat and beat in the butter and vanilla essence. Cover and cool until warm.

5 Spread the pastry cream evenly in the flan case and place on a serving plate. Hull the strawberries and arrange them neatly in concentric circles on the cream. If berries are large, halve them and arrange cut sides downwards on the cream.

6 To make the glaze, place the jam, lemon juice and water in a pan and stir until boiling. Cook for 5 minutes then sieve. Glaze the strawberries, using a soft brush loaded with glaze, and working from the centre. Allow to set for 1 hour before serving. **Serves 6**

Rose Petal Fancies

--- DESSERT ---

(Illustrated on page 63)

100 g/4 oz plain flour
50 g/2 oz butter
4 large eggs
100 g/4 oz castor sugar
175 g/6 oz apricot jam, melted
450 g/1 lb almond paste
icing
450 g/1 lb icing sugar
rose water to taste (optional)
little warm water
few drops red food colouring
decoration
crystallised rose petals

1 Grease a 23-×33.5-cm (9-×13-inch) Swiss roll tin. Line the base and sides with greaseproof paper. Heat the oven to moderate (180 C, 350 F, gas 4).

2 Sift the flour and set aside. Melt the butter until just soft enough to pour and allow to cool. Place the eggs and sugar in a bowl and whisk with an electric mixer until pale and firm enough to leave a thick 'ribbon' when the beaters are lifted. If whisking by hand, set the bowl over a pan of simmering water until the mixture thickens, then remove from the heat and whisk until cold. Fold in half the flour and when evenly blended fold in the remaining flour and then the butter.

3 Transfer to the Swiss roll tin. Tilt the tin until the mixture makes an even layer. Bake for about 25 minutes, or until evenly golden and firm to the touch. If possible leave in the tin for 24 hours before making the fancies.

4 Loosen the sides of the cake and remove from the tin on the lining paper. Using a sharp knife, trim the edges neatly. Spread the jam over the surface. Roll out the almond paste to fit the slab of cake, place it on top and trim. Divide the covered cake into 20 squares. Brush off any loose crumbs and place the cakes well apart on a cake rack over a flat tray.

5 Make up the glacé icing. Sift the icing sugar into a bowl and add the rose water and just sufficient warm water to give a coating consistency. Beat until smooth and add a drop or two of red food colouring to give a pale pink tint. Using a teaspoon, gradually coat each cake with icing, easing it down the sides until evenly covered. Place a rose petal on each and leave to set. Place in paper cases to serve if wished. **Makes 20**

Chocolate and Orange Layer Cake

--- DESSERT ---

(Illustrated on page 63)

150 g/5 oz plain flour
25 g/1 oz cornflour
20 g/$\frac{3}{4}$ oz cocoa powder
2 teaspoons baking powder
$\frac{1}{2}$ teaspoon salt
150 g/5 oz castor sugar
5 tablespoons corn oil
6 tablespoons water
2 large eggs, separated
filling and decoration
175 g/6 oz castor sugar
6 tablespoons water
4 large egg yolks
225 g/8 oz unsalted butter
2 tablespoons orange juice
finely grated rind of 2 oranges
few drops orange food colouring
50 g/2 oz flaked almonds, toasted

1 Grease two 17.5-cm/7-inch sandwich tins and line the bases with greaseproof paper. Heat the oven to moderately hot (190 C, 375 F, gas 5).

2 Sift the flour, cornflour, cocoa, baking powder and salt into a bowl and add the sugar. Mix together the oil, water and egg yolks, add to the dry ingredients and beat well until the batter is smooth. Whisk the egg whites until stiff and fold in evenly.

3 Divide between the two tins and bake for about 25 minutes, or until firm to the touch. Turn out on a wire rack, remove the lining paper and allow to cool.

4 To make the crème au beurre, place the sugar and water in a pan and heat gently until the sugar dissolves. Bring to boiling point and boil gently until the syrup reaches 110 C/225 F on a sugar thermometer. Place the egg yolks in a bowl and whisk lightly. Gradually add the syrup, in a thin stream, beating all the time until the mixture is cold and thick. Place the butter in a separate bowl and beat until creamy. Add the egg mixture a little at a time, beating vigorously. Beat in the orange juice and rind and tint if desired. Chill until firm.

5 Split each cake layer in half horizontally, to make 4 layers altogether. Using just under half the crème au beurre, spread 3 layers and re-form the cake, placing the uncovered layer on top. Use half the remaining filling to cover the sides of the cake. Press on the almonds and put the cake on a serving dish. Spread a little filling on top of the cake and place the remainder in a piping bag fitted with a rose nozzle. Pipe rosettes all round the top outside edge, and round the base if wished. **Serves 8**

May

As spring slips into summer, this is the season
to enjoy the bounty of fresh young produce

Spring is well rung in and summer's on the way, along with some of the special delights which make a brief appearance only at this season. Asparagus is typical. Use the best spears in a creamed chicken dish or in Asparagus mimosa; the less perfect specimens are ideal for soups. The early apricots and cherries which come in now are firm and not too sweet, so include them in savoury recipes such as the Apricot supper dish given in this section. Fish should be good at this season and makes a light main dish suited to the warmer weather. Shellfish is also popular for May-time meals. The weather should be warm enough to get out in the garden for a children's party at Whitsun. But for eating indoors or outside, the emphasis at any children's party is bound to be on an exciting cake; the Parcel cake is particularly easy to make and effective, with its coloured streamers leading to the children's place settings.

Cold Boiled Bacon with Pickled Mushrooms

───── BREAKFAST ─────

1 (1-kg/2¼-lb) bacon collar joint
2 teaspoons powdered gelatine
pickled mushrooms
450 g/1 lb button mushrooms
4 spring onions, trimmed
good pinch of ground allspice
150 ml/¼ pint French dressing (page 186)

1 Place the joint in a large saucepan and just cover with cold water. Bring to the boil, discard the water, refill the saucepan with fresh boiling water to just cover the joint, cover and simmer for 1¼ hours.

2 Remove the pan from the heat and leave the meat to cool in the stock. Lift out the joint, strip off the rind, drain well and chill.

3 Meanwhile boil the stock until reduced by half. Strain into a bowl and chill. When set, scrape off the fat. Reheat the stock and sprinkle in the gelatine, stirring until it is completely dissolved. Cool, and when

the stock becomes syrupy, spoon it over the joint and chill overnight.

4 Meanwhile prepare the pickled mushrooms. Slice each mushroom in half through the centre of the cap and the stalk. Chop the onions. Place together in a polythene container. Whisk the allspice into the French dressing and pour over the mushroom mixture. Seal the container and shake well. Chill and shake again before serving.

5 Serve thick slices of the jelly-coated bacon with the pickled mushrooms. **Serves 4–6**

Note This is an excellent breakfast dish to be prepared the evening before, as the jelly-coated bacon and mushrooms both improve by remaining in the refrigerator overnight.

Prune Velvet

───── BREAKFAST ─────

225 g/8 oz prunes
cold tea
2 tablespoons golden syrup
150 ml/¼ pint natural yogurt

1 Soak the prunes in just enough cold strained tea to cover for 1 hour. Cook in the tea until soft. Remove the pan from the heat and add the golden syrup, stirring until dissolved.

2 Press the mixture through a sieve, discarding the prune stones. Whisk in the natural yogurt. Serve in four small dishes. Alternatively spoon over your favourite cereal. **Serves 4**

VARIATION
Prune and orange velvet Use orange flavoured yogurt instead of natural yogurt and sprinkle with demerara sugar before serving.

Asparagus Mimosa

FIRST COURSE

(Illustrated on page 66)

450 g/1 lb medium asparagus spears
50 g/2 oz butter
100 g/4 oz fresh white breadcrumbs
1 tablespoon finely chopped parsley
1 hard-boiled egg yolk, mashed
salt and pepper
melted butter to serve

1 Trim the asparagus spears to the same length, leaving about 7.5 cm/3 inches before the green part begins. Lay them on a piece of folded foil wide enough to support the spears during cooking, and long enough to extend at each end to form 'lifters'. Pierce the centre of the foil strip. Place the asparagus on the foil in a wide shallow pan and pour over lightly salted water just to cover. Bring to the boil then cook gently for about 25 minutes, depending on the thickness of the spears, or until tender but not broken.

2 Meanwhile, melt the butter in a frying pan, add the breadcrumbs and toss over moderate heat until golden brown. Remove from the heat and stir in the parsley and egg yolk. Season to taste and keep hot.

3 Lift the asparagus spears on the foil and drain well. Arrange neatly on a warm serving dish and sprinkle the topping over the centre of the bundle, leaving the tips and the bases of the stalks uncovered. Serve hot and hand melted butter separately. **Serves 4**

Asparagus Cream Soup

FIRST COURSE

450 g/1 lb asparagus spears, cooked as for
Asparagus mimosa plus cooking liquid
chicken stock
25 g/1 oz butter
25 g/1 oz flour
1 medium onion, chopped
1 teaspoon lemon juice
$\frac{1}{4}$ teaspoon sugar
4 tablespoons single cream
salt and pepper
few drops green food colouring

1 Cut the tips from the asparagus spears and reserve. Chop the stalks roughly. Make up the cooking liquid to 600 ml/1 pint with chicken stock.

2 Melt the butter in a large pan and stir in the flour. Cook for 1 minute then gradually add the stock and bring to the boil, stirring constantly. Add the pieces of asparagus and the onion and bring back to the boil. Cover and cook gently for about 20 minutes, or until the onion is soft.

3 Press through a sieve and return to the pan. Blend in the lemon juice, sugar and cream, bring to boiling point and season to taste. Add a few drops of green food colouring if wished to tint the soup pale green. Stir in the asparagus tips and reheat carefully before serving. **Serves 4**

Apricot Salad Starters

FIRST COURSE

2 ripe apricots
100 g/4 oz white cabbage
$\frac{1}{2}$ small green pepper, deseeded
1 small carrot
6 tablespoons mayonnaise (page 186)
1 tablespoon soured cream
1 tablespoon wine vinegar
1 tablespoon chopped chives
2 teaspoons castor sugar
4 sprigs mint to garnish

1 Cut the apricots in half, remove the stones and chop the flesh roughly. Finely shred the cabbage, dice the pepper and grate the carrot.

2 Spoon the mayonnaise into a bowl, stir in the soured cream, vinegar, chives and sugar. Mix the prepared fruit and vegetables together, stir into the dressing and toss well.

3 Serve in small salad dishes, each garnished with a sprig of mint. **Serves 4**

VARIATION
Rhubarb salad starters Substitute one delicate pink stem of rhubarb for the apricots. First cut in 1-cm/$\frac{1}{2}$-inch lengths, and blanch in boiling water for 30 seconds. Drain well and cool before adding to the remaining ingredients.

Super Veal Stew with Artichoke Hearts

MAIN COURSE

450 g/1 lb stewing veal, diced
2 tablespoons seasoned flour
25 g/1 oz butter
1 medium onion, chopped
450 ml/¾ pint chicken stock
1 (200-g/7-oz) can artichoke hearts
bouquet garni consisting of
parsley, thyme and 2 bay leaves
salt and pepper
225 g/8 oz lean bacon rashers
1 egg yolk
1 tablespoon lemon juice
2 tablespoons single cream

1 Coat the veal with seasoned flour. Melt the butter and add the onion and fry until soft. Fry the veal over a brisk heat until brown on all sides. Remove from the pan and keep warm. Sprinkle in the remaining seasoned flour and stir, gradually adding the stock with the veal, artichoke hearts and liquid from the can. Bring to the boil, add the bouquet garni and seasoning to taste, cover and simmer for 1 hour. Remove the bouquet garni.

2 Roll up the bacon rashers and secure with cocktail sticks. Cook under a medium grill for 5 minutes. Remove the cocktail sticks and add the bacon to the stew. Simmer for a further 15 minutes.

3 Beat together the egg yolk, lemon juice and cream. Add a little of the hot liquid from the stew and beat in until blended. Stir this mixture into the stew and reheat but do not allow to boil. Taste and adjust the seasoning and serve with buttered new potatoes. **Serves 4**

VARIATION

Veal stew with haricot beans (*Illustrated on page 71*) Substitute a 340-g/12-oz can of haricot beans for the artichoke hearts. Add the beans to the stew with the bacon and cook for only 10 minutes before adding the egg, lemon juice and cream mixture.

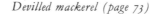

Devilled mackerel (page 73)

Super veal stew with artichoke hearts
and Kidneys in mustard wine sauce (page 72)

Lamb with Spring Cabbage

—— MAIN COURSE ——

25 g/1 oz butter
450 g/1 lb boned lean lamb, diced
1 teaspoon grated lemon rind
½ teaspoon caraway seeds
450 ml/¾ pint beef stock
salt and pepper
1 (675-g/1½-lb) firm cabbage, quartered
4 large potatoes, quartered
2 teaspoons cornflour

1 Melt the butter in a large heavy-based pan and fry the lamb on all sides until sealed. Add the lemon rind, caraway seeds, stock and seasoning and bring to the boil. Cover and simmer for 30 minutes.

2 Core the cabbage quarters and add to the pan with the potatoes. Bring back to the boil, cover and simmer for a further hour, or until the vegetables and meat are tender. Moisten the cornflour with a little cold water, add to the pan and bring to the boil, stirring carefully. Cook gently for a further 5 minutes, taste and adjust seasoning. **Serves 4**

Lamb Chops with Minted Cream

—— MAIN COURSE ——

4 loin of lamb chops
1 medium onion, sliced
1 clove garlic, crushed
250 ml/8 fl oz strained cold tea
150 ml/¼ pint double cream
1 teaspoon vinegar
½ teaspoon salt
¼ teaspoon pepper
1 teaspoon horseradish sauce
1 tablespoon finely chopped mint leaves

1 Place the chops, onion, garlic and tea in a frying pan. Bring to the boil, cover and cook gently for 40 minutes, turning the chops once, until they are tender and the liquid has almost evaporated. Remove the cover and cook for a further 5 minutes to brown.

2 Meanwhile, whisk the cream and vinegar with the seasoning until thick. Fold in the horseradish and mint.

3 Arrange the chops on a warm serving dish and spoon 2 tablespoons sauce on top of each, so that it is melting as it reaches the table. **Serves 4**

Kidneys in Mustard Wine Sauce

—— MAIN COURSE ——

(*Illustrated on page 71*)

225 g/8 oz long-grain rice
100 g/4 oz cooked peas
8 large lamb's kidneys
75 g/3 oz butter
1 medium onion, chopped
100 g/4 oz lean bacon, chopped
150 ml/¼ pint dry red wine
1 tablespoon lemon juice
4 teaspoons French mustard
parsley to garnish

1 Cook the rice in boiling salted water for about 12 minutes, until tender, stirring in the peas 2 minutes before the end of cooking time.

2 Meanwhile, trim and skin the kidneys, leaving them whole. Melt 50 g/2 oz of the butter and sauté the kidneys for 5 minutes, turning them frequently. Remove from the pan and keep hot.

3 Add the onion and bacon to the fat in the pan and cook until the onion is transparent. Pour in the wine and lemon juice, bring to the boil and cook briskly until the liquid is reduced by about one-third. Remove the pan from the heat. Cream the mustard with the rest of the butter and gradually blend into the wine liquid.

4 Drain the rice and peas and place on a warm serving dish. Arrange the kidneys on the rice and spoon over a little of the sauce. Garnish with parsley. Hand the rest of the sauce separately in a warm sauce boat. **Serves 4**

Creamed Chicken with Asparagus

—————— MAIN COURSE ——————

225 g/8 oz asparagus spears, trimmed
40 g/1½ oz butter
50 g/2 oz fresh white breadcrumbs
300 ml/½ pint hot white sauce (page 186)
350 g/12 oz cooked chicken meat, diced
salt and pepper

1 Cook the asparagus in boiling salted water for about 15 minutes, until tender (see Asparagus mimosa, page 69). Drain well, reserving the cooking liquid.

2 Meanwhile, melt the butter, add the breadcrumbs and stir over moderate heat until golden brown.

3 Take 150 ml/¼ pint of the reserved liquid and blend into the hot white sauce. Stir in the chicken and season well to taste. Pour this mixture into a greased oven-proof dish and arrange the asparagus spears on top like the spokes of a wheel. Sprinkle with the buttered crumbs and bake in a hot oven (220 C, 425 F, gas 7) for 10 minutes. **Serves 4**

Curried Shellfish Flan

—————— SUPPER OR SNACK ——————

175 g/6 oz shortcrust pastry (page 184)
300 ml/½ pint white sauce (page 186)
1 teaspoon curry powder
2 tablespoons lemon juice
1 tablespoon tomato chutney, sieved
175 g/6 oz peeled prawns
2 hard-boiled eggs, chopped
salt and pepper

1 Roll out the pastry to line a 20-cm/8-inch flan tin. Line with greaseproof paper and baking beans and bake blind in a moderately hot oven (200 C, 400 F, gas 6) for 15 minutes. Remove the paper and baking beans and return the flan to the oven for a further 10 minutes, or until pale golden brown. Remove from the oven and reduce the heat to moderate (180 C, 350 F, gas 4).

2 To make the filling, heat the white sauce if necessary and blend in the curry powder, lemon juice and chutney. Stir in the prawns and egg and season to taste. Turn this mixture into the prepared flan case and place in the oven for about 15 minutes, until heated through thoroughly. **Serves 4**

Devilled Mackerel

—————— SUPPER OR SNACK ——————

(*Illustrated on page 70*)

2 tablespoons fresh white breadcrumbs
2 tablespoons grated onion
pinch of cayenne pepper
1 tablespoon dry mustard
4 mackerel, filleted
25 g/1 oz flour
50 g/2 oz butter
1 medium onion, sliced

1 To make the stuffing, combine the breadcrumbs, grated onion, cayenne and half the mustard. Spread each mackerel fillet with stuffing and roll up. Secure each mackerel roll with a wooden cocktail stick. Mix the flour with the remaining mustard and use to coat the rolls.

2 Melt the butter in a large frying pan, add the fish rolls and fry over moderate heat for about 12 minutes, turning occasionally.

3 Separate the onion slices into rings. Remove the cocktail sticks from the mackerel rolls and serve hot, topped with the onion rings. **Serves 4**

Sausage and Spring Onion Bake

—————— SUPPER OR SNACK ——————

4 slices white bread
2 teaspoons French mustard
450 g/1 lb large pork sausages
6 spring onions, chopped
3 eggs
300 ml/½ pint milk
150 ml/¼ pint single cream
pinch of ground mace
1 teaspoon Worcestershire sauce
salt and pepper

1 Remove the crusts from the bread and spread thinly with mustard. Cut each slice into quarters. Arrange these in a well-greased shallow ovenproof dish.

2 Place the sausages in a greased frying pan and fry for about 4 minutes, until brown all over. Add the onion and fry for a further 1 minute. Arrange in the dish on the bread. Beat together the eggs, milk, cream, mace and Worcestershire sauce. Season to taste and pour over the sausages and bread.

3 Bake in a moderate oven (180 C, 350 F, gas 4) for about 30 minutes, until golden brown on top. **Serves 4**

Whitsun Children's Party

Cheese and Egg Boats

•

Parcel Cake

•

Ice Cream with Peanut Crunch

•

Iced Chocolate Whizz

Cheese and Egg Boats

(*Illustrated on page 74*)

450 g/1 lb shortcrust pastry (page 184)
6 eggs
salt and pepper
100 g/4 oz Cheddar cheese, grated
2 tablespoons mayonnaise (page 186)
6 processed cheese slices
6 glacé cherries, halved

1 Roll out the pastry and use to line 12 small boat-shaped moulds. Line with small squares of greaseproof paper and baking beans. Bake blind in a moderately hot oven (190 C, 375 F, gas 5) for 10 minutes. Remove the beans and paper and return the cases to the oven for a further 10 minutes.

2 Beat the eggs with the seasoning and scramble in a non-stick pan until the eggs form a soft creamy mixture. Remove from the heat and stir in the grated cheese. Cool and add the mayonnaise.

3 Fill the pastry boats with the egg mixture.

4 Cut triangular sails from the cheese slices and fix one or two on each boat with a cocktail stick. Top each cocktail stick with half a glacé cherry. **Makes 12**

VARIATIONS

Tuna and egg boats Make up half the quantity of scrambled egg. Omit the cheese and add a 198-g/7-oz can of tuna fish, drained and flaked.

Ham and egg boats Make up half the quantity of scrambled egg and flavour it with a little prepared mustard. Add 175 g/6 oz chopped ham in place of the grated cheese.

Parcel Cake

(*Illustrated on page 74*)

350 g/12 oz margarine or butter
350 g/12 oz castor sugar
6 eggs, lightly beaten
350 g/1 lb self-raising flour
100 g/4 oz raspberry jam
buttercream
100 g/4 oz butter
225 g/8 oz icing sugar, sifted
few drops of vanilla essence
pink or blue food colouring
ribbon and postage stamp

1 Line a 20-cm/8-inch square cake tin with grease-proof paper and grease thoroughly. Heat the oven to moderate (160 C, 325 F, gas 3).

2 Cream the margarine or butter with the castor sugar until soft and creamy. Gradually beat in the eggs, adding a little of the flour to prevent the mixture from curdling. Fold in the remaining flour and turn into the prepared tin.

3 Bake in a moderate oven (160 C, 325 F, gas 3) for 2 hours until well risen, golden brown and firm to the touch. Turn out and cool on a wire rack.

4 Slice the cake in half horizontally and sandwich together with the jam. Place on a serving plate or cake board.

5 To make the buttercream, cream the butter with the icing sugar until pale and soft and beat in the vanilla essence. Reserve a quarter of the cream for piping. Colour the remaining buttercream with pink or blue food colouring and spread evenly over the cake marking the sides with a fork.

6 Arrange a piece of ribbon on the cake in the form of a parcel and place a bow on top. Using a small star nozzle and the reserved buttercream pipe a border around the bottom of the cake.

7 Rinse the stamp in a little boiling water and dry thoroughly. Place on the cake as if on a parcel. Place the remaining buttercream in a piping bag fitted with a small plain nozzle and write the name of the child on the cake.

8 Streamers with tiny presents on the end may be attached to the cake and arranged next to each place setting on the table. **Serves 12**

Ice Cream with Peanut Crunch

WHITSUN CHILDREN'S PARTY

(*Illustrated on page 74*)

175 g/6 oz butter
175 g/6 oz fresh peanuts, chopped
6 tablespoons clear honey
1 (1-litre/35-fl oz) carton vanilla ice cream

1 Melt the butter in a saucepan and add the peanuts. Stir over a gentle heat until hot and golden. Add the clear honey and continue stirring until the mixture is well blended. Remove from the heat.

2 Scoop portions of ice cream into twelve individual serving dishes and spoon over the warm peanut crunch sauce. Serve immediately. **Serves 12**

Iced Chocolate Whizz

WHITSUN CHILDREN'S PARTY

(*Illustrated on page 74*)

Mix 4 tablespoons cocoa powder, 1 teaspoon instant coffee and 4 tablespoons light Muscavado sugar in a large bowl. Gradually whisk in 300 ml/$\frac{1}{2}$ pint boiling water until creamy and smooth. Continue whisking and add 2.5 litres/$4\frac{1}{2}$ pints cold milk. Liquidise in batches until foamy. Put a little crushed ice in the bases of 12 small tumblers. Pour the iced chocolate drink from the liquidiser goblet into the glasses and serve at once. **Serves 12**

Lemon Cheese Tart

DESSERT

175 g/6 oz shortcrust pastry (page 184)
100 g/4 oz cream cheese
75 g/3 oz castor sugar
grated rind of 2 lemons
150 ml/$\frac{1}{4}$ pint double cream
2 eggs, separated
pinch of grated nutmeg

1 Roll out the pastry and use to line an 18-cm/7-inch flan ring on a baking sheet. Prick the base with a fork and bake 'blind' in a moderately hot oven (200 C, 400 F, gas 6) for 8 minutes. Remove and reduce the oven temperature to moderate (180 C, 350 F, gas 4).

2 Beat the cream cheese with the sugar, lemon rind, cream and egg yolks until blended. Stiffly whisk the egg whites and fold into the lemon mixture. Turn into the pastry case and sprinkle with nutmeg.

3 Bake in the moderate oven for 40 minutes, until the filling is set. Serve warm or chilled. **Serves 4–6**

VARIATION

Kiwi cheese tart When the cooked cheese tart is quite cold, top with slices of peeled kiwi fruit (Chinese gooseberry) and brush with a little warmed sieved apricot jam.

Krispie Ice Cream Flan

DESSERT

50 g/2 oz butter
2 tablespoons golden syrup
2 tablespoons cocoa powder
75 g/3 oz Rice Krispies
50 g/2 oz seedless raisins
2 firm bananas
1 (500-ml/17.6-fl oz) carton vanilla ice cream
25 g/1 oz walnuts, chopped

1 Place the butter and syrup in a large saucepan and melt over gentle heat. Remove from the heat and stir in the cocoa powder until the mixture is smooth. Add the Rice Krispies and raisins and stir until coated with the chocolate mixture. Press into a greased 23-cm/9-inch flan dish, building up the sides well. Chill until firm.

2 Slice the bananas and arrange in the chocolate case. Spoon the ice cream decoratively over the top and sprinkle with the nuts. Serve immediately, or freeze then allow to soften for 10 minutes. **Serves 4–6**

June

Crisp green salads
and luscious fruits are here
to celebrate
the long summer days

At last the welcome sight of our home-grown summer fruit and vegetables greets us in the shops. This means a drop in prices and fruit in plenty to use with main dishes and salads as well as for dessert. There's even a strawberry salad starter for you to try from this chapter. Imported fruits are in good supply too. Fresh pineapples, avocado pears, summer oranges and apples. Fresh herbs make a delightful change from dried ones and by now most gardens have a clump of refreshing green mint to pick from. New potatoes just seem to cry out for leafy mint and you will enjoy other mint recipes at this season. A special favourite is Minted duck casserole, just as nice with chicken too. Picnic time is here again and our Midsummer picnic features delicious fruits in savoury and sweet dishes, juicy pineapple and succulent raspberries. Variations are given for the raspberries and cream flan so that in other summer months you could make it with peaches or strawberries.

Yogurt with Minted Bananas

BREAKFAST

50 g/2 oz sugar
150 ml/$\frac{1}{4}$ pint water
4 tablespoons mint jelly
1 tablespoon finely chopped mint
450 ml/$\frac{3}{4}$ pint natural yogurt
2 medium bananas, sliced

1 Place the sugar and water in a small saucepan over low heat, and stir until the sugar is completely dissolved. Spoon in the mint jelly and whisk over moderate heat until the mixture is smooth. Stir in the chopped mint and remove from the heat.

2 Meanwhile, divide the yogurt between four small serving dishes. Arrange the bananas on the yogurt. Pour over the hot mint sauce and serve at once. If preferred, make the sauce the previous day, and serve cold spooned over the bananas. **Serves 4**

Sausages with Granary Fingers

BREAKFAST

50 g/2 oz butter
225 g/8 oz beef chipolata sausages
4 large slices Granary bread
1 teaspoon yeast extract spread

1 Melt 15 g/$\frac{1}{2}$ oz butter in a frying pan, add the sausages and fry gently for about 8 minutes until golden brown all over. Drain and keep hot.

2 Meanwhile, spread the slices of bread with the remaining butter and then two of the slices with the yeast extract. Make up into sandwiches, pressing well together. Cut each of the sandwiches into four fingers.

3 Fry quickly in the fat rendered out from the sausages, turning until golden brown and crisp on both sides.

4 Serve each person with two sausages and two Granary fingers. **Serves 4**

Stuffed Apple Salads

FIRST COURSE

(Illustrated on page 81)

4 large dessert apples
juice of $\frac{1}{2}$ lemon
225 g/8 oz cooked chicken meat
50 g/2 oz canned pineapple pieces
75 g/3 oz seedless grapes
100 g/4 oz cottage cheese
1 tablespoon well-seasoned vinaigrette dressing
(page 186), or mayonnaise (page 186)
shredded lettuce

1 Polish the apples and cut off the tops to form caps. Use a grapefruit knife to remove as much apple flesh as possible without breaking the skins. Discard the cores and chop the remaining apple flesh. Place in a bowl and sprinkle with lemon juice to prevent discoloration.

2 Chop the chicken and pineapple and add to the bowl with the grapes. Add the cottage cheese and vinaigrette dressing or mayonnaise and combine with the chicken mixture.

3 Pile up the chicken salad in the scooped out apple. Arrange shredded lettuce on four small plates and top each with filled apple. **Serves 4**

Note If large grapes only are available, halve them and remove the pips before using.

Hanalei pineapple salad (page 82) and Stuffed apple salads

Hanalei Pineapple Salad

FIRST COURSE

(Illustrated on page 81)

2 small pineapples
2 gherkins, chopped
1 small onion, chopped
2 bananas, sliced
juice of ½ lemon
225 g/8 oz cherries
150 ml/¼ pint mayonnaise (page 186)
1 teaspoon French mustard

1 Halve the pineapples lengthways and scoop out all the flesh. Discard the hard part of the core and chop the rest, reserving any juice and the pineapple shells.

2 Mix the chopped pineapple with the gherkins, onion, bananas and lemon juice.

3 Halve and stone the cherries, reserving a few for garnish and mix into the pineapple together with any reserved juice, the mayonnaise and mustard.

4 Toss well to give a lightly dressed salad and arrange with the whole cherries in the pineapple shells. **Serves 4**

Fresh Salmon Pâté

FIRST COURSE

225 g/8 oz cooked fresh salmon
2 tablespoons lemon juice
2 teaspoons Worcestershire sauce
¼ teaspoon salt
150 ml/¼ pint double cream
2 tablespoons mayonnaise (page 186)
pepper
6 stuffed green olives, sliced, to garnish

1 Remove any skin and bones from the salmon. Place the fish in a liquidiser with the lemon juice, Worcestershire sauce, salt, cream and mayonnaise and purée until the mixture is smooth. Add pepper to taste.

2 Divide between four ramekin dishes, smooth the tops and chill. Garnish with olive slices and serve cold with fingers of hot toast. **Serves 4**

Stuffed Whiting Grill

MAIN COURSE

4 large whiting
salt and pepper
2 tablespoons mango chutney
2 tablespoons fresh white breadcrumbs
1 tablespoon chopped chives
1 tablespoon chopped parsley
25 g/1 oz butter, melted

1 Split the fish and remove the backbones. Sprinkle the cavities well with salt and pepper. Chop any large lumps in the chutney and mix it with the breadcrumbs, chives and parsley.

2 Divide this stuffing between the fish and fold them together again to re-form their shape.

3 Brush the fish with melted butter and cook under a moderately hot grill for about 7 minutes. Turn the fish carefully, brush with more butter and cook for a further 7 minutes until the fish are golden brown and crisp. **Serves 4**

Baked Mackerel
with Gooseberry Stuffing

MAIN COURSE

100 g/4 oz gooseberries
2 tablespoons water
4 tablespoons fresh breadcrumbs
1 tablespoon grated onion
salt and pepper
4 medium mackerel, cleaned
1 teaspoon flour
25 g/1 oz butter

1 To make the stuffing, top and tail the gooseberries then cook gently with the water until soft. Rub through a sieve. Place the breadcrumbs in a bowl with the onion and add as much of the gooseberry purée as necessary to make a stiff mixture. Season to taste.

2 Fill the cavities in the fish with the stuffing. Secure with wooden cocktail sticks or sew up the openings. Place the fish, side by side, in a greased ovenproof dish. Sift the flour over the top and dot with the butter.

3 Cover lightly with foil and bake in a moderately hot oven (190 C, 375 F, gas 5) for 30 minutes. Remove the foil, baste with the juices in the dish and return to the oven for a further 10 minutes or until the fish is cooked. **Serves 4**

Cherry-baked Bacon

— MAIN COURSE —

1 (1 to 1.25-kg/2¼ to 2½-lb) bacon collar joint
225 g/8 oz ripe cherries
2 tablespoons vinegar
100 g/4 oz soft brown sugar
1 teaspoon ground mixed spice
150 ml/¼ pint water
2 teaspoons cornflour

1 Place the joint in a saucepan and cover with cold water. Bring to the boil, drain and cover with fresh water. Bring to the boil again, cover and simmer for 20 minutes per 450 g/1 lb and 20 minutes over.

2 Meanwhile, place the cherries in a saucepan with the vinegar, sugar, spice and water. Bring to the boil, stirring, then simmer for about 10 minutes.

3 Drain the joint, strip off the rind and score the fat. Place in an ovenproof dish and brush with some of the cherry syrup. Bake in a hot oven (220 C, 425 F, gas 7) for 20 minutes, basting once with the syrup.

4 Moisten the cornflour with a little cold water, add to the cherries and syrup in the pan. Bring to the boil, stirring constantly. Simmer for 2 minutes and serve with the bacon joint. **Serves 4**

Pork Chops with Curried Apricot Sauce

— MAIN COURSE —

4 pork chops
25 g/1 oz butter
225 g/8 oz apricots
50 g/2 oz seedless raisins
1–2 teaspoons curry powder
3 tablespoons strong chicken stock
4 tablespoons orange juice
salt

1 Trim the chops and brown quickly in the butter on both sides. Remove from the pan and keep warm.

2 Stone and roughly chop the apricots, add to the pan with the raisins and curry powder. Stir over moderate heat for 3 minutes. Add the stock and orange juice and bring to the boil, stirring all the time.

3 Return the chops to the pan, baste with the sauce, cover and simmer for 45 minutes, or until the chops are tender. Season to taste. **Serves 4**

VARIATIONS

Pork chops with curried peach sauce Substitute 2 large ripe peaches, peeled, for the apricots, and use 2 tablespoons lemon juice in place of 2 tablespoons of the orange juice.

Pork chops with curried apple sauce Substitute 1 large cooking apple, peeled, cored and chopped, for the apricots, and add an extra 2 tablespoons orange juice to the sauce.

Pork chops with curried plum sauce Substitute 4 large dessert plums for the apricots and use sultanas instead of the raisins.

Lamb with Lemon-glazed Potatoes

— MAIN COURSE —

(*Illustrated on page 84*)

1 (1-kg/2¼-lb) best end of neck lamb joint
450 g/1 lb medium new potatoes, scraped
2 lemons
25 g/1 oz demerara sugar
salt and pepper
1 chicken stock cube
300 ml/½ pint boiling water
2 teaspoons cornflour

1 Place the joint in a roasting tin and surround with the potatoes. Squeeze the juice from both lemons and mix with the sugar and seasoning to taste. Pour this mixture over the meat and potatoes.

2 Cook in a moderate oven (180 C, 350 F, gas 4) for about 1½ hours, basting occasionally with the juices in the roasting tin. Place the joint on a warm serving dish and arrange the potatoes around it.

3 Make up the stock cube with the boiling water, pour into the roasting tin and stir well, scraping up any sediment. Pour off any excess fat and strain the juices into a small saucepan. Moisten the cornflour with a little cold water, add to the pan and bring to the boil, stirring constantly. Season to taste and simmer for 2 minutes. Serve in a sauce boat with the roast. **Serves 4**

Lamb with lemon-glazed potatoes (page 83)

Liver with Tomato and Orange Sauce

MAIN COURSE

1 tablespoon oil
450 g/1 lb lamb's liver, sliced
1 large onion, sliced
1 (298-g/10½-oz) can condensed cream
of tomato soup
grated rind and juice of 1 orange
1 teaspoon chopped thyme
2 teaspoons chopped chives
salt and pepper

1 Heat the oil and fry the liver slices for 5 minutes on each side. Remove from the pan and keep hot. Add the onion to the fat remaining in the pan and fry gently until soft. Stir in the soup, orange rind and juice, thyme, chives and seasoning to taste. Mix well and bring to the boil, stirring constantly.

2 Return the liver slices to the pan, bring back to boiling point and simmer for about 20 minutes, until the liver is tender. Taste and adjust the seasoning if necessary. **Serves 4**

Minted Duck Casserole

MAIN COURSE

(*Illustrated below*)

4 duck portions
3 tablespoons seasoned flour
2 tablespoons oil
225 g/8 oz mushrooms, chopped
450 ml/¾ pint chicken stock
1 teaspoon grated onion
1 teaspoon chopped mint
225 g/8 oz shelled peas
salt and pepper

1 Coat the duck portions generously in seasoned flour. Heat the oil and fry the portions briskly until evenly browned all over, turning once. Transfer to an ovenproof casserole and add the mushrooms, stock, onion and mint.

2 Cover and cook in a cool oven (150 C, 300 F, gas 2) for 1¼ hours. Add the peas and seasoning to taste, cover and cook for a further 30–45 minutes, or until the duck portions are tender and the flesh comes away easily from the bones. **Serves 4**

Minted duck casserole

Fruited Chicken Mayonnaise

MIDSUMMER PICNIC

(Illustrated on page 78)

1 (1.75-kg/3¾ to 4-lb) chicken, cooked
300 ml/½ pint mayonnaise (page 186)
300 ml/½ pint soured cream
salt and pepper
1 tablespoon lemon juice
1 tablespoon curry paste
2 tablespoons apricot chutney
2 dessert apples, cored
1 medium onion, grated
50 g/2 oz seedless raisins
100 g/4 oz seedless grapes

1 Remove the skin from the chicken. Separate the joints from the body of the chicken and remove all the flesh from the bone. Cut into neat pieces.

2 Mix the mayonnaise with the soured cream, seasoning, lemon juice, curry paste and chutney. Taste the sauce and add extra curry paste or lemon juice to taste. Chop the apples and stir into the sauce with the chicken, onion, raisins, and grapes.

3 Cover with cling film and chill for at least 2 hours. Serve with rice salad and green salad. **Serves 8**

VARIATIONS

Ham and pineapple spiced mayonnaise Substitute 1 kg/2 lb cubed ham for the chicken, and use 225 g/8 oz chopped pineapple (canned or fresh) in place of the apple and grapes.
Egg and seafood spiced mayonnaise Substitute 12 halved hard-boiled eggs for the chicken, and add 175 g/6 oz peeled prawns. The apple and grapes may be omitted if preferred.

Rice and Pepper Salad

MIDSUMMER PICNIC

(Illustrated on page 78)

450 g/1 lb long-grain rice
1 large red pepper, deseeded
dressing
1 tablespoon grated mild onion
1 tablespoon lemon juice
3 tablespoons apple juice
4 tablespoons oil
salt and pepper

1 Cook the rice in lightly salted boiling water for about 12 minutes, or until just tender. Meanwhile, finely chop the pepper.

2 Place the onion, lemon juice, apple juice and oil in a screw-topped container and shake well. Season to taste with salt and pepper.

3 Drain the rice, rinse with hot water and drain well again. While still warm, fork in the dressing and chopped pepper. Cover with cling film and chill for at least 1 hour before serving. **Serves 8**

Cucumber Mousse

MIDSUMMER PICNIC

2 large cucumbers, partially peeled
50 g/2 oz gelatine
300 ml/½ pint strong chicken stock
4 teaspoons lemon juice
350 g/12 oz cream cheese
4 tablespoons mayonnaise (page 186)
few drops green food colouring
salt and pepper

1 Chop the cucumbers roughly then purée in a liquidiser.

2 Dissolve the gelatine in the stock and lemon juice in a small pan.

3 Place the cream cheese in a bowl and beat until soft. Gradually add the mayonnaise and warm gelatine mixture, beating well all the time, until smooth. Blend in the cucumber purée and tint pale green with a few drops of green food colouring. Season to taste with salt and pepper.

4 Divide between 8 individual containers with seals. Chill until set. **Serves 8**

Green Salad

This can be served instead of the cucumber mousse for a simple picnic. Carefully prepare a selection of fresh salad ingredients. Drain well and pack without dressing, otherwise the salad will become limp.

Strawberries and Cream

MIDSUMMER PICNIC

To keep strawberries as fresh and firm as possible, hull them, rinse, if absolutely necessary, in cold water through a colander or sieve, and turn out very gently on to kitchen paper. Handle the fruit as little as possible and pack without squashing down in individual containers. Pack lightly whipped cream and castor sugar separately. At serving time, spoon the cream and sprinkle the sugar over the fruit. If the sugar is added earlier, it will draw juices from the strawberries, creating a syrup and giving them a soft texture. Allow 150 to 175 g/5 to 6 oz strawberries and 50 ml/2 fl oz cream per person.

Picnic Loaves

If it is not practical to serve food which will require forks, it is an excellent idea to prepare a large picnic loaf with an interesting filling. Re-assemble the loaf, wrap tightly in foil and chill for at least 2 hours. When the loaf has taken a firm shape, slice it diagonally into 8 portions and wrap each portion separately in cling film. It is quite easy to eat these unusual 'sandwiches' without using too many paper serviettes.

Frankfurter and Apple Stuffed Loaf

MIDSUMMER PICNIC

1 large French loaf
50 g/2 oz butter
filling
1 dessert apple, cored
½ teaspoon lemon juice
1 (225-g/8-oz) can cannellini beans, drained
2 tablespoons chopped parsley
4 large frankfurters, sliced
4 spring onions, chopped
2 tablespoons peanut butter
1 tablespoon salad cream
salt and pepper

1 Slice the loaf in half lengthways, remove some of the soft crumb and butter both halves lightly.

2 Slice the apple thinly and sprinkle with the lemon juice to prevent discoloration. Mix together the beans, apple, parsley, frankfurter and onion.

3 Beat together the peanut butter and salad cream and season. Pour over the bean mixture and toss lightly.

4 Pack into the lower half of the loaf, press the top half in place and wrap tightly. Chill before cutting.

FILLING VARIATIONS

Egg and tomato stuffing Shell and chop 4 hard-boiled eggs and mix with 50 g/2 oz grated Cheddar cheese and 4 tablespoons mayonnaise. Skin and thinly slice 2 large tomatoes. Shred 6 large lettuce leaves. Fill the bottom half of the buttered French loaf with half the shredded lettuce, half the egg mixture and the tomato slices. Top with the remaining egg mixture and lettuce and press the top half of the loaf in place.
Smoked mackerel filling Remove the skin and any bones from 225 g/8 oz smoked mackerel fillets and flake the fish. Soften 175 g/6 oz cream cheese and mix with 1 tablespoon creamed horseradish sauce, 2 teaspoons lemon juice and 2 tablespoons mayonnaise. Season with salt and pepper to taste. Fill the bottom of the buttered French loaf with the fish. Peel and slice a small cucumber, arrange over the fish. Spread the cheese mixture into the top half and sandwich together.
Pineapple and blue cheese filling Drain a 225-g/8-oz can of pineapple pieces well. Crumble 175 g/6 oz Danish blue cheese, mix with the pineapple pieces and 3 tablespoons mayonnaise. Cut 8 thin slices from a crunchy lettuce of the iceberg type and lay half of them on the bottom half of the buttered French loaf. Cover with the pineapple and cheese mixture, top with the rest of the lettuce slices and press the top half in place.
All loaves serve 8

Raspberry Cream Flan

MIDSUMMER PICNIC

(Illustrated on page 89)

225 g/8 oz shortcrust pastry (page 184)
300 ml/½ pint double cream
grated rind of ½ orange
2 egg whites
50 g/2 oz castor sugar
350 g/12 oz raspberries
toasted flaked almonds to decorate (optional)

1 Roll out the pastry to line a 23-cm/9-inch flan tin. Line with greaseproof paper and baking beans and bake blind in a moderately hot oven (190 C, 375 F, gas 5) for 15 minutes. Remove the paper and baking beans and return the pastry case to the oven for a further 15–20 minutes, until just golden. Allow to cool.

2 Whip the cream with the orange rind until quite thick. Whisk the egg whites with the sugar until the mixture stands in soft peaks. Fold into the cream with half the raspberries. Spoon into the pastry case.

3 Cover the filling with the remaining raspberries and decorate with toasted flaked almonds, if liked. Chill before serving. **Serves 8**

VARIATIONS

Peaches and cream flan Substitute 350 g/12 oz sliced fresh or canned peaches for the raspberries, and flavour the cream with a few drops of almond essence in place of the grated orange rind.
Strawberry and almond cream flan Substitute 350 g/12 oz halved strawberries for the raspberries and add 50 g/2 oz toasted flaked almonds to the whipped cream instead of the orange rind.

For travelling Pack the Fruited chicken mayonnaise salad and rice salad into polythene containers with lids. Pack the flan into a large polythene container or biscuit tin. If you have a 'keep cold box', pack all the food into it to keep it cool.

Gooseberry Crumble

DESSERT

(Illustrated on page 89)

450 g/1 lb gooseberries
2 tablespoons water
100 g/4 oz sugar
75 g/3 oz self-raising flour
pinch of salt
50 g/2 oz margarine
25 g/1 oz rolled oats
50 g/2 oz castor sugar
dessert gooseberries to decorate (optional)

1 Top and tail the gooseberries and place in an ovenproof dish with the water and sugar.

2 Sift the flour and salt into a bowl. Rub in the margarine then stir in the oats and castor sugar. Spoon this mixture over the fruit.

3 Bake in a moderate oven (180 C, 350 F, gas 4) for 1–1¼ hours, until golden brown. Serve warm with cream or custard. **Serves 4**

Fresh Pineapple Sorbet

DESSERT

(Illustrated on page 89)

1½ teaspoons gelatine
600 ml/1 pint water
175 g/6 oz sugar
grated rind and juice of 1 large lemon
1 medium pineapple
1 egg white

1 Mix the gelatine with 2 tablespoons of the water and allow to soften.

2 Place the remaining water in a pan with the sugar and heat gently, stirring, until the sugar has dissolved. Boil for 5 minutes then add the lemon rind and juice with the softened gelatine and stir until the gelatine has completely dissolved. Allow to cool.

3 Peel and remove the flesh from the pineapple, discarding any hard pieces of core. Purée the flesh in a liquidiser or mash thoroughly and combine with the lemon syrup. Freeze until slushy.

4 Turn into a mixing bowl and beat until smooth. Whisk the egg white until stiff and fold into the pineapple mixture. Return to the container and freeze until firm. Scoop into stemmed glasses. **Serves 4**

Fresh pineapple sorbet, Gooseberry crumble
and Raspberry cream flan

Strawberry Yogurt Mould

DESSERT

225 g/8 oz strawberries
about 50 g/2 oz sugar
15 g/½ oz gelatine
2 tablespoons water
finely grated rind and juice of 1 large orange
150 ml/¼ pint natural yogurt

1 Liquidise the strawberries or press through a sieve. Sweeten the purée with sugar to taste.

2 Dissolve the gelatine in the water in a basin over a pan of hot water. Stir in the orange rind and juice and blend in the purée. Leave until beginning to thicken.

3 Whisk the yogurt into the strawberry mixture and pour into a rinsed 600 ml/1-pint mould. Chill until set then turn out on a serving plate. **Serves 4**

VARIATION

Loganberry yogurt mould Substitute 225 g/8 oz ripe loganberries for the strawberries. Sieve to remove the seeds and then sweeten the purée to taste.

Cidered Sausages

SUPPER OR SNACK

450 g/1 lb pork sausages
50 g/2 oz butter
1 bunch spring onions, chopped
1 thick rasher bacon, chopped
2 tablespoons tomato purée
300 ml/½ pint cider
50 g/2 oz soft brown sugar
1 tablespoon Worcestershire sauce
salt and pepper
2 teaspoons cornflour

1 Cook the sausages under a moderately hot grill for about 15 minutes, until cooked through and golden brown all over.

2 Meanwhile, melt the butter and fry the onion and bacon until the onion is soft. Add the tomato purée, cider, sugar and Worcestershire sauce, and bring to the boil, stirring constantly. Season to taste. Moisten the cornflour with a little cold water, add to the pan and stir until the sauce boils and thickens. Simmer for 5 minutes.

3 Place the sausages in a warm serving dish and pour the sauce over them. Serve with pasta shells or elbow macaroni. **Serves 4**

Hubble Bubble

SUPPER OR SNACK

50 g/2 oz butter
450 g/1 lb new potatoes, cooked and diced
100 g/4 oz mushrooms, sliced
2 small tomatoes, peeled
225 g/8 oz cooked peas
4 eggs, beaten
salt and pepper
50 g/2 oz Cheddar cheese, grated

1 Melt the butter in a heavy-based frying pan and use to fry the potato, stirring frequently, until golden brown. Add the mushrooms and cook for 1 minute. Quarter the tomatoes discard the seeds, and add to the pan with the peas.

2 When all the vegetables are bubbling hot, pour in the egg. Season to taste and sprinkle with the cheese. Cover the pan and cook gently until the egg is set. Serve hot cut into wedges. **Serves 4**

VARIATION

Herby hubble bubble Substitute 3 tablespoons chopped mixed herbs (parsley, chives, mint) for the tomatoes and season to taste with salt and freshly ground black pepper.

Egg and Cheese Sunburst Platter

SUPPER OR SNACK

6 hard-boiled eggs
100 g/4 oz cottage cheese, sieved
100 g/4 oz Cheddar cheese, grated
2 tablespoons mayonnaise (page 186)
salt and pepper
1 carton mustard and cress
1 teaspoon paprika pepper

1 Cut the eggs in half lengthways and scoop out the yolks. Blend together the cottage cheese, Cheddar cheese and mayonnaise with seasoning to taste. Divide the filling between the egg white halves, piling it up in the centres.

2 Arrange the stuffed eggs on a bed of snipped mustard and cress. Press the egg yolks through a sieve over the salad, then sprinkle with paprika. **Serves 4**

Ham and Egg Florentine Salad

SUPPER OR SNACK

225 g/8 oz spinach
4 hard-boiled eggs
good pinch of grated nutmeg
2 tablespoons mayonnaise (page 186)
salt and pepper
4 slices ham
finely shredded lettuce

1 Wash the spinach and cook in the water clinging to the leaves until tender. Drain and press out excess water. Press through a sieve and cool.

2 Cut the eggs in half lengthways. Remove the yolks and mash them with the spinach, nutmeg and mayonnaise. Season to taste. Stuff the egg white halves with spinach mixture, then press two halves together, to re-form the eggs.

3 Divide the surplus spinach filling between the ham slices and roll each up tightly. Wrap the rolls in greaseproof paper or foil and chill for 30 minutes.

4 Remove the wrapping and serve the ham rolls and stuffed eggs on a bed of shredded lettuce. **Serves 4**

Peach and Anchovy Rarebits

SUPPER OR SNACK

1 (56-g/2-oz) can anchovies
40 g/1½ oz flour
175 ml/6 fl oz milk
100 ml/4 fl oz light ale
225 g/8 oz Cheddar cheese, grated
freshly ground pepper
4 ripe peaches, peeled
8 slices buttered toast

1 Drain the anchovies. Place the anchovy oil, flour, milk and light ale in a saucepan. Whisk over moderate heat until the sauce boils and thickens. Cook for 1 minute, then remove from the heat and stir in almost all the cheese. Season carefully with pepper.

2 Halve, stone and slice the peaches. Arrange on the toast slices and spoon over the cheese mixture. Arrange the anchovy fillets on top and sprinkle over the remaining cheese.

3 Grill until golden and bubbling. Cut each slice into two triangles and serve hot. **Serves 4**

Apricot Supper Dish

SUPPER OR SNACK

2 eggs
50 g/2 oz butter
4 rashers bacon, chopped
100 g/4 oz apricots, stoned
100 g/4 oz long-grain rice, cooked
salt and pepper
300 ml/½ pint milk
25 g/1 oz flour
100 g/4 oz Gouda cheese, grated

1 Hard boil the eggs, then shell them and slice.

2 Melt half the butter. Fry the bacon and apricots, stir in the rice and season. Turn into a greased ovenproof dish. Arrange the egg slices on top.

3 Place the milk, flour and remaining butter in a saucepan and whisk until the sauce boils and thickens. Stir in half the cheese and season well. Spoon over the mixture and sprinkle with the rest of the cheese.

4 Place under a moderately hot grill for about 8 minutes, until the topping is golden. **Serves 4**

Cheese and Apple Puffs

SUPPER OR SNACK

1 (370-g/13-oz) pack frozen puff pastry, defrosted
15 g/½ oz butter
1 small onion, finely chopped
175 g/6 oz chopped dessert apple
½ teaspoon salt
pinch of freshly ground black pepper
large pinch of grated nutmeg
8 thin processed cheese slices
1 egg, beaten

1 Roll out the pastry thinly to a 40-cm/16-inch square. Divide into 16 10-cm/4-inch squares. Take 8 of the pastry squares, fold each one in half, snip the folded edge 4 times and unfold again.

2 Melt the butter and sauté the onion and apple. Stir in the salt, pepper and nutmeg and leave to cool.

3 Divide the apple mixture between the 8 uncut pastry squares and cover each with a cheese slice. Press lightly. Brush edges with beaten egg. Cover with the snipped pastry squares and press edges well to seal.

4 Brush the puffs with beaten egg, arrange on dampened baking sheets and bake in a hot oven (220 C, 425 F, gas 7) for 15 minutes. Serve hot. **Makes 8**

July
Supper parties and barbecues
add delight to summer,
when meals
can be enjoyed outdoors
in the still-warm evenings

Really hot weather heralds the arrival of the glorious soft fruit season in earnest. Goose-berries and strawberries are joined by other soft fruits – red- and blackcurrants and raspberries. Use these fruits in fools and mousses, perfect for the height of the summer. The list of vegetables at their peak includes globe artichokes, peas and broad beans in the pod. Lettuces are inclined to bolt if not used up quickly enough, so a cold lettuce soup is a useful variation on the better known potato vichyssoise, while the pods from young peas can be used to make another refreshing summer soup. With the long light evenings, even a supper party could be given out in the garden and so our Garden party menu would be just right, served with cold iced coffee in the afternoon or mugs of steaming hot coffee as the evening cools. Save the outer leaves from lettuces used in the Lettuce heart salad to make the vichyssoise, or cook them in the classic French way, braised with peas and spring onions in butter and seasoning.

Strawberry Muesli

— BREAKFAST —

50 g/2 oz rolled oats
150 ml/¼ pint cold water
2 dessert apples
50 g/2 oz sultanas
brown sugar to taste
175 g/6 oz strawberries
150 ml/¼ pint strawberry fruit yogurt

1 Soak the oats in the water overnight. Next morning, drain off any excess water.

2 Core and grate the apples, add to the soaked oats with the sultanas and sugar to taste.

3 Reserve four good strawberries and slice the remainder. Fold into the oat mixture with the yogurt. Divide between four dishes and top each with a strawberry. **Serves 4**

VARIATIONS
Banana bran muesli Add 2 tablespoons unproces-sed bran flakes to the soaked oats with the apple, and use 2 large bananas, sliced, instead of the strawberries.
Hazelnut muesli Substitute 75 g/3 oz chopped toasted hazelnuts for the strawberries and use a hazelnut yogurt. If the mixture is a little dry, add a tablespoon or two of milk.

New Potato and Fennel Omelette

— BREAKFAST —

2 tablespoons finely chopped fennel leaves
1 teaspoon sugar
1 teaspoon malt vinegar
2 tablespoons boiling water
4 eggs
salt and pepper
25 g/1 oz butter
1 teaspoon oil
4 small new potatoes, cooked and diced

1 Place the fennel, sugar and vinegar in a small bowl, pour over the water and allow to stand for several minutes.

2 Whisk the eggs and season to taste. Drain the fennel and stir into the egg mixture.

3 Heat the butter and oil in a frying pan, add the potato and fry until golden. Pour in the egg mixture and stir gently with a fork over moderate heat until the omelette begins to set. Allow to cook for about 2 minutes, then slip the pan under a hot grill for a further minute to brown the top. Serve cut in half. **Serves 2**

Chilled Avocado Soup

FIRST COURSE

(Illustrated on page 98)

25 g/1 oz butter
1 small onion, finely chopped
150 ml/¼ pint chicken stock
2 large ripe avocados
juice of ½ lemon
300 ml/½ pint natural yogurt
150 ml/¼ pint double cream
salt and pepper
sprigs of mint to garnish (optional)

1 Melt the butter in a small saucepan, add the onion and cook until soft but not browned.

2 Add the stock, bring to the boil and cook gently for 10 minutes then leave to cool.

3 Halve, stone and peel the avocados, then sprinkle the flesh with lemon juice.

4 Cut the avocado into chunks and mix with the onion and stock. Liquidise with the yogurt and cream.

5 Taste the soup and adjust the seasoning then chill it thoroughly before serving in individual bowls, garnished with sprigs of mint, if liked. **Serves 4**

Fresh Pea Pod Soup

FIRST COURSE

1 kg/2¼ lb pea pods
1 rasher lean bacon
1 large onion, sliced
few sprigs fresh mint
few sprigs parsley
1 litre/1¾ pints chicken stock
salt and pepper
25 g/1 oz butter
20 g/¾ oz flour
100 g/4 oz cooked peas
about 1 teaspoon sugar
chopped mint to garnish

1 Place the pea pods in a large saucepan with the bacon, onion, mint and parsley and the stock. Season well, bring to the boil, then cover and simmer for about 20 minutes, until the flesh of the pods is soft. Remove the bacon and rub the mixture through a sieve, or liquidise, then sieve.

2 Melt the butter in a clean saucepan and stir in the flour. Cook for 2 minutes over gentle heat, stirring. Gradually add the pea pod purée and bring to the boil, stirring constantly. Add the cooked peas. Cover and simmer for 5 minutes, then add sugar and more seasoning to taste. Sprinkle with mint. **Serves 4**

Lettuce Vichyssoise

FIRST COURSE

outer leaves from 1 large lettuce
1 large onion
2 medium leeks
350 g/12 oz potatoes
50 g/2 oz butter
1 litre/1¾ pints chicken stock
salt and pepper
150 ml/¼ pint single cream
snipped chives to garnish

1 Remove the leaves from the lettuce leaving only the pale heart which should be reserved for a salad. Slice the onion and leeks and dice the potatoes.

2 Melt the butter in a large saucepan, add the onion and leek, cover and cook gently for about 15 minutes, until soft. Add the potato, lettuce and stock and bring to the boil, stirring constantly. Cover and simmer for a further 20 minutes.

3 Sieve or liquidise the soup and season well. Cool, stir in the cream and sprinkle with chives. **Serves 4–6**

Bacon and Broad Bean Salad

FIRST COURSE

450 g/1 lb shelled young broad beans
3 tablespoons French dressing (page 186)
8 rashers streaky bacon
4 spring onions, trimmed
salt and pepper
shredded lettuce

1 Cook the beans in lightly salted boiling water until tender. Drain and, while still hot, pour over the dressing. Allow to cool.

2 Snip the bacon into fine shreds and fry without additional fat until crisp. Drain well on kitchen paper.

3 Chop the spring onions, mix with the dressed beans and season to taste.

4 Arrange a bed of shredded lettuce on four plates. Top with the bean mixture and the bacon. **Serves 4**

Globe Artichokes with Lemon Dressing

FIRST COURSE

(Illustrated below)

4 globe artichokes
½ lemon
4 tablespoons mayonnaise (page 186)
1–2 tablespoons hot water
freshly chopped herbs (optional)

1 Trim the artichokes well, removing the stems, outer leaves and coarse tops of any fully developed leaves. Soak in salted water for 1 hour, then drain.

2 Squeeze the juice from the lemon. Place the artichokes, cut stem ends downwards, in a saucepan. Add boiling salted water to cover and the squeezed lemon half. Bring to the boil and cook for 25–45 minutes, according to the size of the artichokes, until tender. Test by pulling off an outer leaf which should come away easily. Drain the artichokes upside down and allow to cool.

3 To serve, remove the inner mauve leaves and 'chokes' if the artichokes are large. Whisk the strained lemon juice into the mayonnaise with 1–2 tablespoons hot water to give a sauce of pouring consistency. If liked, freshly chopped herbs such as fennel leaves, dill or tarragon may be added to the sauce. Either spoon the sauce into the centres of the artichokes or, if serving smaller ones, hand it separately. **Serves 4**

VARIATIONS

Globe artichokes with yogurt and chive dressing Substitute 4 tablespoons natural yogurt for the mayonnaise, and 2 tablespoons chopped chives for the fresh herbs.
Globe artichokes with wine vinaigrette dressing Substitute a vinaigrette dressing (page 186) for the lemon dressing, using dry white wine instead of vinegar.

Globe artichokes with lemon dressing

Trout with Seedless Grapes

— MAIN COURSE —

(Illustrated on page 99)

40 g/1½ oz butter
50 g/2 oz fresh brown or white breadcrumbs
175 g/6 oz seedless grapes
2 tablespoons chopped mixed herbs
1 small onion, chopped
4 small trout, cleaned
salt and pepper
1 bay leaf
300 ml/½ pint dry cider
1 tablespoon plain flour

1 Grease a shallow ovenproof dish with a little of the butter. Combine half the remaining butter with the breadcrumbs, half the grapes, the herbs and onion. Use to fill the cleaned trout and re-form each of them into a good shape.

2 Arrange the fish side by side in the prepared dish. Sprinkle with a little salt and pepper, put the bay leaf in the dish and pour over the cider. Cover lightly with foil and cook in a moderately hot oven (190 C, 375 F, gas 5) for 20 minutes.

3 Strain off the juices from the dish, taking care not to damage the skin of the fish.

4 To make the sauce, place the remaining butter, the flour and cider stock in a saucepan and whisk together over moderate heat until the sauce boils and thickens. Simmer for 2 minutes. Add the remaining grapes and reheat without allowing the sauce to boil.

5 Arrange the fish on a warm serving dish and spoon a little of the sauce over each one. Hand the rest of the sauce separately. **Serves 4**

Plaice Rolls in Crabmeat Sauce

— MAIN COURSE —

salt and pepper
100 g/4 oz cooked long-grain rice
75 g/3 oz butter, melted
8 plaice fillets, skinned
1 tablespoon flour
150 ml/¼ pint milk
100 g/4 oz crabmeat
1 hard-boiled egg, chopped
¼ teaspoon grated nutmeg
1 egg yolk
8 anchovy fillets to garnish

1 Season the rice and stir in 2 tablespoons of the melted butter. Spread the rice mixture thinly on the skinned sides of the plaice fillets and roll them up with the tail ends inwards.

2 Arrange the rolls, side by side, in a lightly greased ovenproof dish. Sprinkle with salt and pepper, trickle over another tablespoon of the melted butter and place in a moderately hot oven (190 C, 375 F, gas 5) for 15 minutes.

3 Place the remaining melted butter in a saucepan with the flour and cook for 1 minute stirring continuously. Gradually add the milk and bring to the boil, stirring constantly, until the sauce is smooth and thick.

4 Fold in the crabmeat and chopped egg. Reheat the sauce. Add the nutmeg and season to taste. Beat in the egg yolk and remove the pan from the heat.

5 Arrange the plaice rolls on a warm serving dish and mask with sauce. Garnish each one with a coiled anchovy fillet. **Serves 4**

VARIATION

Plaice rolls in carrot and orange sauce Substitute 225 g/8 oz carrot, cooked in orange juice and liquidised or sieved, for the crabmeat. Add extra seasoning and use grated orange rind and chopped parsley to garnish instead of the anchovy fillets.

Chilled avocado soup *(page 95)*
and Raised chicken pie *(page 101)*

Gammon Steaks with Green Pea Purée

——— MAIN COURSE ———

4 gammon steaks
50 g/2 oz butter
1 teaspoon French mustard
1 tablespoon clear honey
450 g/1 lb shelled peas
1 teaspoon sugar
1 sprig mint
salt and pepper

1 Snip the rind and fat on the gammon steaks. Place in the grill pan without the grid. Melt half the butter and use to brush over the lean parts of the gammon steaks. Place under a moderate grill for 7 minutes. Blend together the mustard and honey. Turn the steaks, spoon over the honey mixture then grill for a further 7 minutes, basting twice during this time with the pan juices.

2 Meanwhile, place the peas in a saucepan and add just sufficient salted water to cover. Add the sugar and mint, bring to the boil, cover and simmer for about 10 – 15 minutes, or until the peas are tender. Remove the mint, drain the peas well and rub through a sieve or purée in a liquidiser together with half the remaining butter and seasoning to taste. Reheat before serving if necessary.

3 Serve each gammon steak with a mound of pea purée in the centre. Divide the remaining butter into four pieces and press a piece into each mound of purée. **Serves 4**

VARIATIONS

Gammon steaks with sautéed cucumber dice Peel and dice a 15-cm/6-inch length of cucumber. Sauté in 25 g/1 oz butter with 1 tablespoon chopped mixed herbs until the cucumber dice are tender. Season well and serve on the gammon steaks instead of the pea purée.

Gammon steaks with apple and mint jelly Heat 300 ml/½ pint thick apple purée, beat in 25 g/1 oz melted butter and season well. Serve on the gammon steaks instead of the pea purée and press 1 teaspoon mint jelly into each mound of apple purée just before serving.

Trout with seedless grapes (page 97)

Summer Fruited Chops

─── MAIN COURSE ───

225 g/8 oz redcurrants
2 tablespoons water
2 tablespoons tomato ketchup
2 tablespoons vinegar
50 g/2 oz demerara sugar
4 lamb chump chops
salt and pepper

1 Top and tail the redcurrants and place in a pan with the water. Cook gently until the fruit is soft, then stir in the ketchup, vinegar and sugar.

2 Place the chops in an ovenproof dish and season with salt and pepper. Spoon over the fruit mixture and cook in a moderate oven (180 C, 350 F, gas 4) for about 30 minutes, or until the chops are tender, basting twice during this time with the fruit mixture. Serve with buttered new potatoes. **Serves 4**

─── VARIATION ───

Lamb chops with gooseberries Substitute 225 g/8 oz gooseberries for the redcurrants and add a pinch of ground mixed spice to the fruit mixture before spooning it over the chops.

Lemon Crusted Veal with Courgettes

─── MAIN COURSE ───

75 g/3 oz fresh white breadcrumbs
2 tablespoons chopped fresh parsley
2 teaspoons chopped fresh thyme
grated rind and juice of 1 lemon
1 onion, finely chopped
salt and pepper
150 ml/¼ pint hot water
1 (1.5-kg/3-lb) shoulder of veal joint, boned
75 g/3 oz butter
675 g/1½ lb medium courgettes

1 Mix together the breadcrumbs, 1 tablespoon of the parsley, the thyme, lemon rind, onion and seasoning. Reserve two tablespoons of this mixture and mix the remainder with the hot water. Stuff the pocket in the veal, tie the joint with string and place in a roasting tin.

2 Heat the butter and lemon juice together, stir in the remaining parsley and pour over the joint. Coat with the reserved stuffing mixture.

3 Roast in a moderate oven (180 C, 350 F, gas 4) for 1 hour, basting once during this time.

4 Meanwhile, top and tail the courgettes. Place in a saucepan with salted water to cover, bring to the boil, cover and cook for 5 minutes. Drain well.

5 Arrange the courgettes around the veal, baste the meat and the courgettes with the pan juices and return to the oven for a further hour, basting again after 30 minutes. Remove the string from the joint before serving. **Serves 6**

Baked Veal and Ham Loaf en Croûte

─── MAIN COURSE ───

450 g/1 lb stewing veal
100 g/4 oz fat ham
1 small onion, quartered
salt and pepper
100 g/4 oz cooked long-grain rice
100 g/4 oz mushrooms, chopped
2 eggs, beaten
275 g/10 oz puff pastry (page 185)

1 Mince together the veal, ham and onion. Season well and combine with the cooked rice and the mushrooms. Reserve a little beaten egg for brushing the pastry and add the rest to the veal mixture. Turn into a greased 0.5-kg/1-lb loaf tin and press down well.

2 Cover with foil and cook in a moderate oven (180 C, 350 F, gas 4) for 1 hour. Allow to cool slightly, then turn out of the tin.

3 Roll out the pastry to a thin square large enough to enclose the meat loaf. Trim neatly and reserve the trimmings. Cut pastry shapes from the trimmings to decorate. Enclose the meat loaf in a pastry parcel and seal the edges well, using a little beaten egg.

4 Place on a dampened baking sheet with the seal underneath, brush with beaten egg, arrange the pastry shapes on top and brush again. Chill for 20 minutes.

5 Bake in a hot oven (230 C, 450 F, gas 8) for 15 minutes, or until the pastry is golden brown, then reduce to moderately hot (190 C, 375 F, gas 5) and cook for a further 15 minutes. **Serves 6**

Stuffed Chicken Breasts with Sage

MAIN COURSE

(Illustrated on page 102)

4 chicken breasts, boned
2 tablespoons chopped sage
50 g/2 oz butter
salt and pepper
2 tablespoons seasoned flour
1 tablespoon oil
2 medium carrots, scraped
50 g/2 oz ham
6 spring onions
150 ml/¼ pint dry white wine
150 ml/¼ pint chicken stock

1 Cut a pocket in each of the chicken breasts. Combine the sage with half the butter. Season well and use to fill the pockets in the chicken breasts. Press together firmly. Turn the stuffed chicken breasts in the seasoned flour.

2 Heat the remaining butter and the oil and brown the chicken breasts lightly on both sides.

3 Cut the carrots and the ham into matchstick strips. Trim the spring onions and cut in similar lengths. Add the carrot, ham and spring onion to the pan with the wine and stock.

4 Bring to the boil, cover and simmer for 20 minutes. Remove the chicken to a warm serving dish and keep hot. Boil the contents of the pan until the liquid is reduced by half, then spoon over the chicken. **Serves 4**

Raised Chicken Pie

MAIN COURSE

(Illustrated on page 98)

1 small onion, finely chopped
175 g/6 oz fresh breadcrumbs
2 tablespoons chopped mixed fresh herbs
1 small red pepper, deseeded and chopped
salt and freshly ground black pepper
1 egg, beaten
1 quantity Hot water crust pastry (page 185)
450 g/1 lb uncooked chicken breast
beaten egg to glaze

1 Mix the onion with the breadcrumbs and herbs.

Add the pepper and season well then mix in the egg to bind the ingredients together.

2 Make the pastry according to the recipe instructions and use two-thirds to line a 23-cm/9-in raised pie mould. Keep the remaining pastry hot, wrapped in cling film, in a basin over hot water.

3 Layer the stuffing and the chicken breast in the pie and use the remaining pastry to cover the top.

4 Trim and seal the edges of the pie and use any trimmings to decorate the top. Flute the edges and glaze the pie with a little beaten egg.

5 Stand the pie on a baking tray and cook in a moderate oven (180 C, 350 F, Gas Mark 4) for 45 minutes then remove the sides of the mould and cook for a further 40–50 minutes.

6 Serve warm or cold. **Serves 6**

Pickled Herrings and Beetroot in Cream

SUPPER OR SNACK

2 tablespoons vinegar
175 g/6 oz cooked beetroot, diced
150 ml/¼ pint soured cream
1 dessert apple, peeled and cored
1 small onion
4 pickled herrings
salt and pepper
4 lettuce leaves
garnish
few onion rings
1 teaspoon capers

1 Pour the vinegar over the diced beetroot and allow to stand for at least 1 hour. Drain off the vinegar and combine the beetroot with the soured cream. Grate the apple and onion and stir quickly into the beetroot mixture so that the apple does not have time to discolour.

2 Drain and fillet the herrings, and cut the fillets into strips. Fold into the beetroot mixture and season to taste.

3 Spoon portions of the mixture into lettuce cups, garnishing each one with a few onion rings and capers. Serve with brown bread and butter. **Serves 4**

Note 150 ml/¼ pint double cream mixed with 1 teaspoon lemon juice can be substituted for the soured cream. Whisk until beginning to thicken.

Stuffed chicken breasts with sage (page 101)
and Chilled cherry mousse (page 104)

Hot Potato Salad with Fresh Sardines

――――――――― SUPPER OR SNACK ―――――――――

450 g/1 lb new potatoes, diced
150 ml/¼ pint hot strong chicken stock
2 tablespoons mayonnaise (page 186)
4 spring onions, chopped
225 g/8 oz cooked peas
1 tablespoon finely chopped parsley
450 g/1 lb fresh sardines, cleaned
little olive oil
salt

1 Place the potato in a saucepan, cover with salted water and cook gently until just tender. Drain well and immediately stir in the hot stock, mayonnaise, spring onion, peas and parsley.

2 Meanwhile, brush the sardines with oil and sprinkle with salt. Place under a hot grill for about 10 minutes, turning once, until cooked through.

3 Warm a small pudding basin, pack firmly with the potato salad and turn out straightaway on to the centre of a serving platter. Surround with the sardines. **Serves 4**

Note To prepare sardines yourself, cut almost through the fish behind the head then pull it carefully. The gut should come cleanly away from the body of the fish without further cutting.

――――――――― VARIATION ―――――――――

Hot potato salad with whitebait Substitute 450 g/1 lb fried whitebait for the sardines.

Breadcrumb Omelette

――――――――― SUPPER OR SNACK ―――――――――

1 tablespoon oil
200 g/7 oz streaky bacon, chopped
3 eggs
300 ml/½ pint milk
1 tablespoon chopped parsley
1 teaspoon chopped sage
75 g/3 oz fresh breadcrumbs
salt and pepper

1 Heat the oil in a frying pan and fry the bacon until crisp. Beat the eggs with the milk, herbs and bread-crumbs. Season to taste and pour the mixture into the pan.

2 Cook, stirring gently, until the mixture sets. Brown the top under a hot grill. Serve hot, cut into wedges. **Serves 4**

Almond and Cherry Cheesecake

――――――――― DESSERT ―――――――――

(*Illustrated on page 92*)

base
50 g/2 oz self-raising flour
½ teaspoon baking powder
50 g/2 oz soft margarine
50 g/2 oz castor sugar
1 egg
topping
75 g/3 oz butter
50 g/2 oz castor sugar
1 egg, beaten
½ teaspoon almond essence
50 g/2 oz ground almonds
50 g/2 oz plain flour, sifted
450 g/1 lb cream cheese
300 ml/½ pint double cream
decoration
225 g/8 oz red cherries
50 g/2 oz almond paste
150 ml/¼ pint double cream

1 To make the base, sift the flour and baking powder into a bowl, add all the remaining ingredients and beat with a wooden spoon until smooth. Transfer to a greased 22.5-cm/9-inch loose-bottomed cake tin.

2 Place the butter and sugar for the topping in a bowl and beat until pale and fluffy. Gradually beat in the egg then add the almond essence and almonds. When smooth, fold in the flour. In a separate bowl cream the cheese and gradually beat in the cream. Add to the almond mixture and stir well together.

3 Carefully spoon the topping over the base in the tin. Bake in a cool oven (150 C, 300 F, gas 2) for 1½ hours, or until just set in the centre. Turn off the heat, open the door slightly and leave the cake in the oven until quite cold.

4 Carefully stone the cherries and stuff each cavity with a small piece of almond paste. Whip the cream and place in a piping bag fitted with a star nozzle.

5 Remove the cake tin sides and transfer the cheesecake, still on its metal base, to a serving plate. Decorate the top with alternate rosettes of cream and the almond paste-stuffed cherries. **Serves 10 – 12**

Chilled Cherry Mousse

— DESSERT —

450 g/1 lb red cherries
150 ml/¼ pint orange juice
2 tablespoons port
castor sugar to taste
15 g/½ oz gelatine
2 tablespoons water
300 ml/½ pint double cream
2 egg whites

1 Reserve a few cherries for decoration and cook the remainder in the orange juice and port over low heat until they are soft. Press through a fine sieve. Sweeten to taste if necessary.

2 Dissolve the gelatine in the water in a basin over a pan of boiling water then stir into the cherry purée and allow to cool until beginning to thicken.

3 Lightly whisk the cream and fold into the fruit jelly. Whisk the egg whites until stiff and fold in.

4 Spoon into stemmed glasses and chill until set. Decorate with the reserved cherries before serving. **Serves 4–6**

Banana and Apricot Fool

— DESSERT —

450 g/1 lb ripe apricots
juice of 1 orange
75 g/3 oz castor sugar
2 large bananas, mashed
300 ml/½ pint thick custard
150 ml/¼ pint double cream, whipped

1 Scald the apricots with boiling water, drain and remove the skins. Halve the apricots and stone them. Place in a liquidiser with the orange juice, sugar and banana and blend until smooth.

2 Mix the apricot and banana purée with the custard and fold in the whipped cream.

3 Spoon into stemmed glasses and chill. **Serves 4–6**

VARIATIONS

Strawberry and orange fool Substitute 350 g/12 oz strawberries for the apricots and use 4 tablespoons orange marmalade instead of the mashed banana.
Gooseberry and apple fool Substitute 450 g/1 lb gooseberries for the apricots. Cook them gently in a covered pan in the orange juice for 20 minutes. Add extra sugar if necessary and sieve to remove the seeds if preferred. Use 150 ml/¼ pint sweetened apple purée in place of the mashed banana.
Blackcurrant and apple fool Substitute 450 g/1 lb blackcurrants for the apricots and cook as for gooseberries above. Use 150 ml/¼ pint sweetened apple purée in place of the mashed banana.

Miniature Chicken and Cheese Pasties

— GARDEN PARTY —

175 g/6 oz butter
450 g/1 lb onions, chopped
225 g/8 oz carrots, grated
225 g/8 oz new potatoes, grated
450 g/1 lb Gouda cheese, diced
450 g/1 lb cooked chicken meat, diced
½ teaspoon grated nutmeg
salt and pepper
1.75 kg/4 lb shortcrust pastry (page 184)
beaten egg to brush

1 Melt the butter and fry the prepared vegetables until beginning to soften. Remove from the heat and stir in the cheese, chicken, nutmeg and seasoning to taste.

2 Roll out the pastry in batches on a floured surface and cut 32 circles each 10 cm/4 inches in diameter, re-rolling if necessary. Divide the filling between the pastry circles and brush the edges with beaten egg. Bring up the pastry edges and pinch together over the filling to make a fluted edge.

3 Arrange on greased baking sheets and brush with beaten egg. Bake in a moderately hot oven (190 C, 375 F, gas 5) for 30 minutes, or until golden brown. **Makes 32**

VARIATIONS

Miniature salmon and corn pasties Substitute 2 439-g/15½-oz cans of pink salmon for the cheese and chicken. Drain, remove the bones and flake roughly before using. Use a 326-g/11½-oz can of sweet corn kernels, drained, instead of the grated potato.
Miniature curried egg cream pasties Substitute 8 hard-boiled eggs, roughly chopped, for the cheese. Add 150 ml/¼ pint white sauce (page 186) made with cream instead of milk and blended with 2 tablespoons curry powder. Stir into the vegetable mixture with the chicken and egg.

Prawn Pots

GARDEN PARTY

1 large lettuce, shredded
1 kg/2 lb peeled prawns
450 g/1 lb butter
1 teaspoon grated nutmeg
1 teaspoon freshly ground black pepper

1 Divide the shredded lettuce between 16 small pots, top with the prawns and chill.

2 Melt the butter and stir in the nutmeg and pepper. Spoon a little of the spiced butter over each prawn pot. The pots must be chilled well so that the butter topping sets immediately. **Serves 16**

Majorcan Onion and Tomato Platter

GARDEN PARTY

2 large mild onions
8 large tomatoes
1–2 tablespoons chopped fresh herbs (including mint, chives, marjoram or thyme)

1 Slice the onions into very thin rings. Place the tomatoes in a bowl and cover with boiling water. Leave for 1 minute then remove from the water and peel. Slice the tomatoes thinly.

2 Arrange the tomato and onion on a large platter and scatter generously with the herbs. **Serves 16**

Lettuce Hearts with Caper Dressing

GARDEN PARTY

8 small lettuces
2 tablespoons capers
3 tablespoons single cream
4 tablespoons mayonnaise (page 186)
1 hard-boiled egg to garnish

1 Remove the outer leaves from the lettuces and shred finely. Quarter the hearts. Make a bed of the shredded lettuce on a large platter and arrange the quarters on this in a decorative pattern.

2 Drain and chop the capers. Stir the cream gently into the mayonnaise and then fold in the chopped capers.

3 Spoon the dressing over the lettuce hearts. Finely chop the egg and press through a sieve over the salad. **Serves 16**

Summer Fruit Shortcakes

GARDEN PARTY

450 g/1 lb plain flour
2 teaspoons cream of tartar
1 teaspoon bicarbonate of soda
$\frac{1}{2}$ teaspoon salt
175 g/6 oz margarine
75 g/3 oz castor sugar
2 eggs, beaten
175 ml/6 fl oz milk
butter to spread
filling
600 ml/1 pint whipping cream
50 g/2 oz icing sugar
225 g/8 oz strawberries
2 large peaches, peeled
225 g/8 oz raspberries

1 Sift together the flour, cream of tartar, bicarbonate of soda and salt into a bowl. Rub in the margarine until the mixture resembles fine breadcrumbs. Stir in the sugar. Make a well in the centre, add the egg and half the milk and blend in, adding as much extra milk as is necessary to form a dough which is soft but easy to handle.

2 Turn out on a floured surface and knead lightly until smooth. Divide into two equal portions and shape each into a ball. Pat out to form 23-cm/9-inch circles and place each on a greased baking sheet.

3 Bake in a hot oven (220 C, 425 F, gas 7) for about 20 minutes, until just pale golden. Remove to a board and split in half while still warm. Lightly butter the cut surfaces.

4 To make the filling, whip the cream with the icing sugar until it forms firm peaks. Cut the strawberries in half, reserving some good halves for decoration. Slice the peaches and combine them with the raspberries and remaining strawberries.

5 Spread the bottom layer of each cake with the sweetened cream, cover with the fruit and replace the top layers of shortcake. Place each cake on a serving dish, spread the tops with the remaining cream and use the reserved strawberry halves to decorate. Serve chilled. **Serves 16**

August
Time to dream of holiday weather, idle days and cool, refreshing drinks

The summer sun is hard at work ripening our vegetable crops of courgettes, marrows and beans. Good as these are served as vegetable accompaniments, they can also be the basis of many interesting main dishes. Try the Marrow medley – marrow dice casseroled with bacon, or try the stuffed egg and French bean salad as a starter. Tiny new beetroot also have a special place in this month's recipes. All meat is good at the moment, but if you prefer to forget pork during the warm weather, try rabbit for a change. It makes a very tasty stew, especially in the spicy paprika sauce given here. This holiday month is just right for casual entertaining. If you plan to have a barbecue, you will be able to give your guests a delightful surprise with some of our unusual barbecue ideas. Courgettes, corn, peppers and aubergines make delicious combinations to parcel up in foil and serve with well-basted lamb cutlets, chicken drumsticks and beef sausages. When the fire dies down, finish up with sweet surprises such as Caramelised apple on a skewer.

Scrambled Egg Sandwiches

— BREAKFAST —

4 eggs
25 g / 1 oz butter
salt and pepper
1 tablespoon mayonnaise (page 186)
8 slices buttered brown bread

1 Lightly whisk the eggs together and scramble in the butter.

2 While still warm, season to taste with salt and pepper and gradually beat in the mayonnaise.

3 Divide the scrambled egg mixture between four slices of the bread, and make up into sandwiches. **Serves 4**

Note These are excellent if made the night before, and closely wrapped in cling film, then refrigerated. They remain moist, and taste exactly as if freshly made.

Rasberry and Apple Custard

— BREAKFAST —

100 g / 4 oz castor sugar
225 g / 8 oz raspberries
1 large cooking apple
2 tablespoons water
15 g / ½ oz butter
1 tablespoon custard powder
4 tablespoons milk

1 Sprinkle half the sugar over the raspberries.

2 Peel, core and slice the apple. Place in a saucepan with the water and butter. Cook over a gentle heat, stirring occasionally, until the apple is soft.

3 Add the remaining sugar, stir to dissolve, then beat until smooth. Add the raspberries with their juice and cook for a further minute.

4 Blend the custard powder with a little of the milk, add the remaining milk, and stir into the hot fruit mixture. Cook, stirring constantly, until it boils and thickens. Cool and serve with cereal. **Serves 4**

Summer Turnip Soup

— FIRST COURSE —

2 medium leeks
40 g / 1½ oz butter
1 medium onion, chopped
175 g / 6 oz potatoes, diced
225 g / 8 oz turnip, diced
20 g / ¾ oz flour
salt and pepper
900 ml / 1½ pints water
1 tablespoon lemon juice
1 egg yolk
4 tablespoons single cream
finely chopped watercress to garnish

1 Trim and slice the leeks. Rinse and drain well. Melt the butter in a large saucepan, add the prepared vegetables and stir over moderate heat until softened.

2 Stir in the flour, season well and gradually add the water and lemon juice. Bring to the boil, stirring constantly, then cover and simmer for 30 minutes.

3 Liquidise or sieve the soup and return to the pan. Place over a low heat. Beat the egg yolk with the cream in a small bowl, blend in a little of the hot soup and add this mixture to the pan. Reheat without boiling, adjust the seasoning and serve hot with watercress. **Serves 4**

Stuffed Egg and French Bean Salad

FIRST COURSE

450 g/1 lb French beans
100 ml/4 fl oz French dressing (page 186)
2 hard-boiled eggs
100 g/4 oz crabmeat
2 tablespoons mayonnaise (page 186)
few drained capers to garnish

1 Trim the beans, halve them and place in a saucepan with salted water to cover. Bring to the boil, cover and simmer for about 10 minutes, or until only just tender. Drain well and pour over the French dressing while the beans are still hot. Cool.

2 Shell the eggs and cut in half crossways, scoop out the yolks and reserve. Combine the crabmeat with the mayonnaise and divide between the egg whites.

3 Place each filled egg half in the middle of a small serving plate and arrange the dressed beans to radiate out from the centre. Place one or two capers on each filled egg white and press the yolks of the eggs through a sieve over the beans. **Serves 4**

VARIATION

Stuffed egg and broad bean salad Substitute 450 g/1 lb shelled broad beans for the French beans and garnish the eggs with sliced stuffed green olives instead of capers.

Masked Fish Steaks with Grapes

MAIN COURSE

100 g/4 oz white grapes
4 cod steaks
about 150 ml/¼ pint milk
salt and pepper
½ teaspoon powdered gelatine
1 tablespoon water
20 g/¾ oz butter
15 g/½ oz flour
2 tablespoons mayonnaise (page 186)
1 tablespoon finely chopped mixed herbs

1 Halve the grapes and remove the pips. Arrange the fish steaks in a shallow pan, pour over the milk and season to taste. Cover the pan and poach gently for about 10 minutes, until the fish is cooked. Remove from the pan with a slotted draining spoon, carefully remove the bones and place the fish steaks on a warm serving dish. Fill the cavities in the steaks with grapes and keep hot while you make the sauce.

2 Dissolve the gelatine in the water in a basin over a pan of hot water. Meanwhile, strain and measure the milk liquid and make up to 150 ml/¼ pint again with more milk if necessary. Place in a clean pan with the butter and flour and whisk over a moderate heat until the sauce boils and thickens. Simmer for 2 minutes and adjust the seasoning to taste. Remove from the heat and beat in the mayonnaise, herbs and dissolved gelatine. Spoon the sauce over the fish steaks to mask them completely and garnish with any left-over grapes. This dish is also delicious served cold. **Serves 4**

Stuffed Peppers

MAIN COURSE

(*Illustrated on page 111*)

4 large green peppers
50 g/2 oz butter
1 medium onion, chopped
450 g/1 lb minced beef
salt and freshly ground black pepper
300 ml/½ pint beef stock
2 tablespoons tomato purée
1 teaspoon sugar
1 teaspoon Worcestershire sauce
½ teaspoon ground nutmeg
100 g/4 oz button mushrooms, sliced
4 tomatoes, peeled and chopped
1 bunch spring onions, chopped

1 Cut the tops off the peppers and reserve. Scoop out all the pith and seeds and blanch the tops and shells in boiling water for 2 minutes. Drain thoroughly.

2 Melt the butter in a pan, add the onion and cook until soft then add the minced beef and seasoning and cook, stirring continuously, until well browned.

3 Stir in the stock, tomato purée, sugar, Worcestershire sauce and nutmeg. Bring to the boil then cover and cook for 20–30 minutes or until the liquid is reduced by half.

4 Add the mushroom and tomato and cook for a further 5 minutes. Remove from the heat and stir in the spring onions.

5 Fill the peppers with the mince mixture and replace the reserved caps. Place in a greased ovenproof dish, cover tightly with cooking foil and cook in a moderate oven (200 C, 400 F, gas 6) for 25–30 minutes. **Serves 4**

Roast Lamb with Redcurrant Glaze

MAIN COURSE

1 clove garlic, crushed
2 tablespoons redcurrant jelly
1 tablespoon soy sauce
pinch of ground cinnamon
2 tablespoons orange juice
1 tablespoon dry sherry
1 (1.5-kg/3-lb) loin of lamb joint

1 Place the garlic, redcurrant jelly, soy sauce, cinnamon, orange juice and sherry in a small pan and warm gently, whisking to melt the redcurrant jelly. Do not allow the mixture to boil.

2 Place the joint in a roasting tin, pour over the marinade and allow to stand for 2 hours.

3 Cook in a moderate oven (180 C, 350 F, gas 4) for 1 hour, baste with the pan juices and return to the oven for a further 30 minutes, or until the juices from the meat are colourless when it is pierced with a skewer. Serve with new potatoes tossed in butter and mixed chopped herbs. **Serves 4**

Courgette and Lamb Casserole

MAIN COURSE

25 g/1 oz butter
1 large onion, chopped
350 g/12 oz minced lamb
225 g/8 oz tomatoes, peeled and chopped
150 ml/¼ pint water
350 g/12 oz courgettes, sliced
salt and pepper

1 Melt the butter and cook the onion gently until transparent. Add the meat and cook, stirring occasionally, until it looks brown and crumbly in texture. Add the tomato and water and stir well to mix the ingredients thoroughly.

2 Arrange layers of the meat mixture and the courgette slices in a greased ovenproof pie dish, seasoning each layer with salt and pepper to taste. Pour over any remaining meat mixture to form the top layer of the casserole.

3 Bake in a moderate oven (180 C, 350 F, gas 4) for 45 minutes. **Serves 4**

Holiday burgers with cucumber salad (page 112)

Stuffed peppers (page 109)
and Rabbit in paprika sauce (page 112)

Meatballs with Creamed Cucumber

——— MAIN COURSE ———

450 g/1 lb minced beef
50 g/2 oz white breadcrumbs
2 tablespoons chopped parsley
2 teaspoons chopped thyme
1 egg, beaten
2 tablespoons seasoned flour
50 g/2 oz lard
1 large cucumber
150 ml/¼ pint water
salt and pepper
300 ml/½ pint well-seasoned white sauce (page 186)

1 Mix the beef, breadcrumbs, herbs and egg together. Form into 16 balls and coat with seasoned flour. Melt the lard and fry the meatballs gently for about 15 minutes, until golden brown all over.

2 Meanwhile, peel and dice the cucumber. Place in a saucepan with the water and a little salt. Bring to the boil then simmer for about 10 minutes, until the cucumber is tender.

3 Drain, and add 150 ml/¼ pint of the cucumber cooking liquid to the hot white sauce with the cucumber. Check the seasoning and serve with the meatballs. **Serves 4**

Holiday Burgers with Cucumber Salad

——— MAIN COURSE ———

(*Illustrated on page 110*)

cucumber salad
1 cucumber, peeled
2 teaspoons salt
150 ml/¼ pint soured cream
4 spring onions, finely chopped
burgers
450 g/1 lb minced beef
salt and freshly ground black pepper
oil for brushing
garnish
shredded lettuce
8 spring onions
1 small onion, sliced into rings
1 tomato, sliced
4 gherkins

1 To make the cucumber salad, dice the cucumber and place in a strainer. Sprinkle over the salt and leave for 15–20 minutes then dry on kitchen paper.

2 Place the cucumber in a serving dish, top with the soured cream and garnish with the spring onions.

3 Mix the minced beef with seasoning to taste and shape into four burgers.

4 Brush with a little oil and cook under a hot grill or over a barbecue until browned on the outside and juicy in the middle. Allow 4–6 minutes on each side, according to taste.

5 Arrange the lettuce on four plates. Place a burger on each and add two spring onions. Garnish the burgers with onion rings, slices of tomato and gherkin fans. **Serves 4**

Rabbit in Paprika Sauce

——— MAIN COURSE ———

(*Illustrated on page 111*)

4 large leg portions rabbit
25 g/1 oz seasoned flour
2 tablespoons oil
1 large onion, chopped
2 tablespoons paprika pepper
1 teaspoon sugar
1 teaspoon salt
150 ml/¼ pint tomato juice
150 ml/¼ pint soured cream

1 Coat the rabbit portions well with seasoned flour. Heat the oil and fry the onion until soft. Add the rabbit portions and fry until golden all over. Mix together the paprika, sugar, salt and tomato juice. Pour over the rabbit in the pan and bring to the boil, stirring constantly.

2 Cover and simmer for about 1 hour, or until the rabbit is tender. Stir in the soured cream and reheat without allowing the sauce to boil. Serve with ribbon noodles. **Serves 4**

Apple and loganberry layer pudding
and Hot peach cream pudding (page 115)

Roast Grouse

MAIN COURSE

2 plump young grouse
4 thick rashers rindless streaky bacon
50 g/2 oz butter
100 ml/4 fl oz red wine
4 thick slices white bread
sprigs of watercress to garnish

1   Cover the breast of each grouse with 2 rashers of bacon and tie on with string, trussing each bird to a compact shape and leaving the feet on.

2   Melt the butter and use to brown the birds all over. Place them in a roasting tin and spoon over any remaining juices from the pan. If preferred, melt the butter in a roasting tin and brown the birds in this on top of the stove.

3   Roast in a moderately hot oven (200 C, 400 F, gas 6) for 20 minutes, then pour over the wine and return the birds to the oven for a further 15 minutes, basting once more during this time.

4   Meanwhile, toast the slices of bread and trim off the crusts. Remove the trussing strings and larding bacon.

5   Arrange the toasts in pairs on a warm serving dish and place one grouse on each pair. Stir up the juices in the pan and spoon them over the birds. Garnish with sprigs of watercress. **Serves 4**

Cauliflower Dreams

SUPPER OR SNACK

225 g/8 oz plain flour
$\frac{1}{2}$ teaspoon salt
pinch of pepper
2 eggs, beaten
150 ml/$\frac{1}{4}$ pint milk
1 tablespoon chopped mixed herbs
4 tablespoons beer
1 small cauliflower
1 (200-g/7-oz) can cooked ham, diced
oil for deep frying
25 g/1 oz grated Parmesan cheese

1   Sift the flour into a bowl with the salt and pepper. Blend in the eggs, milk, herbs and beer. Beat well until the batter is smooth, then allow it to stand while you prepare the cauliflower.

2   Divide the cauliflower into florets and place in a saucepan with salted water to cover. Bring to the boil, cover and cook gently for 5 minutes. Drain well.

3   Dip the cauliflower florets and cubes of ham in the batter and fry in deep moderately hot oil for about 4 minutes, until golden brown and crisp. Drain well on kitchen paper and pile up on a warm serving dish. Serve hot, sprinkled with the cheese. **Serves 4**

VARIATION

Courgette dreams   Substitute 225 g/8 oz courgettes for the cauliflower. Top and tail and cut the courgettes into 1-cm/$\frac{1}{2}$-inch slices and parboil as above for 4 minutes. Use a 200-g/7-oz can of chopped ham and pork instead of the ham.

Marrow Medley

SUPPER OR SNACK

1 large marrow
8 thick slices lean bacon, diced
50 g/2 oz butter
generous pinch of garlic powder
generous pinch of grated nutmeg
salt and pepper
2 teaspoons cornflour
2 tablespoons milk

1   Peel and deseed the marrow. Cut the flesh into large dice. Arrange the bacon in the base of a large heavy saucepan and dot with the butter. Put the marrow dice on top, seasoning between the layers with garlic powder, nutmeg and salt and pepper. Do not add any water.

2   Cover the pan closely and place over a high heat for 3 minutes, then reduce the heat to simmer and continue cooking, covered, for about 20 minutes.

3   Blend the cornflour with the milk. When the marrow is tender, stir in the cornflour mixture and cook gently for a further 5 minutes. Check the seasoning and serve hot. **Serves 4**

VARIATION

Marrow with frankfurters   Use only 2 thick slices of bacon and add 1 tablespoon oil to the pan with the butter. Slice 225 g/8 oz frankfurters and stir into the marrow mixture with the blended cornflour. Cook for a further 7 minutes instead of 5.

Buttered Spinach Toss

SUPPER OR SNACK

675 g/1½ lb spinach
65 g/2½ oz butter
salt and pepper
175 g/6 oz garlic sausage, diced
2 thick slices white bread, diced
4 eggs

1 Wash the spinach thoroughly and drain well. Place in a heavy-based saucepan with half the butter and seasoning to taste. Cover and cook over a moderate heat for 5 minutes. Uncover and stir occasionally until the spinach is tender.

2 Meanwhile, melt the rest of the butter in a frying pan and toss the garlic sausage and bread until the bread is crisp and golden brown. Poach the eggs.

3 Roughly chop the spinach in the pan and stir in the bread mixture. Taste and add more seasoning if necessary. Divide between four warmed plates and top with the poached eggs. **Serves 4**

Apple and Loganberry Layer Pudding

DESSERT

(*Illustrated on page 113*)

450 g/1 lb cooking apples
1 tablespoon water
225 g/8 oz ripe loganberries
about 100 g/4 oz castor sugar
150 g/5 oz butter
350 g/12 oz fresh white breadcrumbs
1 teaspoon ground cinnamon
150 ml/¼ pint double cream

1 Peel, core and chop the apples. Place in a saucepan with the water. Cover and cook very gently, stirring occasionally, until the apples are soft. Beat to a smooth purée.

2 Reserve a few good loganberries and press the remainder through a sieve to remove the seeds. Mix the loganberry purée with the apple purée and sweeten to taste with sugar. Allow to cool.

3 Melt the butter in a large saucepan, add the breadcrumbs and stir over a low heat until the crumbs are golden brown and the butter has been absorbed. Stir in the cinnamon.

4 Sprinkle one-third of the spiced crumbs evenly over the base of a greased 20-cm/8-inch cake tin. Spoon over half the loganberry mixture. Sprinkle with another one-third of the spiced crumbs then top with the rest of the loganberry mixture. Finally, sprinkle with the remaining spiced crumbs. Alternatively layer the crumbs and fruit mixture in an ovenproof glass dish, ending with a layer of crumbs.

5 Bake in a moderate oven (180 C, 350 F, gas 4) for 30 minutes. Allow to cool in the tin and chill for at least 4 hours, then turn out on to a serving dish. Alternatively allow to cool in the glass dish.

6 Whip the cream and use to decorate the pudding with the reserved loganberries. **Serves 4**

Hot Peach Cream Pudding

DESSERT

(*Illustrated on page 113*)

4 large ripe peaches
3 tablespoons castor sugar
300 ml/½ pint soured cream
2 eggs
1 tablespoon cornflour
decoration
extra peach slices, dipped in lemon juice
50 g/2 oz soft brown sugar

1 Peel, halve and stone the peaches. Cut the flesh into slices and arrange in the base of a buttered shallow ovenproof dish. Sprinkle with 1 tablespoon of the sugar. Place in a cool oven (150 C, 300 F, gas 2) for 15 minutes.

2 Meanwhile, place the cream and eggs in a bowl and whisk together until blended. Sprinkle in the cornflour and the remaining sugar and whisk thoroughly. Pour over the hot peaches and return to the oven for about 45 minutes, or until golden brown and firm to the touch.

3 Allow to cool, decorate with the peach slices and sprinkle with brown sugar. Chill well. Just before serving place the pudding under a grill, pre-heated to its maximum setting, until the sugar caramelises. **Serves 4**

VARIATIONS

Hot cherry cream pudding Stone 450 g/1 lb ripe cherries and use instead of the peaches. Depending on the tartness of the cherries, you may want to add an extra tablespoon of sugar before heating the fruit. Whisk a pinch of ground cinnamon into the cream topping with the cornflour.

Caramelised apple on a skewer (page 119)

Barbecue

Oriental Basted Lamb Cutlets

•

Red Wine Basting Sauce with
Chicken Drumsticks

•

Corn and Courgette Parcels

•

Rodeo Beans

•

Caramelised Apple on a Skewer

Oriental Basted Lamb Cutlets

——— BARBECUE ———

(Illustrated on page 116)

12 lamb cutlets
sauce
100 ml/4 fl oz chicken stock
3 tablespoons clear honey
3 tablespoons soy sauce
1 clove garlic, crushed
2 tablespoons tomato ketchup
pinch of ground ginger

1 First make the sauce. Place all the ingredients in a saucepan and stir over gentle heat for 10 minutes.

2 Brush the cutlets with the sauce and cook on a grid over the coals for 25–30 minutes, turning and basting occasionally with the sauce. Cooking time depends on the size of the cutlets. **Serves 12**

Red Wine Basting Sauce with Chicken Drumsticks

——— BARBECUE ———

(Illustrated on page 116)

12 chicken drumsticks
sauce
3 tablespoons oil
100 ml/4 fl oz red wine
1 tablespoon grated onion
$\frac{1}{2}$ teaspoon salt
1 tablespoon Worcestershire sauce
$\frac{1}{2}$ teaspoon freshly ground black pepper

1 First make the sauce. Combine all the ingredients, mix well and chill for 1 hour.

2 Place the drumsticks in a shallow dish, pour over the sauce, cover and chill for at least 3 hours.

3 Drain the drumsticks and cook on a grid over the coals for 25–30 minutes, turning and basting occasionally with the sauce. Cooking time depends on the size of the drumsticks. **Serves 12**

Barbecued beef bangers

(Illustrated on page 116)

Use up remaining basting sauces to brush 12 large beef sausages. Cook them over the coals for 20 minutes, turning and basting frequently.

Corn and Courgette Parcels

——— BARBECUE ———

(Illustrated on page 116)

4 tablespoons oil
2 cloves garlic, sliced
675 g/1$\frac{1}{2}$ lb small courgettes, sliced
675 g/1$\frac{1}{2}$ lb cooked or canned sweet corn kernels
salt and pepper

1 Heat the oil in a large saucepan and fry the garlic for 1 minute. Remove from the pan with a slotted draining spoon.

2 Add the courgettes to the pan and cook, stirring, for 5 minutes. Stir in the sweet corn, cover and cook gently for 10 minutes, until the courgettes are just tender.

3 Remove from the heat, season well and divide between 12 large squares of foil. Fold in the foil and crimp edges well together to make airtight parcels.

4 Arrange the parcels around the edges of the barbecue grill to keep hot. **Serves 12**

Rodeo Beans

——— BARBECUE ———

(Illustrated on page 116)

2 (447-g/15$\frac{3}{4}$-oz) cans baked beans
2 teaspoons black treacle
4 teaspoons malt vinegar
2 teaspoons prepared mustard
$\frac{1}{2}$ teaspoon Worcestershire sauce
2 spring onions, chopped

1 Turn the baked beans into a saucepan and stir in the treacle, vinegar, mustard, and Worcestershire sauce. Heat through gently.

2 Sprinkle over the spring onion and serve with the barbecued meats and vegetables. **Serves 12**

Caramelised Apple on a Skewer

BARBECUE

(*Illustrated on page 117*)

12 large dessert apples
175 g/6 oz butter, melted
about 225 g/8 oz demerara sugar

1 Core the apples, peel, if desired, and cut into quarters. Thread four apple quarters on to a skewer for each person.

2 Brush the apple generously with melted butter, holding the skewer over a soup plate to catch the surplus, and sprinkle with the sugar, turning to coat evenly.

3 When the main dishes have been barbecued and the coals are no longer so hot, put a clean grid on the fire and cook the apple-loaded skewers, turning them frequently, until the apple is golden brown. **Serves 12**

VARIATION

Crusted pineapple on a skewer Substitute 12 thick slices of fresh pineapple for the apples. Remove the peel and hard parts of the core and cut each slice into quarters. Brush with melted butter as above and sprinkle with crushed macaroons instead of the demerara sugar. Cook as above.

Summer Coolers

(*Illustrated on pages 106–107*)

Lime cooler

150 ml/$\frac{1}{4}$ pint lime juice cordial
2 tablespoons lemon juice
soda water
green food colouring
castor sugar
ice cubes
slices of lime to decorate

1 Mix the lime juice cordial with the lemon juice in a jug and top up with soda water to taste.

2 Mix a little green food colouring with some water in a saucer. Dip the rim of four glasses first in the colouring and then in castor sugar.

3 Pour the drink into the middle of the glasses, add ice cubes and decorate with slices of lime. **Serves 4**

Raspberry sparkle

150 ml/$\frac{1}{4}$ pint raspberry syrup
150 ml/$\frac{1}{4}$ pint white rum
2 tablespoons orange juice
tonic water or lemonade
fresh fruit such as redcurrants
or grapes to decorate

1 Mix the raspberry syrup with the rum and orange juice and chill thoroughly.

2 Top up with chilled tonic water or lemonade to taste and serve in tall glasses, decorated with small bunches of redcurrants or grapes. **Serves 4**

Creamy blackcurrant shake

150 ml/$\frac{1}{4}$ pint blackcurrant syrup
600 ml/1 pint milk, well chilled
150 ml/$\frac{1}{4}$ pint single cream, well chilled
blackcurrants to decorate

1 Shake or liquidise the blackcurrant syrup with the milk and cream.

2 Serve in tall glasses decorated with small bunches of blackcurrants. **Serves 4**

Orange froth

300 ml/$\frac{1}{2}$ pint orange juice, well chilled
1 egg, separated
50 g/2 oz castor sugar
600 ml/1 pint natural yogurt, well chilled
orange slices to decorate

1 Whisk the orange juice with the egg white until frothy.

2 Whisk the egg yolk with the castor sugar and yogurt. Gradually whisk the orange juice mixture into the yogurt.

3 Serve in tall glasses decorated with orange slices. **Serves 4**

Peach fizz

4 small ripe peaches or nectarines
1 bottle champagne or sparkling white wine

1 Wash the peaches or nectarines and prick all over with a fork. Put one nectarine in each glass.

2 Pour over the champagne or sparkling white wine and serve immediately. Top up as required. The wine-soaked fruit is also delicious to eat. **Serves 4**

September

It's the 'season of fruitfulness',
when the harvest is complete and there's a treasury
of garden riches

As mellow harvest time approaches there may also be a glut of vegetables, especially tomatoes, both home grown and in the shops. Besides your own choice of tomato dishes, try them in two completely new ways; as a sorbet, or fry for breakfast the small green tomatoes you have previously used only in chutney. Courgettes and marrows are still abundant, and home-grown aubergines and peppers are quite a bargain. The fruit basket is piled high with plums, damsons, greengages and peaches. You'll find recipes for all of them in this section. Melons, although imported, should be at their lowest in price at this time of year. Try Melon ice cream, using honeydew or cantaloupe for a subtle contrast in flavour. Finally use diced water melon, which is such a lovely deep pink, to top the scoops of ice cream. Blackberries must surely be the cheapest of all summer fruits since so many can be picked completely free where they grow wild, if you don't mind a few scratches on your hands. The Blackberry meringue cake would make a delightful conclusion to the Harvest Festival supper. In fact the whole menu is truly seasonal, combining cucumber and marrow in one unusual salad and tomatoes stuffed with a diced sweet pepper mixture in the other.

Bacon with Fried Green Tomatoes

———— BREAKFAST ————

25 g/1 oz lard or bacon fat
8 rashers streaky bacon
225 g/8 oz small green tomatoes
salt and pepper
1 thick slice stale bread
1 tablespoon chopped mixed herbs

1 Melt the lard in a frying pan and cook the bacon rashers until crisp. Drain and place on a warm plate.

2 Add the whole tomatoes to the fat remaining in the pan and fry gently on all sides until soft, keeping the tomatoes whole. Sprinkle with salt and pepper to taste.

3 Meanwhile cut the bread into small dice. Add to the pan with the tomatoes and fry, turning occasionally, for 2 minutes. Sprinkle with the herbs.

4 Serve each person with two bacon rashers and a portion of the tomatoes with bread dice. **Serves 4**

VARIATION
Wiltshire breakfast Substitute pork sausages for the bacon rashers, and diced dessert apple for the bread dice.

Peanut butter and bramble jelly on toast

Spread slices of freshly made, warm toast with peanut butter and then with bramble jelly.

Madras Melon Cocktails

———— FIRST COURSE ————

2 teaspoons Madras curry powder
1 teaspoon lemon juice
225 g/8 oz honeydew melon, diced
100 g/4 oz cooked chicken meat, diced
100 g/4 oz small pasta shapes, cooked
150 ml/$\frac{1}{4}$ pint soured cream
good pinch of salt
little shredded lettuce

1 First make the dressing. Blend the curry powder to a paste with the lemon juice and allow to stand for 30 minutes.

2 Meanwhile, combine the melon, chicken and pasta in a bowl and chill well.

3 Beat the curry paste into the soured cream with the salt. Drain off any liquid from the melon mixture and fold in the curried cream.

4 Place a little shredded lettuce in four cocktail glasses and spoon in the melon salad mixture. **Serves 4**

VARIATION
Madras pineapple cocktails Substitute 225 g/8 oz diced pineapple for the melon and use 1 teaspoon pineapple juice instead of the lemon juice.

Fresh Tomato Sorbet

FIRST COURSE

450 g/1 lb ripe tomatoes, chopped
1 small onion, chopped
1 teaspoon powdered gelatine
3 tablespoons lemon juice
1 tablespoon tomato purée
1 tablespoon sugar
$\frac{1}{2}$ teaspoon Worcestershire sauce
1 egg white
mint and parsley sprigs to garnish

1 Put the tomatoes and onion in a saucepan. Place over low heat and bring to the boil without adding any water. Cover and simmer for 15 minutes, or until the onion is soft.

2 Dissolve the gelatine in the lemon juice in a basin over a pan of hot water.

3 Sieve the tomato mixture into a large bowl and stir in the tomato purée, sugar, Worcestershire sauce and gelatine mixture. Cool and place in a shallow polythene container. Freeze until slushy. Turn out and beat thoroughly.

4 Whisk the egg white until stiff and fold into the partially frozen mixture. Return to the container and freeze until firm.

5 Scoop portions of the sorbet into small glasses and garnish with sprigs of mint and parsley. **Serves 4**

Aubergine Niçoise

FIRST COURSE

2 medium aubergines
salt and pepper
3 tablespoons oil
1 medium onion, sliced
4 sticks celery, chopped
1 clove garlic, crushed
350 g/12 oz tomatoes, peeled and sliced
1 (56-g/2-oz) can anchovies
1 tablespoon sugar
2 tablespoons vinegar

1 Slice the aubergines, sprinkle the slices with salt and leave to stand for 30 minutes. Rinse off the salty juices and pat dry with kitchen paper.

2 Heat the oil and fry the onion, celery and garlic until the onion is soft. Then add the aubergine slices and fry for a further 2 minutes, stirring frequently. Add the tomatoes and cook gently for 5 minutes. Chop the

anchovies and add to the pan with the oil from the can, the sugar and the vinegar. Taste and season carefully, adding salt only if necessary. Cook gently for a further 5 minutes and serve hot in individual dishes, or chill and serve cold. **Serves 4**

Fish with Lemon Parsley Sauce

MAIN COURSE

1 small bunch parsley
4 portions white fish fillet
1 large onion, sliced
salt and pepper
675 g/1$\frac{1}{2}$ lb runner beans, sliced
25 g/1 oz butter
25 g/1 oz flour
finely grated rind and juice of 1 large lemon
1 egg yolk

1 Strip the parsley from the stalks and chop the leaves. Place the fish, parsley stalks, onion and some seasoning in a pan. Just cover with water, bring to the boil and simmer for 15 minutes.

2 Meanwhile, cook the beans in boiling salted water for about 10 minutes, until tender.

3 Drain the beans and arrange on a warm serving dish. Lift the fish from the pan with a slotted draining spoon and place on the beans. Keep hot.

4 Strain the fish stock and measure 300 ml/$\frac{1}{2}$ pint of it into a clean saucepan. Add the butter and flour and whisk over moderate heat until the sauce boils and thickens. Beat in the chopped parsley with the lemon rind and juice and cook for 2 minutes. Season to taste, remove from the heat and beat in the egg yolk. Spoon a little of the sauce over the fish and serve the rest separately in a sauce boat. **Serves 4**

VARIATION
Fish with orange parsley sauce Substitute 1 large orange for the lemon and serve on a bed of cooked cauliflower florets, instead of the runner beans.

Pork Chops
with Sugared Courgettes

MAIN COURSE

75 g/3 oz butter
4 pork chops
2 teaspoons French mustard
450 g/1 lb courgettes, sliced
50 g/2 oz sugar

1 Melt the butter in a saucepan. Use a little of it to brush the chops on both sides. Spread them with a little mustard and place under a hot grill for 5–7 minutes on each side, depending on thickness, until the chops are cooked through.

2 Meanwhile, cook the courgettes in a little boiling salted water for about 10 minutes, until just tender. Drain well.

3 Add the sugar to the rest of the melted butter in the saucepan and heat gently until it dissolves. Turn in the courgettes and toss them in the sugar mixture until they are golden brown. Serve with the hot chops.
Serves 4

Beef and Beetroot Stroganoff

MAIN COURSE

(*Illustrated on page 125*)

450 g/1 lb chuck steak, cubed
2 tablespoons seasoned flour
25 g/1 oz butter
450 ml/¾ pint beef stock
225 g/8 oz button onions
4 small cooked beetroot, quartered
150 ml/¼ pint soured cream
salt and pepper

1 Coat the meat in seasoned flour. Melt the butter in a heavy-based saucepan and fry the meat until sealed on all sides. Add the stock and onions and bring to the boil, stirring. Cover and simmer for about 1½ hours, until the meat is tender.

2 Add the beetroot to the saucepan and cook for a further 10 minutes.

3 Blend in the cream, taste and adjust the seasoning. Reheat carefully, stirring, but do not allow to boil. Serve with noodles. **Serves 4**

Vegetable and ham lasagne (page 127)

Ham and cheese pasties (page 133) and Beef and beetroot Stroganoff

Veal with Peach Pockets

MAIN COURSE

4 veal cutlets
4 thin slices ham
1 large peach, peeled and quartered
40 g / 1½ oz butter
toasted breadcrumbs to coat
25 g / 1 oz flour
300 ml / ½ pint milk
50 g / 2 oz Cheddar cheese, grated
salt and pepper

1 Cut through each cutlet from the side into the bone, to make a pocket. Wrap a slice of ham around each piece of peach and press one peach 'parcel' into each veal 'pocket'. Melt the butter in a saucepan and use a little of it to brush the cutlets, then coat with breadcrumbs. Arrange in an ungreased ovenproof dish.

2 Bake in a moderate oven (180 C, 350 F, gas 4) for 30 minutes.

3 Meanwhile, add the flour and milk to the butter in the saucepan and whisk over moderate heat until the sauce boils and thickens. Simmer for 2 minutes then stir in the cheese and season to taste.

4 Pour the sauce over the cutlets and return to the oven for a further 30 minutes. **Serves 4**

VARIATION
Veal with plum pockets Substitute 2 ripe Victoria plums for the peach and add a pinch of ground cinnamon to the cheese sauce before pouring it over the cutlets.

Aubergined Veal Cutlets

MAIN COURSE

75 g / 3 oz butter
4 small veal cutlets
50 g / 2 oz mushrooms, chopped
1 medium aubergine, chopped
4 spring onions, chopped
25 g / 1 oz fresh white breadcrumbs
good pinch of dried thyme
salt and pepper
150 ml / ¼ pint dry cider

1 Melt the butter and fry the cutlets quickly until sealed on both sides. Transfer them to a shallow ovenproof dish.

2 Add the mushrooms, aubergine and onion to the fat remaining in the pan and fry until the onion begins to soften. Stir in the breadcrumbs, thyme and plenty of seasoning. Spoon this mixture on top of the cutlets and pour the cider into the dish around them.

3 Cook in a moderate oven (180 C, 350 F, gas 4), for 35–40 minutes, or until the cutlets are tender. **Serves 4**

VARIATION
Peppered veal cutlets Substitute 1 large green or red pepper for the aubergine. Deseed and then chop it. Use a generous pinch of dried marjoram instead of the thyme.

Tarragon Lamb and Pasta Hotpot

MAIN COURSE

2 tablespoons oil
1 large onion, sliced
675 g / 1½ lb middle neck of lamb, cubed
175 g / 6 oz button mushrooms
600 ml / 1 pint beef stock
2 tablespoons chopped tarragon
finely grated rind and juice of 1 orange
salt and pepper
225 g / 8 oz courgettes
100 g / 4 oz pasta wheels

1 Heat the oil in a large heavy-based saucepan and fry the onion gently until beginning to soften. Add the pieces of lamb and cook until browned on all sides. Add the mushrooms and cook for 2 minutes. Pour in the stock and add the tarragon, orange rind and juice and plenty of seasoning. Bring to the boil, cover and simmer for 1 hour.

2 Cut the courgettes into chunks or leave whole if very small. Add these to the pan, cover again and cook for a further 30 minutes.

3 Stir the pasta into the hotpot, cover the saucepan again and continue to cook gently for a further 25 minutes, or until the pasta is just tender. Taste and adjust the seasoning if necessary. **Serves 4**

Liver and Apple Pie

—————— Main course ——————

350 g/12 oz pig's liver
25 g/1 oz lard
100 g/4 oz fat streaky bacon, chopped
1 large onion, chopped
salt and pepper
1 tablespoon flour
1 large cooking apple, peeled
175 g/6 oz shortcrust pastry (page 184)

1   Thinly slice the liver. Melt the lard and fry the bacon and onion until the onion begins to soften. Add the liver slices and fry until sealed on all sides. Drain and place in a greased pie dish. Sprinkle with salt, pepper and flour.

2   Core and slice the apple, add to the fat remaining in the pan and fry lightly. Spoon the contents of the pan over the liver mixture. Pour in hot water nearly level with the meat and stir well. Insert a pie funnel.

3   Roll out the pastry and cut a lid and a strip to fit the rim of the dish. Place the strip round the moistened rim, moisten it and cover the pie with the lid, sealing the edges.

4   Bake in a moderately hot oven (200 C, 400 F, gas 6) for 30–40 minutes, until golden brown. **Serves 4**

Vegetable and Ham Lasagne

—————— Main course ——————

100 g/4 oz lasagne
3 tablespoons oil
225 g/8 oz onions, sliced
225 g/8 oz carrots, sliced
3 sticks celery, sliced
$\frac{1}{2}$ teaspoon dried mixed herbs
salt and pepper
50 g/2 oz butter
50 g/2 oz flour
600 ml/1 pint milk
pinch of grated nutmeg
175 g/6 oz Cheddar cheese, grated
4 thin slices ham

1   Cook the lasagne in a pan of boiling salted water for 12–15 minutes, until just tender. Drain well.

2   Heat the oil and fry the onion, carrot and celery until soft, stirring occasionally. Add the herbs and seasoning and cook for a further 2 minutes.

3   Place the butter, flour and milk in a saucepan and whisk over moderate heat until the sauce boils and thickens. Simmer for 2 minutes then beat in the nutmeg, half the cheese and seasoning to taste.

4   Layer the vegetable mixture in a greased ovenproof dish with the lasagne, ham and sauce, repeating the layers and ending with a layer of sauce. Sprinkle with the remaining cheese and bake in a moderately hot oven (200 C, 400 F, gas 6) for 45 minutes. **Serves 4**

Roast Chicken with Marrow

—————— Main course ——————

4 chicken portions
salt and freshly ground black pepper
12 button onions
50 g/2 oz butter, melted
350 g/12 oz tomatoes
1 small marrow

1   Season the chicken portions with salt and pepper and place in a shallow ovenproof dish, skin side downwards, with the onions. Spoon over the butter and cook in a moderately hot oven (190 C, 375 F, gas 5) for 25 minutes.

2   Meanwhile, press the tomatoes through a sieve. Peel the marrow and remove the seeds. Cut into chunks.

3   Turn the chicken portions, place the marrow in the dish and baste with the buttery juices. Pour over the tomato pulp and return to the oven for a further 30 minutes, or until the marrow is tender. **Serves 4**

Melon Ice Cream

—————— Dessert ——————

$\frac{1}{2}$ small ripe melon
100 g/4 oz castor sugar
grated rind of 1 lemon
300 ml/$\frac{1}{2}$ pint double cream

1   Peel the melon, discarding the seeds. Chop the flesh and purée in a liquidiser with the sugar and lemon rind until smooth. Make up to 300 ml/$\frac{1}{2}$ pint with water if necessary.

2   Lightly whip the cream and combine with the melon pulp. Pour into a shallow container and freeze until slushy. Turn out and beat until smooth, then return to the container and freeze until firm. Serve scooped into stemmed glasses. **Serves 4–6**

Semolina ring with plums
and Blackberry meringue layer cake

Greengage Crumble

DESSERT

450 g / 1 lb ripe greengages
175 g / 6 oz castor sugar
75 g / 3 oz butter
175 g / 6 oz plain flour

1 Halve the greengages and remove the stones. Place the greengages in an ovenproof dish and sprinkle with one third of the sugar. Bake in a moderately hot oven (190 C, 375 F, gas 5) for 10 minutes.

2 Meanwhile, rub the butter into the flour and stir in the remaining sugar. Sprinkle over the fruit to cover it completely.

3 Return to the oven for a further 40 minutes. Serve warm with custard or cream. **Serves 4–6**

VARIATIONS

Plum crumble Substitute 450 g / 1 lb plums for the greengages and add ½ teaspoon ground cinnamon to the crumble mixture with the sugar.
Damson crumble Substitute 450 g / 1 lb ripe damsons for the greengages and add 2 tablespoons golden syrup to the sugar used for sweetening the fruit.

Blackberry Meringue Layer Cake

DESSERT

(Illustrated on page 128)

4 egg whites
225 g / 8 oz castor sugar
1 teaspoon cornflour
2 teaspoons vinegar
300 ml / ½ pint double cream, whipped
350 g / 12 oz ripe blackberries

1 Whisk the egg whites until stiff. Add half the sugar and whisk once again until stiff. Fold in the cornflour, vinegar and remaining sugar.

2 Grease two baking sheets and line with non-stick cooking paper. Mark a circle on each one 20 cm / 8 inches in diameter. Spread the meringue mixture on each baking sheet to completely fill the circles.

3 Bake in a cool oven (150 C, 300 F, gas 2) for 1 hour, until crisp and pale golden. Allow to cool, then remove the parchment.

4 Sandwich the meringue layers together with some whipped cream and blackberries and decorate with the remaining cream and blackberries. **Serves 4**

VARIATION

Pear and lemon meringue cake Flavour the whipped cream with 2 teaspoons grated lemon rind. Use peeled, cored and chopped ripe pears in place of the blackberries.

Semolina Ring with Plums

DESSERT

(Illustrated on page 128)

1 orange jelly tablet
450 ml / ¾ pint milk
finely grated rind and juice of 1 orange
1 tablespoon castor sugar
40 g / 1½ oz semolina
150 ml / ¼ pint double cream
2 egg whites
filling
350 g / 12 oz plums
2 tablespoons water
4 tablespoons seedless red jam

1 Make the jelly tablet up to 300 ml / ½ pint with water. Stir over gentle heat until dissolved then allow to cool.

2 Place the milk, orange rind and sugar in a saucepan and heat, stirring, until the sugar has dissolved. Sprinkle in the semolina and stir constantly over moderate heat until the mixture boils and thickens. Simmer for 3 minutes, stirring all the time. Remove from the heat and blend in the dissolved jelly and the orange juice. Cool until the mixture is on the point of setting.

3 Whip the cream until thick and, in a separate bowl, whisk the egg whites until stiff. Fold both these evenly into the semolina mixture. Rinse a 1.25-litre / 2-pint ring mould with cold water, pour in the semolina mixture and chill until set.

4 To make the filling, halve and stone the plums. Place in a saucepan with the water and the jam. Cover and cook very gently, stirring occasionally, until the fruit is soft. Allow to cool.

5 Turn the ring out on to a serving dish, pile the plums in the centre and spoon a little of the sauce evenly over them. Any remaining sauce may be handed separately. **Serves 4**

Melon ice cream (page 127)

Harvest Festival Supper

Raised Pork Pies

Sweet Pepper Cups

Cucumber and Marrow Salad

Country Herbed Bread with
Cheese Dice

Raised Pork Pies

HARVEST FESTIVAL SUPPER

(Illustrated on page 130)

filling
2 kg/4½ lb pie pork, chopped
2 large onions, chopped
3 tablespoons chopped sage or 1 tablespoon dried
sage
salt and pepper
pastry
1.5 kg/3 lb plain flour
½ teaspoon salt
450 g/1 lb soft lard
600 ml/1 pint water
2 eggs, beaten
to finish
1 tablespoon powdered gelatine
450 ml/¾ pint hot chicken stock

1 First prepare the filling. Combine the pork, onion and sage in a bowl and season well. Leave to stand while making the pastry cases.

2 Sift the flour and salt into a large bowl. Melt the lard in a saucepan, add the water and bring to the boil. Pour into the dry ingredients and stir well until the mixture forms a dough. Knead quickly until smooth.

3 Divide the mixture between three bowls and cover two with cling film. Work with the remaining pastry, trimming off a quarter for the pie lid. Keep this covered so that it remains warm and pliable. Roll out the remainder and use to line the base and sides of a 15-cm/6-inch loose-bottomed cake tin. Turn in one-third of the pork mixture. Roll out the remaining pastry to make a lid, moisten the edges and seal well together. Trim off excess pastry and reserve.

4 Make up the other two pies in the same way. Flute the edges of the pies and use the reserved pastry trimmings to make leaves. Make a small hole in the centre of each pie; top with a small ball of pastry. Brush the pies with beaten egg and cook in a moderately hot oven (190 C, 375 F, gas 5) for 1½ hours.

5 Cool the pies in the tins, making sure they are completely loosened while still warm.

6 Remove the balls of pastry to leave small holes in the pie lids. Add the gelatine to the hot stock; stir until completely dissolved. Cool until warm then pour into the pies. Replace the pastry balls and leave until the stock has set. Remove the pies from the tins. **Serves 16**

Sweet Pepper Cups

HARVEST FESTIVAL SUPPER

(Illustrated on page 130)

16 tomatoes
1 (56-g/2-oz) can anchovy fillets
juice of ½ lemon
1 tablespoon grated onion
2 large red peppers, deseeded and chopped
2 tablespoons chopped parsley
salt and freshly ground black pepper

1 Cut the tops off the tomatoes and reserve. Scoop out the flesh and seeds, taking care not to damage the shells. Drain the oil from the anchovies and reserve. Chop the anchovies finely.

2 Press the tomato flesh through a sieve and combine with the anchovy oil, chopped anchovies, lemon juice, onion, red pepper and chopped parsley. Season to taste.

3 Spoon the mixture into the tomato shells and replace the reserved lids. **Serves 16**

Cucumber and Marrow Salad

HARVEST FESTIVAL SUPPER

(Illustrated on page 130)

1 large marrow, peeled and deseeded
4 tablespoons oil
2 large onions, chopped
2 cloves garlic, crushed
4 tablespoons cider vinegar
4 tablespoons sweet cider
4 tablespoons oil
½ teaspoon dry mustard
salt and freshly ground black pepper
8 large tomatoes, peeled and chopped
2 cucumbers, diced
freshly chopped herbs (mint, thyme) to garnish

1 Dice the marrow. Heat the oil and gently fry the onion, garlic and marrow for about 5 minutes, until softened. Drain off any surplus oil and allow to cool.

2 Make the dressing by whisking together the cider vinegar, cider, oil and mustard. Season to taste.

3 Place the chopped tomato and cucumber in a large bowl and pour over the dressing. Stir in the marrow mixture and sprinkle with the herbs. **Serves 16**

Country Herbed Bread with Cheese Dice

HARVEST FESTIVAL SUPPER

(Illustrated on page 130)

Slice 3 large crusty white loaves of bread (preferably bloomers), cutting through almost to the bottom. Soften 450 g/1 lb butter, mash and season with salt, pepper, 1–2 crushed garlic cloves and chopped fresh mixed herbs to taste. Spread generously into the cuts in the bread. Press to re-form the loaves and wrap in foil parcels. Before serving, place the parcels in a moderately hot oven (190 C, 375 F, gas 5) for 15 minutes. Serve with cubes of cheese such as Cheddar, Double Gloucester or Stilton. **Serves 16**

Ham and Cheese Pasties

SUPPER OR SNACK

(Illustrated on page 125)

225 g/8 oz puff pastry
1 dessert apple, peeled
225 g/8 oz ham, chopped
100 g/4 oz mild cheese, grated
1 teaspoon dry mustard
1 tablespoon fresh breadcrumbs
2 tablespoons chopped parsley
salt and pepper
2 tablespoons cream
milk or beaten egg to brush

1 Roll out the pastry to a 30-cm/12-inch square and cut into four smaller squares.

2 Core and chop the apple. Mix with the ham, cheese, mustard, breadcrumbs and parsley. Season to taste and moisten with the cream. Divide the filling between the pastry squares and brush the edges with the milk or egg. Fold the pastry over to make triangular pasties and pinch the edges to seal well.

3 Place on a dampened baking sheet and brush with milk or beaten egg. Bake in a moderately hot oven (200 C, 400 F, gas 6) for 20 minutes, then reduce the heat slightly and cook for about a further 10 minutes, until the pasties are well risen and golden brown. **Serves 4**

Cheese-stuffed Courgettes

SUPPER OR SNACK

450 g/1 lb courgettes
25 g/1 oz butter
1 medium onion, chopped
$\frac{1}{4}$ teaspoon dried thyme
25 g/1 oz fresh brown breadcrumbs
salt and pepper
pinch of grated nutmeg
100 g/4 oz Cheddar cheese, grated

1 Trim the courgettes and cut each in half lengthways. Scoop out the centre of each courgette half and chop this flesh finely. Heat a pan of salted water until boiling, add the courgette shells, bring back to the boil and cook for 2 minutes. Drain well and arrange in a greased ovenproof dish.

2 Melt the butter in a saucepan and cook the onion gently until soft but not brown. Stir in the thyme, breadcrumbs and chopped courgette flesh, and season with the salt, pepper and nutmeg. Spoon this mixture into the courgettes and sprinkle with the cheese.

3 Bake in a moderately hot oven (190 C, 375 F, gas 5) for 25 minutes, until the courgettes are tender. **Serves 4**

Toast Tartlets

SUPPER OR SNACK

40 g/1$\frac{1}{2}$ oz butter
1 tablespoon oil
6 slices white bread
2 hard-boiled eggs, chopped
75 g/3 oz salami, diced
300 ml/$\frac{1}{2}$ pint white sauce (page 186)
salt and pepper
4 tablespoons cooked or canned sweet corn kernels
75 g/3 oz Cheddar cheese, grated

1 Heat the butter and oil together until the butter melts. Trim the bread slices and cut each into two pieces, as nearly square as possible. Brush the bread squares with the melted butter mixture on both sides and fit each into a bun tin. Bake in a moderate oven (180 C, 350 F, gas 4) for 10 minutes, or until crisp.

2 Meanwhile, stir the chopped egg and salami into the sauce and season well.

3 Divide the sweet corn between the toast tartlets and spoon over the sauce. Sprinkle with cheese and return to the oven for 10 minutes. Serve hot. **Serves 6**

October

Golden leaves and misty mornings form the backcloth
of autumn and the start of the game season

The leaves on the trees are turning to bronze and rust before sadly fluttering down. It's goodbye to the last of the runner beans, and a warm welcome to the newly matured root vegetables, especially carrots. Hearty dishes are in demand again and beef is the prime favourite meat. Try it with pears or with plums, both of which are superb this month. Pork is in season too, another meat for which plums make a lovely accompaniment, as do damsons. This is the beginning of the game season so there is a recipe for pheasant and also for Hare in damson sauce. If you like the flavour of hare, you might equally enjoy this recipe using saddle of venison, marinated in brown ale. On the sweet side, pears and apples are plentiful and make the most delicious hot puddings as well as cold desserts. For our Hallowe'en party oven-baked pork sausages are served hot with a variety of seasonal dips, including one made with cranberries. Naturally there's Pumpkin pie to finish.

American Pancakes

BREAKFAST

175 g/6 oz plain flour
1½ teaspoons baking powder
1 teaspoon salt
2 eggs, beaten
300 ml/½ pint milk
2 tablespoons oil
oil for frying
225 g/8 oz pork chipolata sausages
butter and maple syrup for serving

1 Sift the flour, baking powder and salt into a bowl. Make a well in the centre and add the eggs, milk and oil. Stir lightly. (Any lumps will disappear during cooking.)

2 Brush a heavy frying pan with oil and heat through evenly. Fry the pancakes one at a time, using 2 tablespoons batter for each pancake. When bubbles form on the uncooked surface, turn the pancake and brown on the other side. Continue in this way until you have 12 pancakes, keeping the cooked pancakes warm.

3 While the pancakes are being cooked, fry or grill the sausages.

4 Serve each person with three pancakes and two chipolata sausages. Top the pancakes with a knob of butter and a generous helping of maple syrup. **Serves 4**

Mixed Melon Chunks

ACCOMPANIMENT

50 g/2 oz sugar
150 ml/¼ pint water
1 teaspoon lemon juice
generous pinch of ground ginger
450 g/1 lb mixed melon flesh, cubed (Honeydew, watermelon, Cantaloupe, Ogen)

1 Dissolve the sugar in the water over a low heat. Add the lemon juice and ginger. Bring to the boil and allow to cool.

2 Pour the syrup over the melon cubes. Chill well and serve in individual glass dishes. **Serves 4**

Peppered Avocado Soup

FIRST COURSE

1 small green pepper, deseeded
25 g/1 oz butter
1 tablespoon grated onion
1 tablespoon flour
600 ml/1 pint chicken stock
1 large ripe avocado
1 tablespoon lemon juice
salt and pepper

1 Shred the pepper finely. Melt the butter and cook the onion and pepper gently until the onion is transparent. Stir in the flour then gradually add the stock and bring to the boil, stirring constantly.

2 Meanwhile, halve and stone the avocado. Scoop out the flesh and mash with the lemon juice. Add to the pan and stir well. Bring back to the boil, cover and simmer for 10 minutes. Taste and adjust the seasoning if necessary. Serve hot in small bowls. **Serves 4**

Beetroot and Orange Soup

FIRST COURSE

450 g/1 lb raw beetroot, peeled
1 large carrot, chopped
1 large onion, chopped
1 bay leaf
2 whole cloves
900 ml/1½ pints beef stock
grated rind and juice of 1 orange
salt and pepper
150 ml/¼ pint natural yogurt

1 Grate the beetroot and place in a large saucepan with the carrot, onion, bay leaf and cloves. Add the stock, bring to the boil, cover and simmer for 30 minutes.

2 Remove the bay leaf and cloves with a slotted spoon and liquidise or sieve the beetroot mixture.

3 Return it to the saucepan with the orange rind and juice and season to taste. Bring to boiling point, carefully stir in the yogurt and reheat but do not allow to boil. Taste and adjust the seasoning if necessary. This soup is also delicious served cold. **Serves 4**

VARIATION

Beetroot and lemon soup Substitute 2 teaspoons grated lemon rind and 2 tablespoons lemon juice for the orange rind and juice. Use chicken stock instead of the beef stock.

Club Mushrooms

FIRST COURSE

225 g/8 oz ripe tomatoes
75 g/3 oz butter
1 tablespoon grated onion
350 g/12 oz button mushrooms
salt and freshly ground black pepper
1 tablespoon sherry
75 g/3 oz cream cheese, softened
1 tablespoon oil
2 slices white bread, trimmed

1 Halve the tomatoes and rub them through a sieve. Melt half the butter in a saucepan, add the onion and cook for 1 minute, stirring, then add the mushrooms. Season well and cook, stirring, for 2 minutes. Add the sherry and tomato pulp and cook gently, stirring occasionally, until the mixture is thick.

2 Gradually stir in the cream cheese until well blended and piping hot, but do not allow the mixture to boil.

3 Heat the remaining butter with the oil and fry the slices of bread on both sides until golden and crisp. Drain well on kitchen paper and cut each slice into four triangles.

4 Serve the mushroom mixture in four small warm serving dishes with the hot fried bread triangles on the side. **Serves 4**

Beef with Pears in Wine

MAIN COURSE

2 large rashers streaky bacon
2 large onions, sliced
450 g/1 lb braising steak, cubed
salt and pepper
300 ml/½ pint strong beef stock
150 ml/¼ pint red wine
225 g/8 oz firm pears, peeled
2 teaspoons cornflour

1 Chop the bacon. Place layers of bacon, onion and steak in a greased ovenproof casserole, seasoning each layer with salt and pepper. Pour over the stock and wine. Add a little water if necessary until the liquid just 'comes through' the meat mixture.

2 Cover and cook in a moderate oven (160 C, 325 F, gas 3) for 1¼ hours.

3 Core and quarter the pears, add to the casserole and stir in gently. Cover again and return to the oven for a further 1 hour. Moisten the cornflour with a little cold water, blend well into the casserole and return to the oven for 10 more minutes, until slightly thickened. Serve with oven-baked potatoes. **Serves 4**

VARIATION

Beef with plums in wine Substitute 225 g/8 oz firm plums for the pears. Halve and stone them before adding to the casserole.

Braised Lamb with Rosemary

MAIN COURSE

2 tablespoon oil
1 large onion, chopped
50 g/2 oz prepared slices cooking apple
1 teaspoon chopped fresh rosemary
or 1 teaspoon dried rosemary
4 large loin of lamb chops
1 tablespoon flour
300 ml/$\frac{1}{2}$ pint beef stock
1 tablespoon tomato purée
salt and pepper

1 Heat the oil and fry the onion and apple until the onion is soft. Drain and place in a shallow ovenproof dish. Sprinkle with the rosemary. Add the chops to the fat remaining in the pan and brown on both sides. Arrange on the onion mixture.

2 Stir the flour into the juices in the pan. Gradually blend in the stock and tomato purée. Bring to the boil, stirring constantly. Season well and pour over the chops.

3 Cover and cook in a moderate oven (180 C, 350 F, gas 4) for 1 hour, or until the chops are tender. **Serves 4**

VARIATION

Braised lamb with plums and thyme Substitute 2 large ripe plums for the apple. Halve, stone and roughly slice them. Add to the onion in the dish but do not fry first. Use 2 teaspoons chopped fresh thyme or 1 teaspoon dried thyme instead of the rosemary.

Pork with Plum Butter

MAIN COURSE

4 large pork shoulder steaks
1 tablespoon oil
450 g/1 lb cooking plums, stoned
2 tablespoons sherry
$\frac{1}{4}$ teaspoon ground cinnamon
1 small onion, grated
salt and pepper
15 g/$\frac{1}{2}$ oz butter
1 tablespoon soft brown sugar
1 tablespoon chopped parsley to garnish

1 Brush the steaks with oil and cook under a moderately hot grill for about 15 minutes, turning them once, until cooked through and golden brown on both sides.

2 Meanwhile, chop the plums and place them in a saucepan with the sherry, cinnamon, onion and a little seasoning. Cover and cook gently for about 10 minutes, or until the fruit is reduced to a pulp. Add the butter and sugar and beat well. Strain in any juices from cooking the pork steaks.

3 Arrange the steaks on a warm serving dish, spoon the sauce over the top and sprinkle with parsley. Serve hot. **Serves 4**

Chicken with Pearl Barley

MAIN COURSE

(*Illustrated on page 139*)

1 (1.5-kg/3-lb) roasting chicken
salt and pepper
25 g/1 oz butter
50 g/2 oz pearl barley
450 g/1 lb white cabbage, shredded
3 sticks celery, chopped
2 tablespoons lemon juice

1 Place the chicken giblets in a pan and add water to cover. Season well, bring to the boil, cover and simmer for 30 minutes, then strain to make about 300 ml/$\frac{1}{2}$ pint strong stock.

2 Melt the butter in a large saucepan and fry the chicken on all sides for about 5 minutes. Transfer to an ovenproof casserole with the pearl barley. Add the cabbage and celery to the fat remaining in the saucepan and toss over moderate heat for 3 minutes. Add to the casserole with the lemon juice, giblet stock and a little seasoning.

3 Cover and cook in a moderately hot oven (200 C, 400 F, gas 6) for $1\frac{1}{4}$ hours. Serve with oven-baked potatoes. **Serves 4**

Chicken with pearl barley
and Hare with Damson Sauce (page 140)

Pheasant in Wine Sauce

——— MAIN COURSE ———

1 plump pheasant
1 large onion, chopped
2 rashers fat streaky bacon, chopped
50 g/2 oz butter
1 tablespoon brandy
150 ml/¼ pint red wine
150 ml/¼ pint beef stock
4 tablespoons single cream
salt and pepper
large croûtons to garnish

1 Chop the pheasant liver, combine with half the onion and place in the pheasant cavity.

2 Put the bacon in a large heavy-based saucepan. Place over a moderate heat until the fat runs. Remove the bacon with a slotted draining spoon and reserve. Add the butter to the fat remaining in the pan and brown the pheasant on all sides. Warm the brandy in a ladle, pour over the pheasant and ignite. When the flames have died down return the bacon to the pan with the rest of the onion, the wine and stock. Bring to the boil, cover and simmer for 1 hour, or until the pheasant is tender.

3 Remove the bird from the pan, cut into portions and arrange on a warm serving dish. Keep hot.

4 Whisk the cream into the juices remaining in the pan and reheat but do not allow to boil. Check for seasoning and spoon the sauce over the pheasant portions. Garnish with croûtons made from triangles of fried bread. **Serves 4**

VARIATION

Partridge in wine sauce Substitute 2 partridges for the pheasant and use 150 ml/¼ pint chicken stock instead of the beef stock.

To roast a pheasant

Season the bird inside and out with salt and pepper. Spread a little butter over the outside and place a small knob inside the cavity. Cover the breast with pork fat and secure with string. Stand on a trivet in a roasting tin and roast in a moderately hot oven (190 C, 375 F, gas 5) for 40 minutes. Remove the pork fat, dredge the breast with a little flour and return the bird to the oven for a further 5 minutes, until browned. Serve garnished with watercress and the tail feather, accompanied by fried breadcrumbs or game chips and rich gravy.

Hare with Damson Sauce

——— MAIN COURSE ———

(*Illustrated on page 139*)

4 hare portions
1 clove garlic, crushed
300 ml/½ pint brown ale
3 tablespoons seasoned flour
2 tablespoons oil
225 g/8 oz carrots, sliced
150 ml/¼ pint strong beef stock
2 bay leaves
sauce
225 g/8 oz damsons, stoned
2 tablespoons water
1 small onion, grated
1 teaspoon soft brown sugar
2 teaspoons cornflour
salt and pepper

1 Place the hare portions and garlic in a dish, pour over the ale, cover and allow to marinate for 24 hours, turning the portions at least once during this time.

2 Lift out the hare portions, dry on kitchen paper and coat with seasoned flour. Heat the oil in a frying pan and fry the hare portions until golden brown on all sides. Drain and reserve the pan to cook the sauce.

3 Place the carrot in an ovenproof dish and arrange the hare portions on top. Strain the marinade into the dish, add the stock and bay leaves, cover and cook in a moderate oven (160 C, 325 F, gas 3) for about 1½ hours, or until the hare is tender. Remove the bay leaves.

4 Meanwhile, cook the damsons in a pan with the water until tender. Press through a sieve or liquidise.

5 Add the onion to the fat left in the frying pan. Fry until transparent. Stir in the damson purée and 150 ml/¼ pint strained stock from the hare dish. Stir in the sugar. Moisten the cornflour with a little cold water, add to the pan and bring to the boil, stirring constantly. Simmer for 2 minutes and season to taste. Serve the sauce poured over the hare and carrots. **Serves 4**

Baked Marrow Boats

SUPPER OR SNACK

1 medium or large marrow, peeled
50 g/2 oz dripping
1 large onion, grated
350 g/12 oz minced beef
40 g/1½ oz flour
1 beef stock cube
150 ml/¼ pint water
salt and pepper
100 g/4 oz Cheddar cheese, grated

1 Halve the marrow lengthways, scoop out the seeds and place the 'boats' in a colander. Pour over about 2 litres/3½ pints boiling water to soften the marrow slightly. Allow to drain.

2 Melt the dripping and fry the onion gently until transparent. Add the beef and fry, stirring, until the mixture looks brown and crumbly. Sprinkle in the flour and crumbled stock cube. Stir until blended then gradually add the water and bring to the boil, stirring constantly. Add a little more water if necessary to give the consistency of a thick sauce. Season to taste.

3 Arrange the marrow 'boats' in a roasting tin, fill them with the beef mixture and sprinkle with the cheese. Pour about 250 ml/8 fl oz boiling water into the roasting tin.

4 Bake in a moderately hot oven (190 C, 375 F, gas 5) for about 45 minutes, until the marrow is tender and the topping golden brown. **Serves 4**

Gammon and Vegetable Medley

MAIN COURSE

2 (225-g/8-oz) gammon steaks
50 g/2 oz lard
2 large onions, sliced
2 bay leaves
350 g/12 oz courgettes, sliced
450 g/1 lb tomatoes, peeled
salt and freshly ground black pepper
2 teaspoons cornflour
150 ml/¼ pint water

1 Remove the rind from the gammon and cut into neat dice. Melt the lard in a large shallow pan and fry the gammon gently for 5 minutes. Add the onion, bay leaves and courgettes and fry for 2 minutes, stirring. Cover the pan and cook gently for 10 minutes.

2 Quarter the tomatoes, add to the pan and season

carefully, adding salt only if necessary. Cover the pan again and cook for a further 10 minutes. Remove the bay leaves.

3 Moisten the cornflour with the water and stir into the gammon mixture. Bring to the boil, stirring constantly, then simmer for 2 minutes. Check the seasoning again and serve with noodles. **Serves 4**

Leeks in Clover

SUPPER OR SNACK

350 g/12 oz leeks, trimmed
150 ml/¼ pint water
salt and pepper
2 eggs
450 g/1 lb hot mashed potato
about 150 ml/¼ pint milk
20 g/¾ oz butter
15 g/½ oz flour
½ teaspoon French mustard
100 g/4 oz Cheddar cheese, grated
1 carton mustard and cress to garnish

1 Slice the leeks and rinse well. Place in a saucepan with the water and a little salt. Bring to the boil, cover and cook for about 10 minutes, until soft. Drain and reserve the cooking liquid.

2 Meanwhile, beat 1 egg into the mashed potato with seasoning to taste. Spread in the base of a greased ovenproof dish. Arrange the cooked leeks on top. Keep hot.

3 Make the reserved liquid up to 300 ml/½ pint with milk and place in a saucepan with the butter and flour. Whisk over moderate heat until the sauce boils and thickens. Simmer for 2 minutes and whisk in the mustard and cheese. When the sauce is smooth, beat in the remaining egg and remove from the heat. Season to taste.

4 Pour the sauce over the leeks and place under a moderately hot grill for about 10 minutes, until piping hot and golden brown on top. Snip the mustard and cress and sprinkle over the top of the bubbling sauce to make the 'clover'. **Serves 4**

Grape jalousie (page 145)

Hallowe'en Party

Hot Cider Punch

⸱

Oven-baked Sausages with Dips

⸱

Pumpkin Pie

Hot Cider Punch

HALLOWE'EN PARTY

(Illustrated on page 142)

1 dessert apple
1 orange
1 lemon
2 tablespoons castor sugar
300 ml/½ pint brandy or sweet sherry
2 bottles dry or sweet still cider

1 Score the surface of the whole fruits with a sharp, pointed knife and rub the sugar into the cuts.

2 Place in a saucepan with the brandy or sherry and cider. Cover and allow to stand for several hours then heat gently before serving. **Serves 12**

Oven-baked Sausages with Dips

HALLOWE'EN PARTY

(Illustrated on page 142)

Grease a roasting tin and arrange 1.5 kg/3 lb pork chipolata sausages in it. Bake in a moderately hot oven (190 C, 375 F, gas 5) for about 20 minutes, until golden brown all over. When cooked, remove at once from the tin and pile up on hot serving plates. Have ready small paper napkins for holding the sausages, and bowls of various dips. Serve with a selection of fresh vegetbles, crisps or French bread. **Serves 12**

Snowy dip

Soften 75 g/3 oz cream cheese and gradually work in 3–4 tablespoons single cream. Season with cayenne pepper and stir in 40 g/1½ oz roughly chopped assorted salted nuts.

Cheesy pineapple dip

Soften 75 g/3 oz cream cheese and beat in 4 tablespoons drained and roughly chopped canned pineapple.

Cranberry dip

Blend 1 tablespoon cornflour and 1 tablespoon wine vinegar in a small saucepan. Stir in 4 tablespoons cranberry sauce and bring to the boil, stirring constantly. Cook for 1 minute and serve hot or cold.

Horseradish dip

Lightly beat 2 tablespoons double cream with a fork then stir in 4 tablespoons horseradish relish.

Pumpkin Pie

HALLOWE'EN PARTY

(Illustrated on page 142)

pastry
350 g/12 oz wholemeal flour
¼ teaspoon salt
175 g/6 oz margarine
2 teaspoons castor sugar
2 egg yolks
cold water to mix
filling
600 ml/1 pint pumpkin purée
225 g/8 oz demerara sugar
4 teaspoons ground cinnamon
2 teaspoons grated nutmeg
2 teaspoons ground ginger
4 eggs, beaten
300 ml/½ pint milk
4 tablespoons brandy
grated rind of 2 lemons
decoration
150 to 300 ml/¼ to ½ pint double cream, whipped

1 First make the pastry. Place the flour and salt in a bowl and rub in the margarine. Stir in the sugar and mix to a pliable paste with the egg yolks and water. Knead lightly, roll out and use to line two 20-cm/8-inch flan dishes. Place the flan dishes on a baking sheet and chill while you make the filling.

2 Beat together the pumpkin purée, sugar and spices. Gradually add the eggs, milk, brandy and lemon rind, beating all the time. Divide the mixture between the pastry cases.

3 Bake in a moderately hot oven (190 C, 375 F, gas 5) for 1 hour. Allow to cool and serve decorated with rosettes of whipped cream. **Serves 12**

Note To make about 600 ml/1 pint of pumpkin purée, steam 500 g/1 lb 2 oz chopped pumpkin flesh for about 25 minutes, until tender, then mash well or liquidise until smooth.

VARIATION
Creamy pumpkin pies Substitute 300 ml/½ pint single cream for the milk and use the grated rind and juice of 2 oranges instead of the lemon rind and brandy.

Toffee-topped Apples

DESSERT

450 g/1 lb dessert apples
300 ml/½ pint cider
50 g/2 oz soft brown sugar

1 Peel and core the apples. Cut each one into eight thick slices.

2 Place the cider in a pan and bring to boiling point. Add the apple slices and poach gently for about 10 minutes, until tender.

3 Remove the apple slices with a slotted draining spoon and place in an ovenproof dish. Sprinkle with the sugar.

4 Boil the cider until reduced to about 3 tablespoons then spoon over the apples and sugar. Place under a hot grill until the topping caramelises. **Serves 4**

Cinnamon Apple Charlotte

DESSERT

450 g/1 lb cooking apples
75 g/3 oz castor sugar
grated rind and juice of 1 lemon
6 large thick slices white bread
butter to spread
3 egg yolks
1 teaspoon cornflour

1 Peel, core and slice the apples. Place in a pan with the sugar, lemon rind and juice. Cover and cook gently until the apple is just tender. Beat until smooth and allow to cool. Add more sugar to sweeten, according to taste.

2 Spread the slices of bread generously with butter and remove the crusts. Cut four of the slices into fingers and leave the other two slices whole.

3 Completely line the sides of a 15-cm/6-inch deep round cake tin with the buttered fingers of bread, buttered surfaces towards the tin. Line the base of the tin with a circle of bread cut from one of the reserved slices, buttered side downwards.

4 Beat the apple purée with the egg yolks and cornflour. Spoon half the mixture into the bread-lined tin. Cover with any remaining fingers of bread, then turn in the rest of the apple mixture. Cut a circle from the remaining slice of bread and fit into the top of the tin, buttered side up.

5 Bake in a moderately hot oven (190 C, 375 F, gas 5) for about 50 minutes. Allow to cool for a few minutes in the tin, then turn out on to a serving dish. Serve hot with cream. **Serves 4–6**

VARIATIONS

Layered banana and prune charlotte Use brown bread instead of white bread. Arrange layers of sliced banana and stoned prunes, soaked overnight, in the bread-lined tin instead of the cooked apple mixture.
Spiced pear charlotte Substitute 450 g/1 lb firm pears for the apples. Peel, core and slice them and cook with the lemon rind and juice. Sweeten to taste. Add ¼ teaspoon ground ginger when beating the purée with the egg yolks and cornflour.

Grape Jalousie

DESSERT

(*Illustrated on page 143*)

225 g/8 oz puff pastry
1 egg, beaten
150 ml/¼ pint double cream
100 g/4 oz black grapes
100 g/4 oz seedless white grapes
4 tablespoons apricot jam, sieved
1 tablespoon water

1 Roll out the pastry to an oblong 13 × 23 cm/5 × 9 inches. Trim off 1 cm/½ in all round the edges. Dampen the edge of the inner oblong and press the trimmings round the edge to make a neat border. Score a decorative pattern with a sharp knife. Place on a dampened baking sheet and brush all over with beaten egg and bake in a moderately hot oven (200 C, 400 F, gas 6) for about 25 minutes, until golden brown. Allow to cool.

2 Whip the cream and spread over the base of the jalousie. Halve and pip the black grapes and arrange on the cream with the white grapes.

3 Mix the apricot jam and water and stir over gentle heat until smooth. Cool slightly and use to glaze the grapes. **Serves 4**

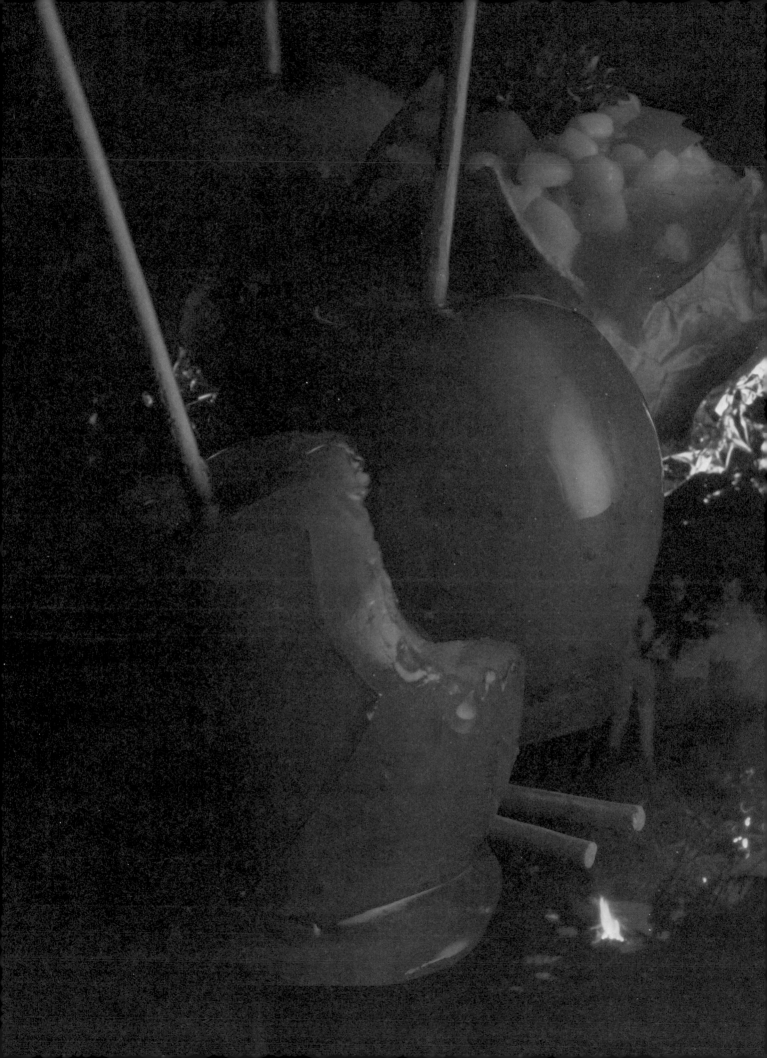

November

With the first sharp frosts of winter
comes the cheer of a Guy Fawkes bonfire
and potatoes baked in the embers

The trees are finally stark and bare and our gardens have gone to sleep for the winter. But there are many consolations – big floury potatoes for baking, comforting hot soups, and home-grown nuts straight from the trees. The Pork and walnut terrine makes an interesting use of them. You may be lucky enough to get hazelnuts and cob nuts too, which could be used as alternatives in this dish. Apples and pears are at their best at this time of year. Try the upside-down pear and ginger pudding for an unusual warming sweet. Now is the time to make your Christmas pudding so that the flavours have time to mature before Christmas day. Let's hope it won't rain and spoil your bonfire party. Just in case, the food for this has been planned so that the more substantial part of the menu can be served indoors afterwards, but there are delicious Scrunchy bars to keep the children happy round the bonfire.

French Toast

BREAKFAST

3 eggs
3 tablespoons milk
salt and pepper
4 large thick slices white bread
butter for frying

1 Beat the eggs with the milk and season lightly to taste.

2 Dip one slice of bread in the egg mixture and fry in a little butter until golden brown underneath. Turn and fry to brown the other side. Drain on kitchen paper and keep hot. Repeat with the remaining pieces of bread, adding more butter to the pan as required.

3 Serve each person with one slice of French toast, cut in half diagonally, with the Hot sweet corn relish. **Serves 4**

VARIATION

Sweet French toast Omit the salt and pepper from the egg mixture and serve the cooked toast with bramble jelly (page 178).

Hot Sweet Corn Relish

ACCOMPANIMENT

25 g/1 oz butter
1 tablespoon soft brown sugar
3 tablespoons marmalade
1 tablespoon white vinegar
1 teaspoon ground ginger
pinch of salt
1 (198-g/7-oz) can sweet corn kernels

1 Melt the butter in a small saucepan. Stir in the sugar, marmalade, vinegar, ginger and salt. Stir over a gentle heat until the mixture is smooth.

2 Drain the can of sweet corn and add the kernels to the pan. Stir until piping hot. **Serves 4**

Beefy Minestrone

FIRST COURSE

2 tablespoons oil
100 g/4 oz minced beef
2 large tomatoes, peeled
1 medium carrot, chopped
2 sticks celery, chopped
1 medium onion, chopped
100 g/4 oz green cabbage, shredded
750 ml/1¼ pints strong beef stock
50 g/2 oz spaghetti
1 (198-g/7-oz) can sweet corn kernels
Parmesan or Cheddar cheese for sprinkling

1 Heat the oil in a large saucepan and fry the beef until brown and crumbly. Chop the tomatoes, add to the pan with the carrot, celery, onion and cabbage. Cook, stirring, for 2 minutes. Pour in the stock and bring to the boil. Cover and simmer for 15 minutes.

2 Break the spaghetti into small pieces, add to the pan with the corn and liquid from the can. Return to the boil and cook for a further 15 minutes. Serve in soup bowls with Parmesan or Cheddar cheese to sprinkle. **Serves 4**

VARIATION

Beefy Minestra Substitute 50 g/2 oz vermicelli for the spaghetti and use 100 g/4 oz diced swede instead of the carrot.

Breton Fish Soup

FIRST COURSE

(Illustrated on page 150)

225 g/8 oz cod or haddock fillet
300 ml/½ pint water
3 teaspoons lemon juice
1 stick celery, sliced
1 medium carrot, sliced
225 g/8 oz potatoes, sliced
1 medium onion, sliced
1 clove garlic, crushed
salt and pepper
25 g/1 oz butter
20 g/¾ oz flour
300 ml/½ pint milk
2 tablespoons chopped parsley

1 Place the fish in a saucepan with the water, lemon juice, celery, carrot, potato, onion, garlic and seasoning. Bring to the boil, cover and cook gently for 20 minutes. Lift out the fish with a slotted spoon, remove the skin and flake roughly.

2 Continue to cook the vegetable mixture for a further 10 minutes, or until the vegetables are soft. Drain off the liquid and reserve.

3 Melt the butter in a large clean saucepan and stir in the flour. Gradually add the milk and reserved stock and bring to the boil, stirring. Cook for 2 minutes. Incorporate the fish and the vegetable mixture and finally stir in the parsley. Taste and adjust the seasoning if necessary. Serve with fresh rolls or Country herbed bread (page 133). **Serves 4**

Pork and Walnut Terrine

FIRST COURSE

450 g/1 lb lean pork, diced
100 g/4 oz streaky bacon
1 small onion, quartered
100 g/4 oz chopped walnuts
50 g/2 oz fresh brown breadcrumbs
generous pinch of ground cloves
1 tablespoon dry sherry
1 egg, beaten
salt and freshly ground black pepper
50 g/2 oz butter

1 Mince together the pork, bacon, onion and walnuts. If a fine texture is required, mince the mixture a second time.

2 Place in a bowl and mix in the breadcrumbs, cloves, sherry and egg. Season generously. Press into a greased small terrine or a 0.5-kg/1-lb loaf tin and smooth the top.

3 Cover with foil and place in a roasting tin half-filled with hot water. Bake in a moderate oven (180 C, 350 F, gas 4) for 2 hours.

4 Remove from the oven and allow to cool in the terrine.

5 Melt the butter, remove the foil and pour over the butter to seal the surface completely. Chill and serve scooped from the terrine. **Serves 4**

Pears Masked with Aspic Mayonnaise

FIRST COURSE

150 ml/¼ pint liquid aspic jelly
150 ml/¼ pint mayonnaise (page 186)
2 large Comice pears
100 g/4 oz cream cheese with pineapple
shredded lettuce
paprika pepper

1 Allow the aspic jelly to become syrupy then beat into the mayonnaise.

2 Peel and halve the pears, scooping out the cores with a teaspoon.

3 Divide the cream cheese with pineapple into four equal portions and press into the cavities in the pears. Place cut sides downwards on a board and spoon over the mayonnaise mixture to coat completely. Chill until set.

4 Arrange a bed of lettuce on four serving plates, top each with a masked pear half and sprinkle lightly with paprika. **Serves 4**

VARIATION
Peaches masked with aspic mayonnaise Substitute 4 large ripe peaches for the pears. Peel and halve them and remove the stones, scooping out just a little of the flesh with a teaspoon. Use 100 g/4 oz cream cheese with chives instead of the cream cheese with pineapple.

Gammon with Onion and Paprika Sauce

─── MAIN COURSE ───

4 gammon steaks
oil for brushing
sauce
2 large onions, chopped
150 ml/¼ pint dry cider
25 g/1 oz butter
25 g/1 oz flour
2 teaspoons paprika pepper
150 ml/¼ pint natural yogurt
salt and pepper

1 Snip the fat on the gammon steaks, brush with oil and cook under a moderately hot grill for about 10 minutes, turning the steaks once.

2 Meanwhile, place the onion and cider in a saucepan. Bring to the boil, cover and cook gently for about 15 minutes, until the onion is soft.

3 Melt the butter in a clean pan and stir in the flour. Cook for 1 minute, stirring. Gradually add the onion mixture and the paprika and bring to the boil, stirring constantly. Cook for 3 minutes then stir in the yogurt and reheat without boiling. Season carefully with salt and pepper and hand the sauce separately with the hot gammon steaks. **Serves 4**

Apple and Bacon Pudding

─── MAIN COURSE ───

(*Illustrated on page 151*)

225 g/8 oz self-raising flour
good pinch of dry mustard
salt and pepper
100 g/4 oz shredded suet
about 150 ml/¼ pint water
1 large cooking apple, peeled
1 large onion, finely chopped
450 g/1 lb streaky bacon, chopped
100 g/4 oz white cabbage, shredded
1 bay leaf
2 tablespoons soft brown sugar

1 Sift the flour, mustard and a pinch of salt into a bowl. Stir in the suet and add sufficient water to make a soft dough. Roll out two-thirds of the pastry to line a 1.5-litre/2½-pint pudding basin.

2 Core and chop the apple. Layer the onion and apple in the pastry case with the bacon, cabbage and bay leaf. Sprinkle with the sugar and pepper. Roll out the remaining pastry to make a lid. Dampen the edges and seal well together.

3 Cover the pudding basin with foil and steam or boil for about 3 hours. Serve the hot pudding from the basin. **Serves 4**

Breton fish soup (page 149) and Country herbed bread (page 133)

Kidney cobbler (page 153)
and Apple and bacon pudding

Pork with Cranberries

MAIN COURSE

450 g/1 lb shoulder of pork, cubed
3 tablespoons seasoned flour
50 g/2 oz lard or pork dripping
1 large onion, chopped
300 ml/$\frac{1}{2}$ pint strong chicken stock
100 g/4 oz cranberries
salt and pepper

1 Coat the pork with seasoned flour. Melt the lard and fry the onion until beginning to soften. Add the pork and fry until sealed on all sides.

2 Stir in any remaining seasoned flour and gradually add the stock. Bring to the boil, stirring constantly. Cover and simmer for 20 minutes.

3 Add the cranberries to the pan, season to taste, cover and cook for a further 10–15 minutes, until the pork is tender and the skins of the cranberries begin to split. **Serves 4**

VARIATION

Pork with pears Substitute 2 firm pears for the cranberries. Peel, quarter and core them before adding to the pan, then cook for a further 20 minutes.

Simmered Spare Rib Chops

MAIN COURSE

1 tablespoon oil
4 spare rib pork chops
1 large onion, sliced
225 g/8 oz swede, diced
4 tomatoes, peeled
$\frac{1}{4}$ teaspoon dried basil
1 (298-g/10$\frac{1}{2}$-oz) can condensed cream of mushroom soup

1 Heat the oil in a large saucepan and fry the chops for 5 minutes on each side. Remove from the pan.

2 Add the onion and swede to the fat remaining in the pan and cook, stirring, until the onion is golden. Quarter the tomatoes, add to the pan with the basil and soup and bring to the boil, stirring constantly.

3 Return the chops to the pan, baste with the sauce, cover and simmer for 45 minutes, or until the chops are tender. Serve with noodles. **Serves 4**

Beef and Apple Pie

MAIN COURSE

450 g/1 lb minced beef
1 large onion, sliced
2 tablespoons flour
about 300 ml/$\frac{1}{2}$ pint beef stock
salt and pepper
2 medium cooking apples, peeled
225 g/8 oz shortcrust pastry (page 184)
milk for brushing

1 Place the minced beef in a large saucepan and cook gently until the fat runs, stirring occasionally. Add the onion and continue cooking, stirring now and then, until the onion is soft.

2 Stir in the flour and when smooth, add the stock and bring to the boil, stirring constantly. Add a little more stock if necessary to give the consistency of a thick sauce. Season to taste. Core and slice the apples and stir into the beef mixture. Transfer to an ovenproof pie dish and insert a pie funnel in the centre.

3 Roll out the pastry and cut a lid and a strip to fit the rim of the dish. Place the strip around the moistened rim, moisten it and cover the pie with the lid, sealing the edges well. Cut a steam vent over the pie funnel and brush the pastry with milk.

4 Bake in a hot oven (220 C, 425 F, gas 7) for 10 minutes, reduce the heat to moderately hot (190 C, 375 F, gas 5) for 20–30 minutes or until the pastry is golden brown. **Serves 4**

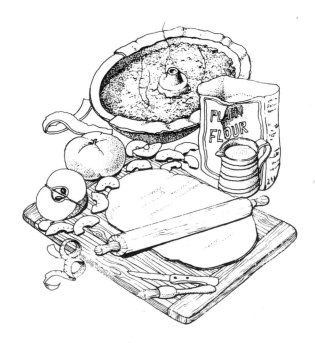

Tomato Liver Bake

—— MAIN COURSE ——

350 g/12 oz lamb's liver
3 tablespoons flour
15 g/½ oz lard
2 medium onions, chopped
4 rashers streaky bacon, chopped
50 g/2 oz mushrooms, sliced
450 g/1 lb tomatoes, peeled and chopped
salt and pepper
1 tablespoon chopped parsley to garnish

1 Cut the liver into thin strips and coat with flour. Melt the lard and fry the onion and bacon for 4 minutes. Drain and place in an ovenproof dish. Add the mushrooms to the fat remaining in the pan and fry until golden. Add the liver strips and fry until sealed on all sides. Stir in the tomato and season to taste.

2 Spoon over the onion mixture, cover and cook in a moderately hot oven (190 C, 375 F, gas 5) for 45 minutes. Serve hot, garnished with parsley. **Serves 4**

Kidney Cobbler

—— MAIN COURSE ——

(*Illustrated on page 151*)

175 g/6 oz self-raising flour
celery salt and pepper
450 g/1 lb lamb's kidneys, halved and cored
1 large onion, chopped
300 ml/½ pint beef stock
1 teaspoon dried mixed herbs
50 g/2 oz butter
milk to mix
1 egg, beaten

1 Well season 2 tablespoons of the flour with celery salt and pepper. Use to coat the kidney and place in a greased pie dish with the onion and stock. Cover and cook in a moderate oven (180 C, 350 F, gas 4) for 40 minutes.

2 Mix the remaining flour with the herbs and more seasoning. Rub in the butter and add sufficient milk to make a soft dough. Roll out on a floured surface and cut into small rounds. Arrange these overlapping on the kidney mixture, brush with beaten egg and return to the oven, uncovered, for a further 30 minutes. **Serves 4**

VARIATION

Kidney and mushroom cobbler Use only 350 g/12 oz kidney and stir 175 g/6 oz sliced button mushrooms into the meat mixture before adding the cobbler topping.

Saffron Chicken

—— MAIN COURSE ——

4 chicken portions
40 g/1½ oz seasoned flour
50 g/2 oz butter
2 green-skinned dessert apples
1 medium onion, chopped
300 ml/½ pint strong chicken stock
generous pinch of powdered saffron
1 teaspoon paprika pepper
salt and pepper

1 Coat the chicken portions with seasoned flour. Melt the butter in a frying pan and fry the chicken portions for about 25 minutes, turning occasionally, until golden brown on both sides and cooked through.

2 Meanwhile, core and chop the apples. Place in a small pan with the onion, chicken stock, powdered saffron and paprika. Bring to the boil, cover and simmer until the onion is tender.

3 Sprinkle any remaining seasoned flour into the chicken pan juices. Stir until blended then gradually add the apple mixture and bring to the boil, stirring constantly. Cover and cook gently for a further 5 minutes, then taste and add salt and pepper if necessary. **Serves 4**

Jellied Apple and Lemon

DESSERT

(Illustrated below)

175 g/6 oz shortcrust pastry (page 184)
450 g/1 lb red and green dessert apples
1 small banana
grated rind and juice of 1 lemon
castor sugar to taste
$\frac{1}{2}$ lemon jelly tablet
grapes to decorate (optional)

1 Roll out the pastry and use to line an 18-cm/7-inch flan ring on a baking sheet. Prick the base with a fork and bake blind in a moderately hot oven (190 C, 375 F, gas 5) for 15 minutes. Remove the baking beans and bake for a further 15–20 minutes until the pastry is cooked. Allow to cool.

2 Halve, core and thinly slice the apples. Slice the banana. Toss the fruit in the lemon rind and juice and stir in sugar to taste. Arrange in the pastry case.

3 Make up the jelly to 300 ml/$\frac{1}{2}$ pint with boiling water. Chill until syrupy. Spoon over the fruit and chill until set. Decorate with grapes. **Serves 4–6**

Grape Macaroon Cream

DESSERT

(Illustrated below)

450 g/1 lb black grapes
300 ml/$\frac{1}{2}$ pint whipping cream
100 g/4 oz almond macaroons, crushed

1 Halve the grapes reserving a few for decoration, and remove the pips. Whip the cream until thick.

2 Put a layer of cream in the base of a glass serving dish. Cover with half the macaroon crumbs and half the grapes. Spread over another layer of the cream and top with the remaining macaroon crumbs and grapes. Finally cover with the rest of the cream.

3 Chill the dessert for at least 2 hours before serving and decorate with the reserved whole grapes. **Serves 4**

VARIATION

Strawberry macaroon cream Substitute 350 g/12 oz strawberries for the grapes. Slice and use to make the dessert with the cream and macaroon crumbs, adding a little sugar to sweeten if liked.

Jellied apple and lemon flan

Upside-down Pear and Ginger Pudding

DESSERT

(Illustrated below)

3 small ripe pears
juice of $\frac{1}{2}$ lemon
150 g/5 oz butter
25 g/1 oz demerara sugar
100 g/4 oz castor sugar
2 eggs, beaten
175 g/6 oz self-raising flour
1 teaspoon ground ginger
pinch of salt

1 Peel, halve and core the pears. Sprinkle with lemon juice. Grease a 15-cm/6-inch cake tin or soufflé dish generously with 25 g/1 oz of the butter and sprinkle the demerara sugar over the base. Place the pear halves on top, rounded sides uppermost.

2 Cream the remaining butter with the castor sugar and gradually beat in the eggs. Sift together the flour, ginger and salt and fold into the creamed mixture. Spoon into the prepared tin and level the top.

3 Bake in a moderate oven (180 C, 350 F, gas 4) for about 45 minutes, or until well risen and golden brown. Invert on to a warm serving dish. **Serves 4**

VARIATIONS

Upside-down prune pudding with cider sauce Soak 100 g/4 oz large prunes in cider overnight. Drain the prunes and use in place of the pear halves. Thicken the cider with a little cornflour to serve as a hot sauce with the pudding.

Upside-down orange pudding with marmalade sauce Use 1 large orange, peeled and cut into thick slices, in place of the pear halves. Add the grated rind from the orange to the sponge mixture. Make a sauce with marmalade and fresh orange juice.

Grape macaroon cream and Upside-down pear and ginger pudding

Christmas Pudding

DESSERT

(Illustrated on page 175)

50 g/2 oz plain flour
½ teaspoon salt
½ teaspoon ground nutmeg
½ teaspoon ground mixed spice
½ teaspoon ground cinnamon
100 g/4 oz currants
100 g/4 oz sultanas
100 g/4 oz seedless raisins
50 g/2 oz glacé cherries, chopped
50 g/2 oz mixed peel
50 g/2 oz ground almonds
25 g/1 oz chopped almonds
225 g/8 oz shredded suet
175 g/6 oz fresh white breadcrumbs
75 g/3 oz soft brown sugar
1 medium carrot, finely grated
3 large eggs, beaten
2 tablespoons brandy
100 ml/4 fl oz milk

1 Sift the flour, salt and spices into a bowl then add the fruit, peel and ground and chopped almonds. Working with your hands, mix the ingredients until the fruit is coated with the flour and spice mixture. Add the suet, breadcrumbs, sugar and carrot and when well combined stir in the egg, brandy and milk. Mix really well. The pudding mixture should be of a dropping consistency.

2 Transfer to a well-buttered 1.5 litre/2½ pint pudding basin. Cover with a double thickness of pleated foil and tie round the rim with string.

3 Stand the basin in a large saucepan and pour in boiling water to come two thirds up the sides of the basin. Bring to the boil, cover the pan and keep the water boiling for 6 hours, adding more boiling water during the cooking time, as required.

4 Remove the basin from the pan and cover the pudding with fresh foil. Store in a cool dry place until needed.

5 When required for serving, boil the pudding again for a further 4 hours. Turn out of the basin on a heated serving dish and decorate with a sprig of holly.

6 To serve the pudding with a flourish, spoon 2 tablespoons warmed brandy over the top and ignite it as the dish is carried to the table. **Serves 6–8**

VARIATION

To make a round Christmas pudding, instead of cooking the mixture in a basin, boil it in a large square pudding cloth. Dip the cloth in boiling water and lay it in a mixing bowl. Dredge well with flour. Spoon in the pudding mixture and draw up all four corners of the cloth evenly, to give the pudding a round shape. Tie the top of the cloth securely with string. Heat the pan of water to boiling, put in the pudding, bring back to the boil and cook as above.

Beef~stuffed Tomato Cups

SUPPER OR SNACK

4 large firm tomatoes
salt
4 tablespoons double cream
4 tablespoons mayonnaise (page 186)
1 teaspoon grated orange rind
1 tablespoon orange juice
2 tablespoons grated fresh horseradish
100 g/4 oz cold roast beef, finely diced
1 tablespoon chopped chives to garnish

1 Halve the tomatoes. Carefully scoop out the seeds and some of the flesh without breaking the cups. Sprinkle inside the tomato cups with salt and stand them upside down on a plate to drain.

2 Whip the cream until thick and combine with the mayonnaise. Dice the tomato flesh, discarding the seeds and liquid. Fold into the mayonnaise mixture with the orange rind and juice and the horseradish. Finally fold in the beef.

3 Pile up in the tomato cups and serve sprinkled with chives. Arrange two filled tomato cups on each small plate. **Serves 4**

VARIATION

Prawn-stuffed tomato cups Substitute 100 g/4 oz peeled prawns for the beef and use 2 tablespoons finely chopped cucumber instead of the horseradish. This variation would also be suitable for a meal starter.

Creamy Onion Bake

SUPPER OR SNACK

225 g/8 oz small onions
25 g/1 oz butter
20 g/$\frac{3}{4}$ oz flour
150 ml/$\frac{1}{4}$ pint milk
100 g/4 oz cottage cheese, sieved
salt and freshly ground pepper
225 g/8 oz cooked beef or lamb, minced
1 tablespoon oil
2 tablespoons fresh breadcrumbs

1 Place the onions in a pan with salted water to cover. Cook gently until the onions are tender. Drain and reserve 150 ml/$\frac{1}{4}$ pint of the cooking liquid.

2 Place the butter, flour, milk and reserved liquid in a saucepan and whisk over moderate heat until the sauce boils and thickens. Simmer for 2 minutes, then stir in the cottage cheese and plenty of seasoning.

3 Place the meat in an ovenproof pie dish, top with the onions and pour the sauce over. Heat the oil and use to fry the breadcrumbs until golden. Spoon them over the sauce in the dish.

4 Bake in a moderately hot oven (190 C, 375 F, gas 5) for 20 minutes. **Serves 4**

VARIATION
Creamy celery bake Substitute 225 g/8 oz sliced celery for the onions and use celery cooking stock in the sauce.

Capered Chicken Snack

SUPPER OR SNACK

25 g/1 oz butter
100 g/4 oz button mushrooms, sliced
25 g/1 oz flour
300 ml/$\frac{1}{2}$ pint milk
2 tablespoons lemon juice
2 tablespoons capers
salt and pepper
350 g/12 oz cooked chicken meat, diced

1 Melt the butter and cook the mushrooms for 2 minutes, until beginning to soften. Stir in the flour and when smooth, gradually add the milk and bring to the boil, stirring constantly. Simmer for 2 minutes, stir in the lemon juice and capers and season to taste.

2 Carefully fold in the chicken and reheat thoroughly,

stirring occasionally. Serve hot with triangles of crisply fried bread. **Serves 4**

VARIATION
Chicken and olive snack Substitute 2 tablespoons sliced stuffed green olives for the capers and season to taste with salt and freshly ground black pepper.

Sausages with Corn Fritters

SUPPER OR SNACK

2 tablespoons oil
450 g/1 lb pork sausages
50 g/2 oz self-raising flour
1 egg
175 g/6 oz cooked or canned sweet corn kernels
milk
salt and pepper
2 small bananas

1 Heat the oil and fry the sausages for about 12 minutes, until cooked through and golden brown all over.

2 Meanwhile, beat together the flour, egg and sweet corn with enough milk to make a thick batter. Season well.

3 Remove the sausages from the pan, place on a warm serving dish and keep hot. Cut the bananas in half lengthways and fry briskly in the fat remaining in the pan for 2 minutes, turning them once. Drain and add to the sausages.

4 To make the fritters, beat up the batter and drop spoonfuls of it into the remaining hot fat. Cook until golden brown and crisp on both sides. Drain well and serve with the sausages and fried bananas. **Serves 4**

Bonfire Party

Celery and Tomato Soup

Sausages in Rolls

Spicy Spare Ribs

Cheesy Scotch Eggs

Campus Jacket Potatoes

Scrunchy Bars

Toffee Apples

Celery and Tomato Soup

———— BONFIRE PARTY ————

(Illustrated on title page)

2 small heads celery
50 g/2 oz butter
3 medium onions, chopped
2 tablespoons plain flour
1.75 litres/3 pints chicken stock
2 (397-g/14-oz) cans tomatoes, chopped
salt and freshly ground black pepper
600 ml/1 pint milk
4 tablespoons chopped parsley (optional)

1 Trim and wash the celery and chop finely. Melt the butter in a large saucepan, add the celery and onion and cook gently until soft but not browned.

2 Sprinkle with flour and gradually add the stock, stirring continuously. Add the tomatoes and bring to the boil. Cover and cook over a low heat for 30 minutes.

3 Remove from the heat and purée the soup in a liquidiser. Taste and adjust the seasoning. Stir in the milk and reheat thoroughly without boiling. Serve sprinkled with parsley. **Serves 12**

VARIATION

Tomato and celery soup with ham *(Illustrated on page 158)* Use ham stock instead of chicken stock and add 225 g/8 oz diced cooked ham with the milk before reheating. Garnish with finely chopped raw celery and chopped parsley.

Sausages in Rolls

———— BONFIRE PARTY ————

(Illustrated on page 158)

1.5 kg/3 lb thick pork sausages
12 long bread rolls
150 g/5 oz butter
1 small lettuce
selection of chutney and pickles for serving

1 Grill the sausages until cooked through and crisp and brown on the outside. Split the rolls and spread with butter. Place a lettuce leaf and 2 sausages in each roll.

2 Serve each roll wrapped in a paper napkin with a selection of chutneys and pickles. **Serves 12**

Spicy Spare Ribs

———— BONFIRE PARTY ————

(Illustrated on page 158)

1.5 kg/3 lb pork spare ribs
2 tablespoons soft brown sugar
1 medium onion, grated
1 teaspoon ground ginger
2 cloves garlic, crushed
2 tablespoons tomato purée
150 ml/$\frac{1}{4}$ pint orange juice
salt and freshly ground black pepper
raw onion rings to garnish

1 Place the spare ribs in a large roasting tin. Mix all the remaining ingredients together and season well. Pour evenly over spare ribs. Cook in a moderately hot oven (200 C, 400 F, gas 6) for 45–50 minutes. Turn and baste the spare ribs frequently during cooking.

2 Alternatively cook the spare ribs over a barbeque, basting frequently with the sauce. **Serves 12**

Cheesy Scotch Eggs

———— BONFIRE PARTY ————

(Illustrated on page 158)

675 g/1$\frac{1}{2}$ lb pork sausagemeat
75 g/3 oz mature Cheddar cheese, finely grated
3 tablespoons chopped parsley
1 tablespoon freshly chopped mixed herbs
salt and freshly ground black pepper
6 hard-boiled eggs
1 egg
1 tablespoon water
40 g/1$\frac{1}{2}$ oz plain flour
175 g/6 oz dry white breadcrumbs
oil for deep frying

1 Mix the sausagemeat with the cheese, parsley, herbs and seasoning and divide into six equal portions. Shell the eggs and place one on top of each portion of sausagemeat. Mould the meat mixture evenly round each egg to coat completely.

2 Beat the egg lightly with the water. Dust each scotch egg with a little flour, dip in the egg mixture and coat thickly and evenly with the breadcrumbs.

3 Deep fry until golden brown then drain on kitchen paper. Allow to cool and cut in half just before serving. **Serves 12**

Campus Jacket Potatoes

BONFIRE PARTY

(Illustrated on page 146)

12 large old potatoes
100 g/4 oz butter, melted
4 tablespoons tomato purée
2 teaspoons Worcestershire sauce
2 teaspoons soft brown sugar
1 medium onion, grated
2 (200-g/7-oz) cans corned beef, diced
salt and pepper

1 Scrub the potatoes, prick them and brush with a little of the butter. Bake in a moderately hot oven (200 C, 400 F, gas 6) for about 1 hour, or until the potatoes feel tender when pressed.

2 Meanwhile, place the remaining butter in a saucepan with the tomato purée, Worcestershire sauce, sugar and onion and cook for 1 minute. Add the corned beef and cook gently for about 5 minutes, stirring occasionally, until bubbling. Season to taste.

3 Cut a deep cross in the top of each potato and open out with a fork. Place in an ovenproof serving dish. Spoon the corned beef filling into the potatoes, cover lightly with foil and return to the oven for a further 10 minutes. Serve hot. **Serves 12**

VARIATION

Pepper and corn potatoes *(Illustrated on page 146)* Bake the potatoes as above. Instead of the corned beef filling melt 50 g/2 oz butter in a saucepan and gently sauté 2 finely chopped onions with two finely chopped red or green peppers. Add 1 (425-g/15-oz) can sweet corn, drained, and heat through gently. Cut the potatoes and fill with sweet corn mixture. Serve at once. Garnish with sprigs of parsley, if liked.

Scrunchy Bars

BONFIRE PARTY

(Illustrated on page 158)

175 g/6 oz margarine
75 g/3 oz soft brown sugar
50 g/2 oz golden syrup
25 g/1 oz ground rice
250 g/9 oz rolled oats
$\frac{1}{2}$ teaspoon salt
soft brown sugar for sprinkling

1 Place the margarine, sugar and syrup in a saucepan and heat gently until the margarine has melted. Do not allow the mixture to boil.

2 Remove from the heat, add the ground rice, oats and salt and mix well.

3 Spread the mixture evenly in a greased Swiss roll tin then sprinkle the top with a layer of brown sugar.

4 Bake in a moderate oven (180 C, 350 F, gas 4) for about 35 minutes, or until golden brown. Cut into bars while still warm then leave to cool in the tin.
Serves 12

Toffee Apples

BONFIRE PARTY

(Illustrated on page 146)

12 red dessert apples
675 g/1$\frac{1}{2}$ lb sugar
450 ml/$\frac{3}{4}$ pint water

1 Wash and dry the apples and stick them onto wooden skewers.

2 Mix the sugar and water together in a saucepan and heat gently, stirring continuously, until the sugar dissolves. Bring to the boil, without stirring, and boil steadily until the syrup turns golden brown.

3 Remove the caramel from the heat immediately it turns golden – do not allow it to overcook or it will become too dark before the apples are coated.

4 Dip the apples in the caramel, twisting them to coat them evenly then place them on an oiled baking sheet. Dip each apple several times in the caramel, working quickly before it hardens then allow them to cool completely. These apples are best made on the same day as serving as the caramel becomes soft and sticky if kept any longer. **Serves 12**

Merry Christmas

December

Christmas preparations
and tea by the fire – such seasonal delights
shut out the dark evenings

A sparkle of frost on the window panes is often to be seen on Christmas Eve. It's cold, but who cares, with all the delights of the festive season in store. The winter vegetables such as Brussels sprouts (delicious in salads and soups), cabbage, cauliflower and fennel are quite as tempting to the palate in their own way as the delicate green vegetables of summer. Fennel in curry cream makes a pleasant starter to a meal. Then there is the arrival of beautiful winter citrus fruits — oranges and grapefruit galore. Try Orange corn cups as another seasonal meal starter. Strangers at other times, but right in season for Christmas, are satsumas, clementines, tangerines and mandarins. These are not winners for cooking, but make a satisfying dessert course after such substantial main dishes as Beef and bacon suet roll, or a snack of Leeks in cheese custard.

Every household has its favourite menu for the roast turkey feast, but help is appreciated with ideas for an appetising meal on Boxing Day. Cold turkey goes well with Prune stuffing balls and Horseradish mayonnaise and the meal is appropriately rounded off with mincepies.

Golden Glazed Grapefruit

--- BREAKFAST ---

Cut 2 large grapefruit in half and loosen the segments with a grapefruit knife. Spread 2 teaspoons orange jelly marmalade over the cut surface of each half and place under a hot grill for 3–4 minutes, until bubbling and golden. Serve at once. **Serves 4**

Smoked Haddock with Poached Eggs

--- BREAKFAST ---

4 portions smoked haddock fillet
150 ml/$\frac{1}{4}$ pint milk
pepper
4 eggs

1 Place the fish in a shallow pan and cover with water. Bring to the boil and immediately drain off the water. Pour over the milk, season with pepper, cover the pan and cook gently for 5–8 minutes, depending on the thickness of the fillet, until the fish flakes easily when tested with a fork.

2 Meanwhile poach the eggs until lightly set.

3 Serve each haddock portion topped with a poached egg. **Serves 4**

Brussels Sprout and Cheese Soup

--- FIRST COURSE ---

675 g/1$\frac{1}{2}$ lb Brussels sprouts
40 g/1$\frac{1}{2}$ oz butter
1 tablespoon flour
900 ml/1$\frac{1}{2}$ pints chicken stock
salt and pepper
4 tablespoons single cream
50 g/2 oz Cheddar cheese, grated

1 Cook the sprouts in plenty of boiling salted water for about 15 minutes, until soft. Drain well.

2 Melt the butter in a large saucepan, add the sprouts and sprinkle with the flour. Stir well until blended. Gradually add the stock and bring to the boil, stirring constantly. Cover and cook gently until the sprouts are really soft.

3 Liquidise the soup or rub through a sieve and return to the saucepan. Add seasoning to taste, stir in the cream and reheat but do not allow to boil. Just before serving, stir in the cheese. **Serves 4**

VARIATION
Brussels sprout and bacon soup Substitute 3 rashers streaky bacon for the grated cheese. Chop and fry gently until crisp, then stir into the soup when it is reheated.

Chicken and Almond Soup

— FIRST COURSE —

1 chicken portion
1 large onion, chopped
175 g/6 oz turnip, diced
175 g/6 oz carrot, diced
1 bouquet garni
salt and pepper
600 ml/1 pint water
about 300 ml/$\frac{1}{2}$ pint milk
25 g/1 oz ground almonds
2 tablespoons fresh white breadcrumbs
few drops of almond essence

1 Place the chicken, onion, turnip, carrot, bouquet garni and seasoning in a pan with the water. Bring to the boil, cover and simmer for about 30 minutes, or until the chicken is cooked.

2 Strain off the liquid and reserve. Discard the bouquet garni. Strip the chicken flesh from the bones.

3 Purée the chicken and vegetables in a liquidiser to make a smooth purée and return it to the pan.

4 Make the reserved stock up to 600 ml/1 pint with milk, add to the purée with the ground almonds and breadcrumbs. Bring to the boil, stirring constantly. Cover and simmer for 20 minutes, stirring occasionally.

5 Add the almond essence, taste and adjust the seasoning. Either serve small portions as a thick creamy soup or, if preferred, add 150 ml/$\frac{1}{4}$ pint hot chicken stock to thin the soup before serving. **Serves 4**

VARIATION
Fish and almond soup Substitute 175 g/6 oz skinned and boned firm white fish fillet for the chicken portion, and use 2 bay leaves and a strip of lemon rind instead of the bouquet garni.

Cauliflower in Curry Cream

— FIRST COURSE —

(*Illustrated on page 167*)

1 small cauliflower
1 tablespoon lemon juice
1 canned red pimiento, chopped
150 ml/$\frac{1}{4}$ pint double cream
1 teaspoon curry paste
salt
ground turmeric to sprinkle

1 Divide the cauliflower into florets. Cook in boiling salted water to cover with the lemon juice for about 10 minutes, until just tender. Drain well and mix with the pimiento.

2 Meanwhile, whisk the cream with the curry paste until thick. Add salt to taste.

3 Top the cauliflower mixture with the curry cream while it is still warm. Chill well and sprinkle with turmeric before serving. **Serves 4**

VARIATION
Fennel in curry cream Substitute 350 g/12 oz cooked chopped fennel for the cauliflower florets and sprinkle the tops with ground mace or grated nutmeg.

Orange Corn Cups

— FIRST COURSE —

2 large oranges
1 (198-g/7-oz) can sweet corn kernels, drained
4 spring onions, chopped
5-cm/2-inch length cucumber, diced
2 tablespoons French dressing (page 186)
50 g/2 oz Gouda cheese, diced
1 carton mustard and cress to garnish

1 Cut the oranges in half and spoon the flesh into a bowl, discarding the pips. Scrape out the remaining pith and reserve the orange 'cups'.

2 Add the sweet corn to the bowl with the onion and cucumber. Pour over the dressing and chill.

3 Just before serving fold in the cheese dice and pile up in the orange cups. Place each one in a glass dish and sprinkle with snipped mustard and cress. **Serves 4**

Danish Baked Fish

—— MAIN DISH ——

finely grated rind and juice of $\frac{1}{2}$ lemon
50 g/2 oz cooked long-grain rice
1 medium onion, chopped
1 teaspoon soy sauce
salt and pepper
4 thick cod steaks
4 slices fat streaky bacon, halved

1 Mix the lemon rind and juice with the rice, onion and soy sauce. Season well.

2 Remove any bones from the fish. Place each steak on a square of foil, fill the cavities with the rice mixture, then cover with two half slices of bacon. Fold in the foil and crimp the edges together.

3 Place the parcels on a baking sheet and cook in a moderately hot oven (190 C, 375 F, gas 5) for 20 minutes. Fold back the foil and return the parcels to the oven for a further 10 minutes to brown and crisp the bacon. Serve with baked or creamed potatoes. **Serves 4**

Haddock with Golden Sauce

—— MAIN COURSE ——

1 tablespoon custard powder
2 teaspoons dry mustard
300 ml/$\frac{1}{2}$ pint milk
450 g/1 lb thick haddock fillet
450 g/1 lb leeks, sliced
65 g/2$\frac{1}{2}$ oz butter
salt and pepper

1 Blend the custard powder and mustard with 2 tablespoons of the milk.

2 Place the fish in a saucepan and pour over the remaining milk. Poach gently for about 15 minutes.

3 Meanwhile, rinse the leek in a colander and drain well. Melt 50 g/2 oz of the butter in a saucepan, add the leek and a little seasoning and cook gently, stirring frequently, for about 10 minutes, until soft.

4 Strain the fish cooking liquid into a clean saucepan and bring to the boil. Pour into the custard powder mixture and stir until smooth. Return to the pan and bring to the boil, stirring constantly. Cook for 3 minutes, stirring all the time, then beat in the remaining butter, a little at a time, and season to taste.

5 Place the leeks on a warm serving dish, top with the fish and pour over the golden sauce. **Serves 4**

Beef and bacon suet roll (page 168)

Leeks in cheese custard (page 173)
and Cauliflower in curry cream (page 167)

Steaks with Brussels Sprout Salad

MAIN COURSE

225 g/8 oz Brussels sprouts
150 ml/¼ pint natural yogurt
juice of ½ lemon
salt and pepper
oil for frying
4 thin slices frying steak
1 lettuce heart, shredded

1 Finely shred the raw Brussels sprouts and place in a bowl. Blend together the yogurt and lemon juice and season well with salt and pepper. Pour over the shredded sprouts and toss until coated. Chill.

2 Heat a little oil in a frying pan and cook the steaks for 1–2 minutes on each side, according to thickness.

3 Mix together the lettuce and sprout salad and serve with the hot steaks. **Serves 4**

Beef and Bacon Suet Roll

MAIN COURSE

(*Illustrated on page 166*)

225 g/8 oz self-raising flour
salt and pepper
100 g/4 oz shredded suet
175 g/6 oz beef skirt, chopped
100 g/4 oz bacon, chopped
1 tablespoon chopped parsley

1 Sift the flour and 1 teaspoon salt into a bowl, stir in the suet and add sufficient water to make a soft dough. Turn out on a floured surface and knead lightly until smooth. Then roll out to a rectangle about 25 × 30 cm/ 10 × 12 inches.

2 Combine the beef, bacon and parsley and sprinkle with pepper. Spread this filling over the pastry, leaving a rim all round. Dampen the edges and roll up like a Swiss roll, pressing to seal.

3 Enclose the roll in a foil parcel, allowing room for the pastry to expand and sealing the edges of the foil to make a watertight parcel. Place in a large saucepan and add boiling water to come halfway up the sides of the roll. Cover the pan and boil gently for 2 hours, adding more boiling water to the pan during this time if necessary. **Serves 4**

Savoy Beef and Leek Parcels

MAIN COURSE

2 large leeks, sliced
50 g/2 oz butter or dripping
350 g/12 oz cooked beef, minced
1 beef stock cube, crumbled
150 ml/¼ pint boiling water
salt and pepper
8 large Savoy cabbage leaves
2 teaspoons soft brown sugar
2 teaspoons Worcestershire sauce

1 Rinse the leek in a colander and drain well. Melt half the butter and cook the leek gently until soft. Stir in the meat, stock cube, water and seasoning to taste.

2 Blanch the cabbage leaves in a saucepan of boiling water for 1 minute. Drain well and cut out the thick parts of stem.

3 Divide the meat filling between the cabbage leaves, fold in the sides then roll up to make neat parcels. Arrange with the joins underneath side by side in a greased ovenproof dish.

4 Melt the remaining butter and stir in the sugar and Worcestershire sauce. Sprinkle over the savoy parcels in the dish.

5 Cover and cook in a moderately hot oven (190 C, 375 F, gas 5) for 1 hour. **Serves 4**

VARIATION

Savoy lamb and apple parcels Substitute 1 large cooking apple for the leeks. Peel, core and chop it before cooking. Use 350 g/12 oz minced cooked lamb instead of the beef.

Pork Chops with Raisin Dumplings

MAIN COURSE

2 tablespoons seedless raisins
450 ml/¾ pint hot chicken stock
50 g/2 oz pork dripping or lard
4 small pork chops
50 g/2 oz white breadcrumbs
1 small onion finely chopped
1 tablespoon chopped parsley
½ teaspoon dried sage
25 g/1 oz self-raising flour
50 g/2 oz shredded suet
salt and pepper

1 Soak the raisins in the stock until required.

2 Melt the dripping in a pan just large enough to take the chops side by side in the base. Add the chops and fry for 10 minutes, turning them once, until golden brown on both sides.

3 Meanwhile, combine the breadcrumbs, onion, parsley, sage, flour, suet and seasoning to taste. Drain the raisins and add to the dry ingredients with sufficient stock to make a soft dough. Pour the remaining stock over the chops and bring to the boil.

4 Divide the dumpling mixture into eight portions with floured hands and shape each into a ball. Arrange these in the pan with the chops. Cover and cook gently for about 15 minutes, or until the dumplings are well risen and fluffy and have absorbed most of the stock.
Serves 4

VARIATION

Pork chops with apricot dumplings Substitute 1 large apricot for the raisins. Halve and stone it and chop roughly. Add to the dry ingredients without soaking in the stock. Use ½ teaspoon dried thyme instead of the sage.

Mushroom and Chicken Risotto

MAIN COURSE

4 tablespoons oil
1 large onion, chopped
350 g/12 oz long-grain rice
1.25 litres/2¼ pints chicken stock
450 g/1 lb cooked chicken meat, diced
75 g/3 oz butter
350 g/12 oz button mushrooms, sliced
salt and pepper
grated cheese for sprinkling

1 Heat the oil in a large saucepan and cook the onion until soft.

2 Stir in the rice and cook for 1 minute. Add the stock and bring to the boil. Stir well, cover and simmer for 20 minutes.

3 Stir in the chicken, cover again and continue cooking for about a further 5 minutes, until the rice is tender and the stock absorbed.

4 Meanwhile, melt the butter and sauté the mushrooms until golden. Stir into the risotto and season to taste. Serve with grated cheese handed separately.
Serves 6

Liver Fritters

MAIN COURSE

1 packet savoury herb stuffing mix
salt and pepper
450 g/1 lb calf's or lamb's liver, thinly sliced
1 egg, beaten
1 medium cooking apple, peeled
50 g/2 oz lard
1 large onion, sliced

1 Season the stuffing mix with salt and pepper. Dip the liver slices in egg, then coat all over with the stuffing mix.

2 Core and slice the apple. Melt the lard and fry the apple and onion until soft but not brown. Drain and keep hot.

3 Add the liver slices to the fat remaining in the pan and fry over moderate heat for about 3 minutes on each side, until brown and crisp.

4 Drain well. Place on a warm serving dish and top with the onion and apple mixture. Serve hot with creamed potatoes. **Serves 4**

Apple Bread and Butter Pudding

DESSERT

(Illustrated below)

2 medium cooking apples
juice of 2 lemons
6 large slices white bread
butter for spreading
75 g/3 oz demerara sugar
50 g/2 oz sultanas
3 eggs
450 ml/¾ pint milk

1 Peel, core and slice the apples. Toss in the lemon juice.

2 Spread the slices of bread generously with butter and cut diagonally into quarters, removing the crusts if preferred.

3 Arrange half the bread triangles in the base of a greased shallow ovenproof dish. Top with the apple slices, drained of excess lemon juice, and sprinkle with half the sugar and the sultanas. Arrange the remaining bread triangles, overlapping, on the top of the apple.

4 Beat the eggs with the milk and pour over the bread and apple. Sprinkle with the remaining sugar. Bake in a moderately hot oven (190 C, 375 F, gas 5) for 40–45 minutes, until golden brown on top. **Serves 4–6**

VARIATIONS

Cranberry bread and butter pudding Cook 225 g/8 oz fresh cranberries with a little water and sugar to taste, until soft. Use in place of the apple. Omit the sultanas and lemon juice.

Citrus bread and butter pudding Use the segments from 2 oranges in place of the apple. Add the grated rind of 1 lemon and 1 orange to the eggs and milk. Omit the sultanas and lemon juice.

Apple bread and butter pudding and Steamed apple and date pudding

Steamed Apple and Date Pudding

DESSERT

(Illustrated below)

100 g/4 oz butter, softened
100 g/4 oz castor sugar
2 eggs, beaten
225 g/8 oz self-raising flour
pinch of salt
pinch of ground mixed spice
1 dessert apple, peeled, cored and grated
75 g/3 oz stoned dates, chopped
about 4 tablespoons apple juice

1 Cream the butter and sugar together until light and fluffy, and gradually beat in the egg. Sift together the flour, salt and spice and fold into the creamed mixture with the apple, dates and sufficient apple juice to give a dropping consistency.

2 Spoon into a greased 1-litre/1¾-pint pudding basin. Cover with a circle of greased greaseproof paper, then completely cover the top of the basin with foil.

3 Steam over boiling water for 1½ hours. Turn out and serve hot with custard or cream. **Serves 4**

VARIATIONS

Orange and raisin pudding Substitute 100 g/4 oz seedless raisins for the grated apple and dates, and use the juice and grated rind of 2 oranges instead of the apple juice. Omit the mixed spice.

Lemon and ginger pudding Substitute 100 g/4 oz chopped crystallised ginger for the grated apple and dates and use the grated rind and juice of 2 lemons instead of the apple juice. Add an extra 25 g/1 oz castor sugar to the butter when creaming.

Latticed apple and apricot flan (page 172)

Latticed Apple and Apricot Flan

DESSERT

(Illustrated on page 171)

350 g/12 oz shortcrust pastry (page 184)
450 g/1 lb cooking apples
100 g/4 oz dried apricots, soaked overnight
100 g/4 oz castor sugar
beaten egg or milk to glaze

1 Use two-thirds of the pastry to line a 25-cm/10-inch flan dish.

2 Peel, core and slice the apples. Chop the apricots and mix with the apples and sugar. Fill the pastry case with this mixture.

3 Roll out the remaining pastry and cut into 1-cm/½-in strips. Arrange the strips to form a lattice pattern on top of the fruit filling. Brush with a little beaten egg or milk and bake in a moderately hot oven (200 C, 400 F, gas 6) for 40–45 minutes until golden brown. **Serves 4–6**

Sausages with Spicy Apple Mash

SUPPER OR SNACK

450 g/1 lb pork or beef sausages
25 g/1 oz butter
1 tablespoon chopped parsley
150 ml/¼ pint thick apple purée
1 tablespoon lemon juice
generous pinch of curry powder
450 g/1 lb mashed potatoes
salt and pepper

1 Cook the sausages under a moderate grill for about 15 minutes, turning them occasionally, until cooked and brown all over.

2 Meanwhile, beat the butter, parsley, apple purée, lemon juice and curry powder into the potato. Reheat until piping hot and season to taste.

3 Mound up the potato mixture on a warm serving dish and arrange the sausages propped up round it. **Serves 4**

Walnut Fish Pasties

SUPPER OR SNACK

450 g/1 lb shortcrust pastry (page 184)
225 g/8 oz smoked cod or whiting, cooked and flaked
2 hard-boiled eggs, chopped
50 g/2 oz walnuts, chopped
300 ml/½ pint white sauce (page 186)
salt and pepper
1 egg, beaten

1 Roll out the pastry and cut into four 18-cm/7-inch circles.

2 Combine the fish, chopped egg, nuts and sauce and season well. Divide the fish filling between the pastry circles, draw up the pastry edges over the filling, brush with egg and seal well together. Flute the edges.

3 Place the pasties on a greased baking sheet and brush all over with beaten egg.

4 Bake in a moderately hot oven (190 C, 375 F, gas 5) for about 40 minutes, until golden brown. **Serves 4**

Worcester Beef Rissoles

SUPPER OR SNACK

350 g/12 oz cooked beef, minced
350 g/12 oz mashed potato
50 g/2 oz Cheddar cheese, grated
1 teaspoon Worcestershire sauce
1 teaspoon dry mustard
salt and pepper
1 egg
2 tablespoons water
toasted breadcrumbs for coating
oil for frying

1 Mix together the beef, potato, cheese, Worcestershire sauce, mustard and seasoning to taste.

2 Divide the mixture into eight equal portions and shape each into a round flat cake with floured hands.

3 Beat the egg with the water. Use to coat the rissoles, then cover them with breadcrumbs.

4 Shallow fry the rissoles in a little hot oil for about 4 minutes on each side, until golden brown. Drain well on kitchen paper and serve hot. **Serves 4**

Chicken with Cheese Toppers

SUPPER OR SNACK

175 g/6 oz self-raising flour
generous pinch of salt
generous pinch of pepper
$\frac{1}{2}$ teaspoon dry mustard
50 g/2 oz butter
40 g/1$\frac{1}{2}$ oz Cheddar cheese, grated
1 egg, beaten
milk to mix
225 g/8 oz cooked chicken meat, diced
450 ml/$\frac{3}{4}$ pint white sauce (page 186)

1 Sift the flour, salt, pepper and mustard into a bowl and rub in the butter. Stir in the cheese. Reserve 2 teaspoons of the egg and add the rest to the dry ingredients with sufficient milk to make a soft dough. Turn out on a floured surface and knead lightly. Roll out and cut into eight 5-cm/2-inch rounds, re-rolling if necessary.

2 Combine the chicken and white sauce. Season well and place in a greased ovenproof pie dish. Arrange the toppers on the chicken mixture and brush with the reserved egg.

3 Bake in a hot oven (220 C, 425 F, gas 7) for 30 minutes, until the toppers are golden brown. **Serves 4**

VARIATION

Chicken with herbed toppers Increase the butter to 75 g/3 oz and omit the cheese. Use $\frac{3}{4}$ teaspoon dried mixed herbs instead of the mustard.

Leeks in Cheese Custard

SUPPER OR SNACK

(Illustrated on page 167)

8 small leeks, trimmed
8 rashers streaky bacon, chopped
15 g/$\frac{1}{2}$ oz butter
15 g/$\frac{1}{2}$ oz flour
300 ml/$\frac{1}{2}$ pint milk
50 g/2 oz Cheddar cheese, grated
salt and pepper
2 egg yolks
2 tablespoons breadcrumbs to garnish

1 Clean the leeks and wash well. Cook in boiling salted water for about 10 minutes, until just tender. Drain well.

2 Meanwhile, place the bacon in a frying pan, cook gently until the fat runs then fry until cooked but not crisp. Drain on kitchen paper.

3 Grease an ovenproof dish with bacon fat and arrange the leeks and bacon in it.

4 Place the butter, flour and milk in a small saucepan and whisk over a low heat until the sauce thickens and boils. Stir in the cheese and season to taste. Remove the pan from the heat and beat in the egg yolks.

5 Pour the sauce over the leeks and sprinkle with breadcrumbs. Cook in a moderate oven (180 C, 350 F, gas 4) for about 30 minutes, or until well browned. **Serves 4**

VARIATION

Celery hearts in cheese custard Substitute 2 small heads of celery for the leeks. Trim and quarter them, then wash well. Cook in boiling salted water for about 20 minutes, until just tender.

Water Chestnut Coleslaw

ACCOMPANIMENT

175 g/6 oz canned water chestnuts, drained
350 g/12 oz white cabbage, finely shredded
1 small onion, grated
5 tablespoons mayonnaise (page 186)
1 teaspoon lemon juice
salt and freshly ground black pepper

1 Cut the water chestnuts into fine dice and place in a bowl with the cabbage and onion.

2 Add the mayonnaise, lemon juice and plenty of seasoning. Mix well.

3 Cover and chill for at least 2 hours. Serve with cold meats such as turkey, ham, tongue or pork. **Serves 4**

VARIATIONS

Apple coleslaw Peel, core and slice 2 dessert apples. Add to the coleslaw in place of the water chestnuts. If liked, add a small pinch of ground cloves to the salad before mixing.
Carrot slaw Substitute 450 g/1 lb grated carrot for the cabbage and water chestnuts, 2 tablespoons orange juice for the lemon juice, and reduce the mayonnaise to 3 tablespoons.
Cheesy coleslaw Substitute 100 g/4 oz grated Cheddar cheese for the water chestnuts.

Christmas pudding (page 156)

Boxing Day Party

Cold Turkey Platter

•

Prune Stuffing Balls

•

Creamy Horseradish Mayonnaise

•

Almond Mince Pies

Cold Turkey Platter

BOXING DAY PARTY

(Illustrated on page 174)

Thinly slice 450 g/1 lb cooked turkey. Set aside the best slices of white meat. Dice the remainder, combine with the Creamy horseradish mayonnaise and fold in an equal weight of diced cooked potato. Arrange the sliced white meat in the centre of a large serving platter and surround with the Prune stuffing balls, the diced turkey and potato mixture and slices of Danish and Hungarian salami. Garnish with parsley. **Serves 8**

Prune Stuffing Balls

BOXING DAY PARTY

(Illustrated on page 174)

1 medium onion, chopped
4 rashers streaky bacon, chopped
75 g/3 oz butter
100 g/4 oz prunes, soaked overnight
175 g/6 oz fresh white breadcrumbs
grated rind and juice of $\frac{1}{2}$ lemon
2 eggs, beaten
salt and pepper
seasoned flour for coating
fat for brushing

1 Fry the onion and bacon gently in the butter until soft. Stone and chop the prunes and add to the onion with the remaining ingredients. Shape into 16 balls.

2 Coat lightly in seasoned flour, place on a greased baking sheet and brush with melted turkey fat or butter. Bake in a moderately hot oven (190 C, 375 F, gas 5) for 20 minutes, or until golden. Cool. **Serves 8**

Creamy Horseradish Mayonnaise

BOXING DAY PARTY

(Illustrated on page 174)

Combine 150 ml/$\frac{1}{4}$ pint mayonnaise (page 186) with 150 ml/$\frac{1}{4}$ pint lightly whipped double cream. Add 1–2 teaspoons lemon juice to taste, and 4 tablespoons grated fresh horseradish, or omit the lemon juice and stir in 2 tablespoons bottled horseradish sauce. **Serves 8**

Almond Mince Pies

BOXING DAY PARTY

(Illustrated on page 174)

225 g/8 oz almond pastry (page 184)
450 g/1 lb mincemeat
castor sugar to sprinkle

1 Set the oven to moderately hot (190 C, 375 F, gas 5). Roll out the pastry thinly and cut out 24 circles using a 7-cm/$2\frac{3}{4}$-inch cutter and 24 circles using a 6-cm/$2\frac{1}{2}$-inch cutter.

2 Line the base of bun or patty tins with the larger circles of pastry. Fill each one with a heaped teaspoon of mincemeat. Dampen the edges of the pastry with water and place the smaller circle of pastry on top, pressing to seal the edges.

3 Using a skewer, make a small hole in the centre to allow the steam to escape. Decorate the pies with pastry scraps cut into the shapes of holly leaves and berries. Chill in the refrigerator for 10 minutes before baking in the heated oven for 20 minutes. Sprinkle with castor sugar and keep warm. **Makes 24**

Chocolate Truffles

225 g/8 oz almond or coconut macaroons
4 tablespoons rum
4 tablespoons single cream
175 g/6 oz plain chocolate
100 g/4 oz maraschino or glacé cherries
chocolate vermicelli or toasted desiccated coconut
to coat

1 Crush the biscuits and sprinkle over the rum. Stir in the cream and leave to stand for 10 minutes.

2 Melt the chocolate in a basin over a saucepan of hot water and pour it over the macaroon mixture. Mix together thoroughly and leave in a cool place until stiff enough to shape.

3 Take a small spoonful of the mixture, press a cherry into the middle and shape into a ball to enclose the cherry completely.

4 Roll each truffle in chocolate vermicelli or a little toasted desiccated coconut. Place the truffles in petit four cases and leave in a cool place until set. Makes approximately 30.

Recipes for Round the Year

Preserving

General Instructions for Making Jam and Jelly

1 Choose unblemished fruit, preferably slightly under-ripe, prepare and place in a large preserving pan with the water. Cook gently until soft. (Some soft berry fruits are not cooked before the sugar is added.)

2 Strain the pulp through a fine cloth or a jelly bag overnight if making jelly.

3 Measure or weigh the pulp or fruit juice, return to the pan and add preserving or granulated sugar, usually in the proportion of a 450 g/1 lb to each 600 ml/1 pint. Heat gently, stirring, until the sugar has completely dissolved, then bring to a full rolling boil and cook until setting point is reached.

4 Three tests for setting point
- ☐ The mixture reaches a temperature of 105 C/220 F on a sugar thermometer.
- ☐ A little of the mixture spooned on to a cold plate and allowed to cool, forms a skin which wrinkles when pushed with a fingertip.
- ☐ The cooled mixture on the plate separates into two distinct parts, without running together again, when a fingertip is drawn through the centre.

Remember to remove the pan from the heat while testing for a set to avoid over-boiling.

5 Skim off any scum and pour the jam or jelly into clean, warm, dry jars and seal with screw-on lids or cover the surface of the jam with waxed discs and seal the pots with squares of cling film, or circles of cellophane secured with rubber bands. Label the pots. If the jam has large pieces of fruit in it, leave to stand for about 20 minutes and stir well before potting to distribute the fruit. Leave until cold before sealing.

Apricot Jam

1.5 kg/3½ lb apricots
juice of 1 lemon
450 ml/¾ pint water
1.5 kg/3 lb preserving or granulated sugar

1 Halve the apricots, remove the stones and quarter the fruit. Place in a preserving pan with the lemon juice and water. Bring to the boil then simmer until the fruit is reduced to a pulp.

2 Add the sugar and heat gently, stirring, until it has completely dissolved. Bring to a full rolling boil and cook until the jam sets when tested.

3 Skim, pot, cover, seal and label. **Makes about 2.25 kg/5 lb**

Note To give a subtle nutty flavour some of the kernels may be added to the jam. Crack a few of the stones and blanch the kernels in boiling water for 1 minute. Drain and rinse under cold water. Slip off the skins and split the kernels in half. Add to the pan with the fruit.

VARIATION
Peach or plum jam Substitute peaches or plums for the apricots.

Pineapple and Lemon Jam

2 medium pineapples
preserving or granulated sugar
grated rind and juice of 4 lemons

1 Peel the pineapples. Chop all the flesh, discarding hard parts of the core. Measure the pineapple pulp and set aside 450 g/1 lb sugar for each 600 ml/1 pint of pineapple pulp. Place the pulp in a preserving pan with the lemon rind and juice. Bring to the boil and cook gently for 10 minutes.

2 Add the sugar and heat gently, stirring, until it has completely dissolved. Bring to a full rolling boil, then cook until the jam sets when tested.

3 Pot, cover, seal and label. **Makes about 1.5 kg/3 lb**

Note Yield will vary according to size of fruit.

Strawberry Preserve

1.5 kg/3½ lb small firm strawberries
1.5 kg/3 lb preserving or granulated sugar
75 ml/3 fl oz lemon juice
15 g/½ oz butter

1 Hull the strawberries and layer them in a preserving pan with the sugar. Sprinkle over the lemon juice and leave to stand in a warm place for about 8 hours, until the fruit juice runs freely.

2 Heat gently, stirring, over low heat, until the sugar has completely dissolved. Bring to a full rolling boil and cook until the syrup sets when tested. Stir in the butter until melted.

3 Leave the jam to stand for 20 minutes, or until a very thin skin forms. Stir for 2 minutes so that the strawberries are well distributed then pot and cover. Seal when cold. **Makes about 2.25 kg/5 lb**

Note This preserve does not set like ordinary jam. The berries remain whole, suspended in a thick syrup.

Bramble Jelly

4 medium cooking apples
2 kg/4½ lb blackberries
600 ml/1 pint water
preserving or granulated sugar

1 Cut up the apples but do not peel or core them. Place in a preserving pan with the blackberries and water. Cook gently until the fruit is very soft.

2 Strain through a fine cloth or jelly bag overnight then measure the juice and return to the pan with 450 g/1 lb sugar to each 600 ml/1 pint.

3 Heat gently, stirring, until the sugar has completely dissolved. Bring to a full rolling boil and cook until the syrup sets when tested.

4 Pot, cover, seal and label. **Makes about 3 kg/7 lb**

Clear Jellied Marmalade

8 large sweet oranges
8 Seville oranges
2 lemons
8 litres/14 pints water
preserving or granulated sugar

1 Thinly slice the oranges and lemons. Tie the pips together in a piece of muslin. Put the fruit and bag of pips in a preserving pan and pour over the water. Bring to the boil then simmer, uncovered, for about 4 hours, or until the liquid has reduced by half.

2 Strain through a fine cloth or jelly bag overnight but do not squeeze the bag or the jelly will be cloudy. Measure the juice and return to the pan with 450 g/1 lb sugar to each 600 ml/1 pint.

3 Heat gently, stirring, until the sugar has dissolved. Bring to a full rolling boil and cook until the jelly sets when tested.

4 Skim, pot, cover, seal and label. **Makes about 3.5 kg/8 lb**

Simple Chunky Marmalade

12 Seville oranges
water
preserving or granulated sugar

1 Chop the oranges roughly, remove the pips and tie these in a piece of muslin. Measure the chopped orange and place in a large preserving pan with 1.75 litres/3 pints water to every 600 ml/1 pint of orange and the bag of pips. Cover and leave to stand overnight.

2 Uncover and cook gently for about 4 hours, or until very soft. Pour into a bowl and leave overnight.

3 Measure the pulp again and add 0.5 kg/1¼ lb sugar to every 600 ml/1 pint.

4 Heat gently, stirring, until the sugar has completely dissolved. Bring to a full rolling boil and cook until the marmalade sets when tested.

5 Skim, pot, cover, seal and label. **Makes about 3.5 kg/8 lb**

Lemon Curd

finely grated rind and juice of 4 lemons
450 g/1 lb castor sugar
100 g/4 oz butter
4 eggs

1 Place the lemon rind and juice with the sugar and butter in the top of a double boiler, or in a basin standing over a pan of simmering water. Stir with a wooden spoon until the sugar has dissolved.

2 Beat in the eggs, one at a time, and continue cooking until thick enough to coat the back of the spoon.

3 Remove from the heat and allow to cool then pot, cover, seal and label. **Makes about 1 kg/2 lb**

Damson Butter or Cheese

1.5 kg/3 lb damsons
250 ml/9 fl oz water
preserving or granulated sugar

1 Place the fruit in a pan with the water and cook gently until really soft.

2 Sieve the pulp, measure it and return it to a clean, dry pan with sugar, allowing 350 g/12 oz sugar per 600 ml/1 pint if making a butter, or 450 g/1 lb per 600 ml/1 pint if making a cheese.

3 Heat gently, stirring, until the sugar has dissolved, then bring to the boil and cook gently until the correct consistency is reached. As the mixture gets thick, stir frequently to prevent sticking. For damson butter boil until thick and creamy; for damson cheese boil until so thick that a wooden spoon drawn through the centre leaves a clean division.

4 Pot the butter as for jam, cover, seal, label and use in the same way.
Pack the cheese into small straight-sided pots or moulds brushed with olive oil. Cover, seal and label. Store for 3 months before using. Turn out of the mould and serve sliced with game, meat or poultry.

Note Other strongly flavoured stone fruits such as plums, can be used in this recipe.

Mint and Apple Jelly

1.5 kg/3 lb green cooking apples
1 litre/1$\frac{3}{4}$ pints water
2 tablespoons lemon juice
large bunch of fresh mint
preserving or granulated sugar
few drops green food colouring

1 Quarter the apples and place in a preserving pan with the water and lemon juice. Wash the mint and add half to the pan. Bring to the boil then simmer until reduced to a thick pulp.

2 Strain through a fine cloth or jelly bag overnight. Measure the juice and return to the pan with 450 g/1 lb sugar to each 600 ml/1 pint. Chop the remaining mint and add to the pan with a few drops of food colouring.

3 Heat gently, stirring, until the sugar has completely dissolved. Bring to a full rolling boil and cook until the jelly sets when tested.

4 Skim, pot, cover, seal and label. **Makes about 1.5 kg/3 lb**

Apricot Brandy

12 ripe apricots
600 ml/1 pint brandy
225 g/8 oz castor sugar

1 Chop the apricots and place in a large screw-topped jar. Crack the stones, remove the kernels and blanch them in boiling water for 1 minute. Drain and slip off the brown skins. Crush the kernels and add to the apricots.

2 Pour over the brandy and add the sugar. Screw the lid on the jar tightly then shake well.

3 Leave to stand for 1 month, shaking the jar frequently.

4 Strain carefully and pour into a suitable bottle.
Makes about 900 ml/1$\frac{1}{2}$ pints

VARIATION
Peach brandy Substitute 8 ripe peaches for the apricots.

Apple and Plum Chutney

1 kg/2 lb cooking apples
450 g/1 lb plums
1.5 kg/3 lb onions, chopped
225 g/8 oz sultanas
225 g/8 oz seedless raisins
600 ml/1 pint malt vinegar
0.75 kg/1$\frac{1}{2}$ lb demerara sugar
1 tablespoon ground mixed spice
1 teaspoon salt
finely grated rind and juice of 2 lemons

1 Peel, core and chop the apples and halve and stone the plums. Place together in an aluminium or stainless steel preserving pan with the remaining ingredients. Heat gently, stirring, until the sugar has dissolved, then simmer, uncovered, stirring occasionally, until the mixture is smooth and thick, with no excess liquid.

2 Pot then cover with vinegar-proof discs and seals. Label and store for at least 6 weeks before using.

Green Tomato Chutney

1.5 kg/3 lb green tomatoes
2 tablespoons salt
100 g/4 oz prunes
100 g/4 oz pressed dates
225 g/8 oz onions, chopped
225 g/8 oz cooking apples
350 g/12 oz soft brown sugar
2 teaspoons mustard seed
1 teaspoon mixed pickling spices
600 ml/1 pint malt vinegar

1 Quarter the tomatoes and cut out the hard stalk ends. Chop roughly and place in layers with the salt in an aluminium or stainless steel preserving pan. Cover the prunes with cold water. Leave overnight.

2 Next day, drain the salty liquid from the tomatoes. Drain the prunes, remove the stones and chop roughly. Chop the dates and onions and peel, core and slice the apples. Place all the ingredients in the pan and heat gently, stirring, until the sugar has dissolved. Bring to the boil then simmer, stirring occasionally, until the mixture is reduced to a thick pulp.

3 Pot then cover with vinegar-proof discs and seals. Label and store for at least 6 weeks before using.

Marrow and Rhubarb Chutney

1 large marrow
rhubarb (can be mature stems)
salt
300 ml/½ pint vinegar
1 large onion, chopped
100 g/4 oz sultanas
100 g/4 oz currants
100 g/4 oz soft brown sugar
1 teaspoon ground ginger
1 teaspoon mustard seed

1 Peel the marrow, remove the seeds and cut the flesh into cubes. Weigh the cubes and add enough cubed rhubarb to make 1.25 kg/2½ lb. Place in a bowl, sprinkle with salt and leave to stand overnight.

2 Place the vinegar in a large pan and add the onion, dried fruit, sugar, ginger and mustard seed. Heat gently, stirring, until the sugar has dissolved.

3 Drain the salty liquid from the marrow and rhubarb cubes, add them to the pan and bring to the boil, stirring. Simmer until reduced to a thick pulp.

4 Pot then cover with cellophane discs and seals. Label and store for at least 1 month before using.

Home-grown Herbs

Gather a selection of the following from your garden on a dry sunny day, if possible just before they flower – dill, fennel, marjoram, mint, oregano, parsley, rosemary, sage, tarragon, thyme. They may be preserved in any of the following four ways. Alternatively use to make unusual flavoured herb vinegars.

Air drying

Tie the herbs in bunches according to their kind and hang them up indoors away from a bright light and in a current of air to encourage the moisture to dry out. After a few weeks when the leaves are sufficiently brittle to crumble when crushed between the fingers, strip them away from any woody stem, reduce almost to a powder, mix together if required and store in small screw-topped jars.

Branches of bay leaves should be hung up in the same way and the dried leaves stripped from the branches as required. After two months, remove all remaining leaves from the branch and pack together in a screw-topped jar.

Oven drying

To dry herbs more quickly, spread them in a thin layer in one or more roasting tins and place in the oven at very low residual heat after cooking two or three times, or until completely dry. Store as above.

Drying by microwave

To dry herbs by microwave, either strip the leaves from the stems beforehand or discard woody stems after the process is completed. Spread small sprigs or single leaves of herbs on a sheet of absorbent kitchen paper. Cover with another sheet and microwave on full power for 2 minutes. The kitchen paper will become quite damp and aids considerably in speeding up the drying process. Strip the leaves from the stems if necessary, crumble between your fingers and store as above. (Woody stemmed herbs such as rosemary may require turning over and processing for a further 30 seconds before becoming completely dry.)

To freeze herbs

Pick just before flowering, strip off and discard any woody stems and pack the leaves or leafy sprigs in small polythene bags or containers. Alternatively lay them flat on one half of a sheet of foil and press the other half over to form a flat pack, crimping the edges tightly. When required, thaw whole leaves, or crumble frozen leaves to save chopping.

Herb vinegars

Use tarragon, mint, basil, marjoram or dill. Gather the leafy tips from the plants just before they flower. Bruise with a pestle or wooden masher and pack into a wide-necked jar. Pour over boiling white wine vinegar or cider vinegar to within 5 cm/2 inches of the top. Seal the jars. Allow to stand for about 10 days, shaking the jars once each day if possible. Taste and if a stronger herb flavour is required, strain the same liquid over a fresh supply of bruised leaves and leave to stand for a further 10 days, shaking each day as before. Finally, strain the vinegar through a very fine cloth and store in glass bottles. Seal with vinegar-proof materials and label.

Unusual Ways of Preserving Fruit

To candy citrus fruit peel

Save the peel of all citrus fruits when you squeeze the juice or remove the flesh without grating the rind from the peel, and store in a polythene bag in the freezer until you have a sufficient quantity – about 450 g/1 lb weight of prepared peel, with as much of the white pith as possible removed.

Defrost the peel and place in a large basin. Dissolve 15 g/$\frac{1}{2}$ oz bicarbonate of soda in 150 ml/$\frac{1}{4}$ pint hot water and spoon over the pieces of peel. Add sufficient boiling water to cover the peel and leave to stand for 20 minutes. Drain and wash well under running water. Place the peel in a pan and cover with cold water. Bring to the boil, then reduce the heat and simmer until the peel is tender. Drain and place in a large basin.

Dissolve 450 g/1 lb granulated sugar in 450 ml/$\frac{3}{4}$ pint hot water. Pour over the peel and leave to stand for 2 days. Strain the syrup into a pan, add a further 225 g/8 oz granulated sugar and heat gently, stirring occasionally, until the sugar has completely dissolved. Bring slowly to the boil, add the peel and simmer in the syrup until it looks clear. Remove the pieces of peel with a slotted draining spoon, arrange on baking sheets and dry out slowly in a cool oven. Reduce the remaining syrup by boiling for about 30 minutes.

Dip the pieces of peel in the syrup, return to the trays and place in the oven again until dry. Boil up the remaining syrup until it is cloudy and thick. Spoon a little into each candied peel 'cup' and leave to dry. Store in airtight containers.

To crystallise flower petals

Pick flowers on a dry, sunny day. According to the season, choose primroses, violets, roses and the blossom of plums, apples, cherries and pears. Not all flowers are edible so do not be tempted to experiment unless you are certain the flower is not poisonous.

Put 25 g/1 oz gum arabic in a small bowl and cover with triple-strength rosewater. Leave for 24 hours. When the gum arabic has melted, carefully paint it over each flower petal, using a fine paint brush. Make sure that the petals are completely coated on both sides. Sprinkle all over with castor sugar and arrange on sheets of greaseproof paper. Allow to dry out overnight then store in airtight containers, in layers divided by sheets of greaseproof paper.

Enriched White Milk Bread

4 teaspoons castor sugar
600 ml / 1 pint warm milk
2 tablespoons dried yeast
1.5 kg / 3 lb strong white flour
1 tablespoon salt
100 g / 4 oz butter
2 eggs, beaten
to finish
1 egg, beaten
40 g / 1½ oz butter, melted
little milk
poppy seeds or sesame seeds

1 Dissolve the sugar in the milk then sprinkle the yeast over the top. Leave to stand in a warm place for about 10 minutes, until frothy.

2 Sift the flour and salt into a bowl and rub in the butter. Make a well in the centre and add the eggs and yeast liquid. Mix to a dough, gradually drawing in the dry ingredients, until the sides of the bowl are clean.

3 Turn out on a floured surface and knead for 10 minutes, until the dough is smooth and pliable.

4 Grease the bowl, return the dough to it and turn once so that it is coated. Cover with polythene and leave in a warm place for about 1 hour, until doubled in size.

5 Turn out again on to a floured surface and knead briefly until dough is firm. Reserve 1 kg / 2 lb dough for the rolls, keep 0.5 kg / 1¼ lb for the small loaf and use the rest for the large loaf.

Rolls Use 50 g / 2 oz dough each time, roll out to a sausage shape about 20 cm / 8 inches long. Tie in a single knot and place on a greased baking sheet, leaving room between the rolls for them to expand during cooking. After proving, brush with beaten egg.

Small loaf Roll out the dough to a rectangle measuring 15 × 30 cm / 6 inches × 12 inches and brush all over with melted butter. Roll up, starting from one short side and place in a greased 450-g / 1-lb loaf tin with the join underneath. After proving, brush the top with butter.

Large loaf Shape the dough to fit a greased 1-kg / 2-lb loaf tin. After proving, brush the top with milk and sprinkle with poppy seeds or sesame seeds.

6 Cover the shaped dough with greased polythene and leave in a warm place for about 30 minutes for the rolls, 40 minutes for the small loaf and 50 minutes for the large loaf, or until almost doubled in size. Uncover, finish as directed, and bake in a moderately hot oven 200 C, 400 F, gas 6) allowing about 20 minutes for the rolls, 35 minutes for the small loaf and 45 minutes for the large loaf. When cooked, bread sounds hollow when tapped on the base with the knuckles. Cool on a wire rack. **Makes 16 rolls, 1 small loaf, 1 large loaf**

VARIATIONS

Plaited cheese loaf Take 0.5 kg / 1¼ lb of dough after it has been kneaded the second time, and work in 75 g / 3 oz grated strong Cheddar cheese and ¼ teaspoon garlic salt. Divide into 3 equal portions and shape each to a sausage about 40 cm / 16 inches long. Place the strands side by side and plait from the centre to one end and then from the centre to the other end. Place on a greased baking sheet and tuck the ends under neatly. Cover with greased polythene and leave in a warm place until almost doubled in size. Uncover, brush with beaten egg and bake in a moderately hot oven as above, for 30 minutes, or until golden brown.

Sweet fruited buns Use 1 kg / 2 lb of dough after it has been kneaded the second time. Roll out to a rectangle measuring 40 × 25 cm / 16 × 10 inches. Brush with 25 g / 1 oz melted butter and sprinkle with 75 g / 3 oz sultanas, 25 g / 1 oz chopped candied peel, 50 g / 2 oz soft brown sugar and 1 teaspoon ground cinnamon. Roll up carefully, starting from one long side, and cut the roll into 16 equal slices. Arrange these flat, side by side in a greased roasting tin, leaving a small space between each. (When risen and baked, the buns should be just touching.) Cover with greased polythene and leave in a warm place until almost doubled in size. Uncover, brush with 25 g / 1 oz butter and sprinkle with 25 g / 1 oz soft brown sugar. Bake in a moderately hot oven as above for about 25 minutes, or until golden brown. Leave to cool slightly in the tin then pull apart and serve warm.

Simple Wholemeal Bread

4 tablespoons clear honey
850 ml/1 pint 8 fl oz warm water
4 tablespoons dried yeast
1 kg/2¼ lb wholemeal flour
1 tablespoon salt
6 tablespoons oil
to finish
little milk
little flour

1 Dissolve the honey in the water and sprinkle on the yeast. Leave in a warm place for about 10 minutes, until frothy.

2 Meanwhile, put the flour in a heatproof bowl and place in a moderate oven until thoroughly warm.

3 Make a well in the flour, add the salt, oil and yeast liquid and mix, drawing in the dry ingredients, until the dough leaves the sides of the bowl clean.

4 Reserve 1 kg/2 lb dough for the rolls, and use the remainder to make the loaf.
Rolls Using 50 g/2 oz dough each time, shape into a ball and place on a greased baking sheet, leaving room between the rolls for them to expand during cooking. Cut a deep cross in the top of each roll with a sharp knife. After proving, brush with milk.
Loaf Shape the dough to a flat round to fit a greased 20-cm/8-inch cake tin. After proving, sprinkle very lightly with flour.

5 Cover the shaped dough with greased polythene and leave in a warm place for about 30 minutes for the rolls and 45 minutes for the loaf, or until almost doubled in size. Uncover, finish as directed, and bake in a moderately hot oven (200 C, 400 F, gas 6) allowing about 20 minutes for the rolls and 40 minutes for the loaf. When cooked, bread sounds hollow when tapped on the base with the knuckles. Cool on a wire rack.
Makes 16 rolls and 1 medium loaf

VARIATION

Fruit and nut loaf Take 0.75 kg/1¾ lb of the freshly mixed dough and work in 50 g/2 oz seedless raisins, 50 g/2 oz chopped walnuts and, if liked, a pinch of caraway seeds. Shape the dough to fit a greased 1-kg/2-lb loaf tin. Cover with greased polythene and leave in a warm place until almost doubled in size. Uncover, brush with melted butter and bake in a moderately hot oven as above for about 35 minutes, or until well risen and browned. Cool on a wire rack.

Orange Teabread

275 g/10 oz plain flour
1½ teaspoons baking powder
½ teaspoon salt
200 g/7 oz butter
350 g/12 oz castor sugar
finely grated rind of 1 large orange
100 g/4 oz chopped walnuts
3 eggs
200 ml/6 fl oz milk
to finish
juice of 1 large orange
1 tablespoon clear honey

1 Sift the flour with the baking powder and salt into a bowl. Rub in the butter and stir in the sugar, orange rind and nuts. Make a well in the centre. Beat up the eggs with the milk, add to the dry ingredients and mix quickly until the dough forms but do not beat.

2 Transfer to a greased 1-kg/2-lb loaf tin and bake in a moderate oven (180 C, 350 F, gas 4) for about 1¼ hours, or until the centre is firm to the touch.

3 Meanwhile, warm the orange juice slightly then stir in the honey until it dissolves.

4 Remove the teabread from the oven and immediately spoon over the orange juice mixture. Leave in the tin for 10 minutes then cool on a wire rack. Serve sliced and buttered. **Makes 1 loaf**

Pastry

Shortcrust Pastry

225 g/8 oz plain flour
$\frac{1}{4}$ teaspoon salt
50 g/2 oz lard
50 g/2 oz butter or hard margarine
2–3 tablespoons cold water

1 Sift the flour and salt into a bowl and rub in the fat until the mixture resembles breadcrumbs. Sprinkle over 2 tablespoons of the water and mix with a round-bladed knife until lumps are formed. Gather the dough together, pressing with the fingers and adding more water if necessary, to make a firm dough.

2 Turn out on a floured surface and knead very lightly until smooth. If possible, chill for 30 minutes before using.

VARIATION
Wholemeal pastry Use 100 g/4 oz each wholemeal flour and plain flour and increase the salt to $\frac{1}{2}$ teaspoon.

Cheese Pastry

225 g/8 oz plain flour
$\frac{1}{4}$ teaspoon salt
pinch of dry mustard
pinch of cayenne pepper
50 g/2 oz lard
50 g/2 oz butter
75 g/3 oz Cheddar cheese, grated
3–4 tablespoons water

1 Sift the flour, salt, mustard and cayenne pepper into a bowl. Rub in the fat until the mixture resembles fine breadcrumbs. Stir in the cheese. Sprinkle over 3 tablespoons of the water and mix until lumps are formed. Gather into a dough, adding more water, if necessary.

2 Turn out on a floured surface and knead very lightly until smooth. Chill for 30 minutes before using.

Almond Pastry

225 g/8 oz plain flour
pinch salt
150 g/5 oz butter
50 g/2 oz ground almonds
100 g/4 oz castor sugar
1 egg beaten

1 Sieve the flour and salt into a mixing bowl and rub in the butter until the mixture resembles fine breadcrumbs.

2 Stir in the ground almonds, sugar and egg and mix quickly to a firm dough. Wrap and chill in the refrigerator for 15 minutes before using.

French Flan Pastry

225 g/8 oz plain flour
pinch of salt
100 g/4 oz butter, diced
1 egg
3 tablespoons water

1 Sift the flour and salt into a cold bowl, make a well in the centre and put in the butter, egg and water.

2 Mix with the fingertips of one hand, gradually drawing in the dry ingredients, until the dough forms a ball.

3 Knead lightly until smooth then wrap in foil or cling film and chill for 30 minutes before using.

Sweet Flan Pastry

225 g/8 oz plain flour
pinch of salt
50 g/2 oz castor sugar
100 g/4 oz butter, diced
2 egg yolks
3 tablespoons water
$\frac{1}{4}$ teaspoon vanilla essence (optional)

1 Sift the flour and salt into a cold bowl. Stir in the sugar. Make a well in the centre and put in the butter, egg yolks and water with the vanilla essence added, if using.

2 Mix with the finger tips of one hand, gradually drawing in the dry ingredients, until the dough forms a ball.

3 Knead lightly until smooth, then wrap in foil or cling film and chill for 30 minutes before using.

Puff Pastry (Blitz Method)

200 g/7 oz strong flour
pinch of cream of tartar
$\frac{1}{4}$ teaspoon salt
150 g/5 oz butter, cut in 1.5 cm/$\frac{1}{2}$ inch dice
175 ml/6 fl oz water, chilled

1 Sift together the flour, cream of tartar and salt. Add the butter and rub in lightly. (Large lumps of butter should still be visible.) Fork in the water. Gather up the dough and roll out on a lightly floured surface.

2 Roll out to a rectangle measuring about 30 × 10 cm/12 inches × 4 inches with a long side towards you. Mark a centre crease across the short side. Fold in the short sides to meet in the centre, then lift the left fold over the right fold.

3 Keeping the side with one fold on the left, roll out again towards the right, to make a long strip as before. Repeat the folding process then cover and chill for 15 minutes.

4 Repeat the double rolling and folding operation, cover and chill for a further 15 minutes.

5 Roll out again to the long strip and fold once. The layered pastry should now measure about 15 × 10 cm/6 × 4 inches and is ready for use.

Hot Water Crust Pastry

450 g/1 lb plain flour
1 teaspoon salt
1 egg yolk
150 ml/$\frac{1}{4}$ pint water
175 g/6 oz lard

1 Sift the flour and salt into a bowl and make a well in the centre. Drop in the egg yolk and sprinkle over a little of the flour.

2 Place the water and lard in a pan and heat gently until the fat has melted. Bring to the boil and remove from the heat. Pour into the dry ingredients and mix quickly with a wooden spoon until the dough is cool enough to handle.

3 Turn out on a floured surface and knead until smooth. Return the ball of dough to the mixing bowl and cover with a plate. Leave in a warm place for 10 minutes before using.

Note It is essential to keep the pastry warm and covered until required, otherwise it will dry out and crack when being rolled out.

Savoury White Pouring Sauce

Place 600 ml/1 pint milk in a pan with 40 g/1½ oz each of butter and flour, and 1 crumbled chicken stock cube. Place over gentle heat and whisk steadily until the sauce boils and thickens. Cook gently, stirring, for 3 minutes then season to taste with salt and pepper if necessary.

VARIATIONS

Thick white sauce For a sauce of coating consistency use 50 g/2 oz butter and 50 g/2 oz flour to 600 ml/1 pint of milk.

Cheese and mustard sauce Omit the stock cube and when the sauce is cooked, stir in 1 tablespoon French mustard and 100 g/4 oz grated strong Cheddar cheese. As soon as the sauce is smooth again, remove from the heat and add salt and pepper to taste.

Parsley and lemon sauce Omit the stock cube and when the sauce is cooked, stir in 4 tablespoons chopped parsley, the finely grated rind of 1 lemon and 2 tablespoons lemon juice. Simmer for 2 more minutes then remove from the heat and season to taste.

White wine sauce Place 150 ml/¼ pint dry white wine in a pan with a piece or slice of onion. Boil until reduced by about half. When the sauce is cooked, beat in 1 egg yolk and simmer for a further 1 minute, stirring all the time. Remove from the heat and strain in the reduced wine, reheat if necessary and season to taste.

French Dressing

Place 1 teaspoon dry mustard in a screw-topped jar with 1 teaspoon castor sugar, ¾ teaspoon salt and ¼ teaspoon pepper. Add 150 ml/¼ pint oil (olive oil if possible) and 4 tablespoons wine vinegar. Put on the lid and shake vigorously until the sugar has dissolved and the dressing thickens. Store in a sealed container and shake well before each use. This dressing keeps for up to 3 weeks in a cool place.

VARIATIONS

Vinaigrette dressing Add 1 tablespoon very finely chopped shallot or spring onion and 2 tablespoons chopped mixed fresh herbs (such as parsley, thyme, marjoram, chervil or tarragon) to the jar before shaking.

Garlic dressing Peel 2 cloves garlic and add to either of the above dressings before mixing. Leave them in the dressing but note that the storage life is shortened to about 1 week in a refrigerator.

Mayonnaise

Start with all ingredients at room temperature. Place 1 egg and 1 egg yolk in a bowl with 1½ teaspoons dry mustard, 1½ teaspoons salt, ½ teaspoon pepper and 1½ teaspoons sugar. Whisk well until blended. Gradually whisk in 200 ml/7 fl oz oil, adding it in quantities of no more than ½ teaspoon at a time, and whisking vigorously and constantly until the mayonnaise thickens. Then, still whisking, add 3 tablespoons white vinegar and then a further 200 ml/7 fl oz oil. You will probably find you are able to add the last of the oil in quantities of about 1 tablespoon. Store in a screw-topped jar.

This classic method is much speeded up by using an electric hand mixer. The blender method is quickest of all.

Blender mayonnaise

Use the same ingredients as above. Place the egg and egg yolk in the blender goblet with the mustard, salt, pepper, sugar and vinegar. Blend on high speed until mixed. Leave the machine switched on high and add the oil in a trickle until the mayonnaise is smooth and thick. Switch off from time to time and scrape down the sides so that all the ingredients are blended.

Note If by any chance the mayonnaise curdles, whether being made by the hand or the blender method, remove it to a jug. Place a further egg yolk in the bowl or blender goblet and beat well or blend, gradually adding the curdled mixture and beating or blending it in as above.

Unusual Sauces and Salad Dressings

Fennel cream sauce

Whip 150 ml/¼ pint double cream with 1 teaspoon clear honey until thick. Blend in 1 tablespoon lemon juice and 2 tablespoons finely chopped fennel leaves. Season to taste with salt and pepper. A delicate sauce ideal to serve with cooked white fish.

Boiled mustard and dill sauce

Blend together 2 teaspoons dry mustard, 1 teaspoon anchovy essence and 2 teaspoons vinegar. Place 25 g/1 oz butter, 25 g/1 oz flour and 250 ml/9 fl oz milk in a saucepan and whisk over gentle heat until the sauce boils and thickens. Whisk in the mustard mixture and about 3 tablespoons chopped dill. Season to taste with salt and simmer for 5 minutes, stirring occasionally. Makes a tasty accompaniment to hot cooked tongue or silverside of beef.

Beetroot, apple and horseradish cream

Mix together 2 tablespoons each finely diced beetroot, grated peeled dessert apple and grated horseradish. Whip 150 ml/¼ pint double cream until thick and fold in the apple mixture. Season to taste with salt and pepper. Serve with hot fried fish in batter.

Mint and cream cheese dressing

Very finely chop 2 tablespoons mint leaves and 1 garlic clove. Soften 225 g/8 oz cream cheese and gradually work in the mint and garlic. Add salt and pepper if wished. Slash open potatoes baked in their jackets and serve with this creamy dressing.

Honey salad dressing

Place ¼ teaspoon each salt, freshly ground black pepper and sweet paprika in a screw-topped jar and stir in 50 ml/2 fl oz cider vinegar and 1 tablespoon clear honey. When blended, add 125 ml/4 fl oz oil and shake well until thickened. Store in a refrigerator and shake before each use. This dressing keeps well and enlivens many different vegetable, rice or pasta salads.

Creamed horseradish and apple sauce

Whip 150 ml/¼ pint double cream with 2 teaspoons clear honey until thick. Peel and grate 1 small cooking apple and fold into the mixture with 2 tablespoons grated horseradish. Lay cling film over the surface and leave to stand for 1 hour before serving. This allows the flavours to develop fully. A tangy cream sauce to serve with hot or cold roast beef or lamb.

Avocado mayonnaise

Soften 75 g/3 oz cream cheese and gradually beat in 2 tablespoons mayonnaise, 4 tablespoons double cream, 2 tablespoons finely chopped parsley and 1 tablespoon grated onion. Peel, halve and stone 1 ripe avocado and mash the flesh. Combine well with the cream cheese mixture and season to taste with salt and pepper. This is a good thick dressing to serve with crunchy mixed vegetable salads.

Soured cream and coconut dressing

Combine 1 tablespoon clear honey with 150 ml/¼ pint soured cream. Place 50 g/2 oz grated fresh coconut in a basin and sprinkle over 2 teaspoons lemon juice. Allow to stand for 20 minutes. Gradually beat in 1 tablespoon clear honey and 150 ml/¼ pint soured cream. Serve with salads which combine fresh fruit and vegetables.

Aïoli

Peel 2 cloves of garlic and pound with ¼ teaspoon salt using a pestle and mortar. Transfer to a basin and add 1 egg yolk. Whisk until smooth. Add 1½ teaspoons lemon juice and whisk again. Gradually trickle in 150 ml/¼ pint olive oil, whisking all the time, then season to taste with freshly ground black pepper. The consistency should be slightly thinner than ordinary mayonnaise. This strongly-flavoured sauce is a traditional accompaniment to cold fish dishes.

Gourmet slimmer's dressing

Place 100 g/4 oz cottage cheese in a blender goblet with 1 teaspoon lemon juice and 2 tablespoons tomato juice. Switch on high until smooth then season to taste with salt, pepper and Worcestershire sauce. Chill and just before serving stir in 2 tablespoons very finely chopped sweet red pepper.

Vegetable and Fruit Freezing Chart

Vegetable	Preparation	Blanching time	Packing
Artichokes			
Globe	Remove outer leaves, trim, wash well. Add lemon juice to blanching water.	7–10 minutes	Polythene bags
Jerusalem	Cook, purée and freeze. Use in soups.	Boil 30 minutes	Polythene containers
Asparagus	Wash, trim, grade and blanch. Pack all lying in one direction.	2–4 minutes	Rectangular polythene containers
Beans			
Broad	Pod, grade and blanch.	3 minutes	Polythene bags
French	Top and tail, slice or leave whole and blanch. Freeze young, tender beans unblanched for 3 months only.	3 minutes	Polythene bags
Runner	Trim, slice thickly, blanch.	2 minutes	Polythene bags
Beetroot	Cook until tender. Peel slice or dice.	Boil 40–50 minutes	Polythene containers
Broccoli	Select compact head with tender stalks. Trim, wash in salted water, blanch, drain well.	3–5 minutes, depending on size	Polythene bags, overwrap
Brussels Sprouts	Select small firm sprouts. Peel, trim and wash thoroughly. Blanch.	3–5 minutes	Polythene bags overwrap
Cauliflower	Trim to small florets. Wash and blanch in salted water. Open freeze. Store 3 months.	3 minutes	Polythene bags
Celeriac	Wash, peel, slice and steam until almost tender, or cut into strips and blanch for use in salads.	Steam 25 minutes; blanch 1 minute	Polythene containers
Courgettes	Wash, trim and slice. Blanch or sauté in butter. Freeze whole, unblanched 3 months only.	1 minute	Polythene containers
Kohlrabi	Peel and dice. Blanch and open freeze.	2 minutes	Polythene bags
Leeks (*For use in cooked dishes*)	Remove tops, roots and stalks. Wash well and slice. Sauté in butter 3–4 minutes.		Polythene containers
Marrow	Use small young marrow. Peel, cut in to rings and remove seeds. Blanch.	3 minutes	Polythene containers
Parsnips	Trim, peel, slice or dice and blanch. Can also be frozen cooked, as a purée.	2 minutes	Polythene bags
Peas	Select young peas, shell and grade. Blanch and open freeze for free-flow pack. Freeze unblanched 3 months only.	1 minute	Polythene bags
Peppers	Wash, remove stems, pips and pith. Halve or slice and blanch.	3 minutes	Polythene containers
Pumpkin	Peel, slice and remove seeds. Steam until tender and mash.	Steam 35–40 minutes	Polythene containers
Spinach	Select young leaves, trim and wash well. Blanch and press out excess water. Freeze washed but unblanched for 3 months only.	2 minutes	Polythene containers Tightly packed in polythene bags
Swedes	Trim, peel and dice. Blanch. Can also be frozen cooked as a purée.	3 minutes	Polythene bags Polythene containers
Tomatoes (*Use for cooking*)	Wipe, remove stem and freeze whole unblanched for three months.		Polythene bags
Turnips	Trim, peel and dice. Blanch. Can also be frozen cooked as a purée.	3 minutes	Polythene bags Polythene containers

Fruit	Preparation	Packing
Apples (*cooking*)	Peel, core and slice into cold salted water. Blanch 1 minute or steam blanch 2 minutes. Freeze dry with sugar. Can also be frozen cooked as a purée, with or without sugar.	Polythene bags or containers
Apricots	Freeze whole, or halved and stoned or sliced, in syrup pack; add ascorbic acid.	Polythene containers
Blackberries	Wash fruit only if necessary and hull. Freeze in dry sugar or syrup pack. Can be frozen as purée.	Polythene bags or containers
Cherries	Remove stalks, wash and stone. Open freeze then pack in dry sugar or syrup pack. White cherries freeze best in syrup. Red cherries freeze better than black.	Polythene bags
Cranberries	Remove stalks, wash and drain. Open freeze and pack dry or in syrup pack.	Polythene containers or bags
Currants – black, red or white	Sprigs – wash, drain, open freeze then pack in dry sugar pack. Or, top and tail and freeze whole, with or without sugar, or purée with sugar and little or no water.	Polythene bags or polythene containers
Figs	Wash gently, leave whole and freeze wrapped individually, or peel and freeze in syrup pack.	Foil Polythene containers
Gooseberries	Wash, dry, top and tail. Freeze in dry sugar or syrup pack. Slightly under-ripe fruit freezes best.	Polythene bags or polythene containers
Grapefruit	Wash, peel, segment or slice. Open freeze segments then pack in dry sugar or syrup pack. Juice can be frozen and packed as ice cubes. Grate zest and mix with sugar then freeze.	Polythene containers
Lemons/Limes	Leave whole, or slice or segment, and freeze in dry sugar or syrup pack. Open freeze lemon slices and pack dry for drinks. Juice can be frozen and packed as ice cubes. Grate zest and mix with sugar then freeze.	Polythene bags or polythene containers
Loganberries	Wash only if necessary, drain, then hull. Open freeze and pack dry or purée with or without sugar. Pick on a dry day when ripe but firm. Mildew develops within hours on wet fruit.	Polythene containers
Oranges	Segment or slice: freeze in dry sugar or syrup pack. Juice can be frozen and packed as ice cubes. Grate zest and mix with sugar then freeze. In season, freeze Seville oranges whole and make marmalade later.	Polythene containers
Peaches	Skin, halve and stone. Freeze halved or sliced in syrup pack with ascorbic acid. Can be frozen as purée with lemon juice and sugar.	Polythene containers
Pears	Peel, core and slice. Poach in boiling syrup $1\frac{1}{2}$ minutes. Drain, cool and freeze with syrup, or prepare straight into cold syrup with ascorbic acid. Choose perfect, slightly under-ripe fruit.	Polythene containers
Pineapple	Peel, core and slice, dice or crush. Freeze slices in layers with dividers. Freeze in dry sugar or syrup pack.	Polythene containers
Plums and Damsons	Wash, halve and stone. Freeze in dry sugar or syrup pack. Can be frozen as cooked purée, with or without sugar.	Polythene containers
Raspberries	Wash only if necessary, drain and then hull. Open freeze and pack dry in dry sugar pack. Can be frozen as purée, with or without sugar. Pick on a dry day when ripe but firm. Mildew develops within hours on wet fruit.	Polythene containers
Rhubarb	Wash, trim and cut into 2.5-cm/1-inch lengths, blanch in boiling water for 1 minute, and cool. Freeze in dry sugar or syrup pack. Can be frozen as cooked purée, with or without sugar. Blanching is necessary as rhubarb is the stem of the plant not the fruit.	Polythene containers
Strawberries	Wash only if necessary, drain and then hull. Open freeze and pack dry in dry sugar or syrup pack. Can be frozen as purée, with or without sugar. Choose firm, dry fruit.	Polythene containers

Index

Aïoli 187
Almond:
  Almond and cherry cheesecake 103
  Almond mincepies 176
  Almond pastry 184
  Chicken or fish and almond soup 165
  Orange and almond pudding 49
American pancakes 136
American turkey and rice salad 18
Anchovy:
  Jerusalem artichoke soup with anchovies 12
  Pan pizza with anchovy topping 19
  Peach and anchovy rarebits 91
Apple:
  Apple and bacon or chicken pudding 150
  Apple bread and butter pudding 170
  Apple coleslaw 173
  Apple and loganberry layer pudding 115
  Apple and plum chutney 179
  Apple and treacle tart 22
  Beef and apple pie 152
  Caramelised apple on a skewer 119
  Cheese and apple puffs 91
  Cinnamon apple charlotte 145
  Fruity apple batter pudding 31
  Gammon steaks with apple and mint jelly 99
  Jellied apple and lemon flan 154
  Lamb and apple casserole 42
  Latticed apple and apricot flan 172
  Maraschino apple dumplings 62
  Mint and apple jelly 179
  Pork chops with curried apple sauce 83
  Sherried apple dumplings 62
  Spiced apple compote 12
  Steamed apple and date pudding 171
  Stuffed apple salads 80
  Tipsy apple dumplings 62
  Toffee apples 161
  Toffee-topped apples 145
  Yorkshire apple pie
Apricot:
  Apricot brandy 179
  Apricot choux puffs 63
  Apricot dumplings 169
  Apricot jam 177
  Apricot salad starters 69
  Apricot-stuffed lamb 46
  Apricot supper dish 91
  Banana apricot fool 104
  Pork chops with curried apricot sauce 83
Artichoke:
  Globe artichokes with lemon dressing 96
  Globe artichokes with wine vinaigrette dressing 96
  Globe artichokes with yogurt and chive dressing 96
  Jerusalem artichoke soup with anchovies 12
  Super veal stew with artichoke hearts 70
Asparagus:
  Asparagus cream soup 69
  Asparagus mimosa 69
  Creamed chicken with asparagus 73
Aubergine:
  Aubergine niçoise 123
  Aubergined veal cutlets 126
  Corn and aubergine parcels 118
Avocado:
  Avocado with herb dressing 32
  Avocado mayonnaise 187
  Chilled avocado soup 95
  Pasta cocktail with avocado sauce 53
  Peppered avocado soup 136

Bacon:
  Apple and bacon pudding 150
  Bacon and broad or green bean salad 95
  Bacon and celery soup 39
  Bacon and chicken cassoulet 57
  Bacon and chicken liver rolls with mushrooms 38
  Bacon with fried green tomatoes 122
  Bacon hotpot 16
  Beef and bacon suet roll 168
  Braised bacon with Madeira or sherry gravy 42
  Cherry-baked bacon 83
  Cold boiled bacon with pickled mushrooms 68
  Marrow medley 114
Banana:
  Banana and apricot fool 104
  Banana bran muesli 94
  Caramel bananas with rum 49
  Layered banana and prune charlotte 145
  Yogurt with minted bananas 80
Barbecue party 116—19
Bean:
  Bacon and broad or green bean salad 95
  Rodeo beans 118
  Smoked haddock and bean salad 13
  Veal stew with haricot beans 70
Beef:
  Baked marrow boats 141
  Beef and ale hotpot 22
  Beef and apple pie 152
  Beef and bacon suet roll 168
  Beef and beetroot Stroganoff 124
  Beef and chestnut casserole 22
  Beef and paprika pancakes 47
  Beef with pears or plums in wine 137
  Beef and pickled beetroot pot 28
  Beef and pickled walnut pot 28
  Beef spice boats 30
  Beef-stuffed tomato cups 156
  Beefy minestrone or minestra 148
  Beefy pop-over 35
  Boiled brisket with parsnips 30
  Cidered beef and prune hotpot 22
  Holiday burgers with cucumber salad 112
  Jellied beef consommé 60
  Meatballs with creamed carrots 112
  Meatballs with creamed cucumber 112
  Savoy beef and leek parcels 168
  Steaks with brussels sprout salad 166
  Worcester beef rissoles 172
Beetroot:
  Beef and beetroot Stroganoff 124
  Beetroot, apple and horseradish cream 187
  Beetroot and orange or lemon soup 137
Biscuit hearts 31
Black Forest cheesecake 61
Blackberry meringue layer cake 129
Blackcurrant:
  Blackcurrant and apple fool 104
  Creamy blackcurrant shake 119
Bonfire party 158—61
Boxing Day party 174—6
Bramble jelly 178
Bread:
  Bread and rolls 182—3
  Country herbed bread with cheese dice 133
  Miniature bread knots 60
  Picnic loaves 87
  Scalloped bread dice 49
  Bread and butter puddings 170
  Breadcrumb omelette 103
Breton fish soup 149

Broccoli:
  Broccoli in lemon butter 46
  Ham and broccoli pancakes 57
Brussels sprout:
  Brussels sprout and cheese or bacon soup 164
  Rice ring with brussels sprouts 35
Buns:
  Hot cross buns 52
  Sweet fruited buns 182

Cake:
  Chocolate and orange layer cake 65
  Glazed strawberry sponge 65
  Lemon kiwi gâteau 65
  Parcel cake 76
  Rose petal fancies 65
Candied citrus fruit peel 181
Candlelight supper buffet 20—2
Caramel bananas with rum 49
Caramelised pink grapefruit 46
Carrot:
  Carrot and celery salad 32
  Carrot and haddie flan 19
  Carrot slaw 173
  Chilled carrot cream 39
Cauliflower:
  Cauliflower in curry cream 165
  Cauliflower dreams 114
  Corn and cauliflower pancakes 57
Celeriac with mustard mayonnaise 27
Celery:
  Carrot and celery salad 32
  Celery hearts in cheese custard 173
  Celery and tomato soup 160
  Creamy celery bake 157
Cheese:
  Cheese and apple puffs 91
  Cheese-crusted fish 35
  Cheese and egg boats 76
  Cheese and mustard sauce 186
  Cheese pastry 184
  Cheese-stuffed courgettes 133
  Cheesy coleslaw 173
  Cheesy pineapple dip 144
  Cheesy Scotch eggs 160
  Egg and cheese sunburst platter 90
  Leeks in cheese custard 173
  Miniature chicken and cheese pasties 104
  Peach and anchovy rarebits 91
  Plaited cheese loaf 182
  Cheesecakes 61,103
Cherry:
  Cherry-baked bacon 83
  Chilled cherry mousse 104
  Hot cherry cream pudding 115
Chicken:
  Apple and chicken pudding 150
  Bacon and chicken cassoulet 57
  Bacon and chicken liver rolls with mushrooms 38
  Baked chicken in sharp sauce 18
  Capered chicken snack 157
  Chicken and almond soup 165
  Chicken breasts in tarragon aspic 60
  Chicken with cheese toppers 173
  Chicken drumsticks with red wine basting sauce 118
  Chicken liver terrine 38
  Chicken mousse towers 39
  Chicken and olive snack 157
  Chicken with pearl barley 138
  Chicken and rice salad 18
  Chicken tonnato 61
  Creamed chicken with asparagus 73
  Crusted coq au vin 32
  Fruited chicken mayonnaise 86
  Lovers' pie 32
  Miniature chicken and cheese pasties 104
  Mushroom and chicken risotto 169
  Mustard glazed chicken 43

  Raised chicken pie 101
  Roast chicken with marrow 127
  Saffron chicken 153
  Stuffed chicken breasts with sage 101
  Welsh pie 32
Children's party 74—7
Chinese leaves, veal casserole with 41
Chinese-style fish and prawns 13
Chinese-style fish strips 13
Chocolate:
  Chocolate and orange layer cake 65
  Chocolate truffles 176
  Iced chocolate whizz 77
Choux puffs with pineapple filling 63
Christmas pudding 156
Chutneys 179—80
Cider punch, hot 144
Cidered beef and prune hotpot 22
Cidered sausages 90
Cinnamon apple charlotte 145
Citrus bread and butter pudding 170
Coconut raisin pudding 23
Cod:
  Danish baked fish 168
  Tuna and cod cream 53
Coleslaws 173
Consommé 60
Corn see **Sweet corn**
Courgette:
  Cheese-stuffed courgettes 133
  Corn and courgette parcels 118
  Courgette dreams 114
  Courgette and lamb casserole 110
  Lemon-crusted veal with courgettes 100
  Pork chops with sugared courgettes 124
  Tuna-stuffed courgettes 133
Crabmeat sauce, plaice rolls in 97
Cranberry:
  Cranberry bread and butter pudding 170
  Cranberry dip 144
  Pork with cranberries 152
Crofter's roastie 16
Crystallised flower petals 181
Cucumber:
  Cucumber and marrow salad 132
  Cucumber mousse 86
  Cucumber salad 112
  Gammon steaks with sautéed cucumber dice 99
Curried shellfish flan 73

Damson:
  Damson butter or cheese 179
  Damson crumble 129
  Hare with damson sauce 140
Desserts see **Puddings and desserts**
Devilled mackerel 73
Dips for sausages 144
Drinks:
  Hot cider punch 144
  Summer coolers 119
Duck:
  Duckling with green pea sauce 56
  Minted duck casserole 85
Dumplings:
  Apple dumplings 62
  Apricot dumplings 169
  Potato dumplings 17
  Raisin dumplings 169

Easter Sunday lunch 44—7
Egg:
  Breadcrumb omelette 103
  Cheese and egg boats 76
  Cheesy Scotch eggs 160
  Egg and cheese sunburst platter 90
  Egg and seafood spiced mayonnaise 86
  Egg and tomato stuffed loaf 87

Egg tonnato 61
Ham and egg boats 76
Miniature curried egg cream
pasties 104
New potato and fennel omelette
94
Paprika baked eggs 26
Scalloped bread dice 49
Scrambled egg sandwiches 108
Smoked haddock with poached
eggs 164
Spring soufflé omelette 57
Stuffed egg and broad or French
bean salad 109
Tuna and egg boats 76

Fennel:
Fennel cream sauce 187
Fennel in curry cream 165
Lamb's liver with fennel 17
Minted fennel starters 53
New potato and fennel omelette
94
Saffron fennel cream 26
Saffron fennel soup 26
Fish. *See also* **Cod, Haddock etc.**
Breton fish soup 149
Cheese-crusted fish 35
Chinese-style fish and prawns 13
Chinese-style fish strips 13
Danish baked fish 168
Fish and almond soup 165
Fish with lemon or orange parsley
sauce 123
Masked fish steaks with grapes 109
Piquant fish puffs 34
Smoked fish bake 41
Walnut fish pasties 172
Flan pastry 184—5
Flower petals, crystallised 181
Franfurter and apple stuffed loaf 87
Freezing fruit and vegetables 188—9
French dressing 186
French toast 148; sweet 148
Fruit. *See also* **Apple, Apricot etc.**
To freeze fruit 189
Fruit and nut loaf 183
Summer fruit shortcakes 105
Unusual ways of preserving fruit
181
Winter fruit salad 33
Fruited chicken mayonnaise 86
Fruity apple batter pudding 31
Fudge brownie pear flan 22

Gammon:
Gammon with onion and paprika
sauce 150
Gammon steaks with apple and
mint jelly 99
Gammon steaks with green pea
purée 99
Gammon steaks with sautéed
cucumber dice 99
Gammon and vegetable medley
141
Garlic dressing 186
Ginger and rhubarb kissel 47
Gooseberry:
Baked mackeral with gooseberry
stuffing 82
Gooseberry and apple fool 104
Gooseberry crumble 88
Lamb chops with gooseberries 100
Gourmet slimmer's dressing 187
Grape:
Grape jalousie 145
Grape macaroon cream 154
Masked fish steak with grapes 109
Trout with seedless grapes 97
Grapefruit:
Caramelised pink grapefruit 46
Golden glazed grapefruit 164
Grapefruit baskets 27
Green salad 86
Greengage crumble 129
Grouse:
Roast grouse 114

Haddock. *See also* **Smoked
haddock**
Carrot and haddie flan 19
Corn and haddie flan 19
Haddock with golden sauce 166
Halloween party 142—5
Ham:
Fried ham and gherkin sandwiches
48
Glazed ham joint 14
Ham and broccoli pancakes 57
Ham and cheese pasties 133
Ham and egg boats 76
Ham and egg florentine salad 91
Ham and pineapple spiced
mayonnaise 86
Turkey and ham cassoulet 57
Hare with damson sauce 140
Harvest festival supper 130—1
Hazelnut muesli 94
Hazelnut pear pie 23
Herb vinegars 181
Herbs, to dry and freeze 180—1
Herby hubble bubble 90
Herring:
Oaty herrings 12
Pickled herrings and beetroot in
cream 101
Honey salad dressing 187
Horseradish:
Creamed horseradish and apple
sauce 187
Creamy horseradish mayonnaise 176
Horseradish dip 144
Hot cross buns 52
Hot water crust pastry 185
Hubble bubble 90

Ice cream with peanut crunch 77
Iced chocolate whizz 77

Jams and jellies 177—9

Kidney:
Grilled mustard kidneys 52
Kidney cobbler 153
Kidney and mushroom cobbler
153
Kidneys in mustard wine sauce 72
Lamb and kidney hotpot 43
Lamb, kidney and mushroom
hotpot 43
Kiwi fruit:
Kiwi cheese tart 77
Lemon kiwi gâteau 64
Kohlrabi croquettes 27
Krispie ice cream flan 77

Lamb:
Apricot-stuffed lamb 46
Braised lamb with plums and
thyme 138
Braised lamb with rosemary 138
Casseroled lamb noisettes 54
Courgette and lamb casserole 110
Crofter's roastie 16
Lamb and apple casserole 42
Lamb chops with gooseberries 100
Lamb chops with minted cream 72
Lamb en croûte 46
Lamb and kidney hotpot 43
Lamb, kidney and mushroom
hotpot 43
Lamb with lemon-glazed potatoes
83
Lamb and plum casserole 42
Lamb with rosemary 46
Lamb with spring cabbage 72
Oriental basted lamb cutlets 118
Roast lamb with recurrant glaze
110
Savoy lamb and apple parcels 168
Summer fruited chops 100
Sweet and spicy lamb 43
Tarragon lamb and pasta hotpot
126
Lamb's liver with fennel 17

Leek:
Leek chowder 13
Leeks in cheese custard 173
Leeks in clover 141
Savoy beef and leek parcels 168
Lemon:
Beetroot and lemon soup 137
Lemon butter 46
Lemon cheese tart 77
Lemon croissants 31
Lemon crusted veal with
courgettes 100
Lemon curd 178
Lemon curd toasts 38
Lemon and ginger cheesecake 61
Lemon and ginger pudding 171
Lemon kiwi gâteau 64
Lemon parsley sauce 123
Lemon sultana pudding 23
Lemon sole in spinach sauce 54
Lettuce hearts with caper dressing
105
Lettuce vichyssoise 95
Lime cooler 119
Liver:
Chicken liver terrine 38
Lamb's liver with fennel 17
Liver and apple pie 127
Liver fritters 169
Liver with tomato and orange
sauce 85
Mexicali liver 48
Tomato liver bake 153
Loganberry yogurt mould 90
Lovers' pie 32

Mackerel:
Baked mackerel with gooseberry
stuffing 82
Devilled mackerel 73
Maraschino apple dumplings 62
Marmalade 178
Marrow:
Baked marrow boats 141
Cucumber marrow salad 132
Marrow with frankfurters 114
Marrow medley 114
Marrow and rhubarb chutney 180
Roast chicken with marrow 127
Mayonnaise 186; in blender 186
Meat. *See also* **Beef, Lamb etc.**
Three-meat family loaf 56
Meatballs with creamed carrots 112
Meatballs with creamed cucumber
112
Melon:
Madras melon cocktails 122
Melon ice cream 127
Mixed melon chunks 136
Mexicali liver 48
Minestrone or minestra 148
Mint and apple jelly 179
Mint and cream cheese dressing 187
Minted duck casserole 85
Minted fennel starters 53
Mocha cheesecake 61
Muesil 94
Mushroom:
Bacon and chicken liver rolls with
mushrooms 38
Club mushrooms 137
Mushroom and chicken risotto 169
Mushroom soufflé omelette 57
Pickled mushrooms 68
Viennese mushroom puffs 27
Mustard and dill sauce, boiled 187
Mustard-glazed chicken 43

Oaty herrings 12
Omelette *see* **Egg**
Onion
Creamy onion bake 157
Gammon with onion and paprika
sauce 150
Majorcan onion and tomato platter
105
Turkey-stuffed onions 18
Orange:
Baked clove oranges 14

Beetroot and orange soup 137
Chocolate and orange layer cake
65
Orange and almond pudding 49
Orange corn cups 165
Orange croissants 31
Orange curd 178
Orange froth 119
Orange parsley sauce 123
Orange and raisin pudding 171
Orange teabread 183
Upside-down orange pudding with
marmalade sauce 155

Pancakes:
American pancakes 136
Beef and paprika pancakes 47
Corn and cauliflower pancakes 57
Ham and broccoli pancakes 57
Paprika baked eggs 26
Parcel cake 76
Parsley and lemon sauce 186
Parsnip:
Boiled brisket with parsnips 30
Roast pork with parsnips 16
Patridge in wine sauce 140
Pasta cocktail with avocado sauce 53
Pastry 184—5
Pâté:
Fresh salmon pâté 82
Pea:
Fresh pea pod soup 95
Gammon steaks with green pea
purée 99
Peach:
Hot peach cream pudding 115
Peach and anchovy rarebits 91
Peach brandy 179
Peach fizz 119
Peach jam 177
Peaches and cream flan 88
Peaches masked with aspic
mayonnaise 149
Pork chops with curried peach
sauce 83
Veal with peach pockets 126
Peanut butter and bramble jelly on
toast 122
Pear:
Beef with pears in wine 137
Fudge brownie pear flan 22
Hazelnut pear pie 23
Pear and lemon meringue cake 129
Pears masked with aspic
mayonnaise 149
Pork with pears 152
Spice pear charlotte 145
Upside-down pear and ginger
pudding 155
Pepper, red or green:
Corn and pepper parcels 118
Peppered avocado soup 136
Peppered veal cutlets 126
Stuffed peppers 109
Sweet pepper cups 132
Pheasant:
To roast a pheasant 140
Pheasant in wine sauce 140
Picnic loaves 87
Pineapple:
Choux puffs with pineapple filling
63
Crusted pineapple on a skewer 119
Fresh pineapple sorbet 88
Ham and pineapple spiced
mayonnaise 86
Hanalei pineapple salad 82
Madras pineapple cocktails 122
Pineapple and blue cheese stuffed
loaf 87
Pineapple and lemon jam 177
Pizza in the pan 19; with anchovy
topping 19
Plaice:
Plaice rolls with carrot and orange
sauce 97
Plaice rolls in crabmeat sauce 97
Plaice tonnato 61
Plum:
Apple and plum chutney 179